The Problems and Prospects
of
American–East Asian Relations

Westview Special Studies on China and East Asia

The Problems and Prospects of American-East Asian Relations
Edited by John Chay

This issue-oriented, multidisciplinary approach to American–East Asian relations asks provocative questions and presents a thoughtful appraisal of the situation today. Using a wide range of sources—among them, recently declassified government documents—the authors examine U.S. relations with China, Japan, and Korea. Issues discussed include the "new policy" toward the People's Republic of China (Was there, in fact, a sudden shift in U.S. policy?); the attitudes of the American people and Congress toward the Republic of China; the friction between the United States and Japan and the implications of the existing imbalance in trade between the two countries; and the potential for continuing and increasing problems in U.S.–Korean relations. Throughout, the authors present an analysis of past and current conditions as a tool for use in formulating sound, effective policy for the future.

John Chay is professor of history and chairman of the Department of History at Pembroke State University. Since 1974 Dr. Chay has been executive director of the North Carolina Southeastern Consortium for International Education.

Other Titles in This Series

Women in Changing Japan, edited by Joyce Lebra, Joy Paulson, and Elizabeth Powers

Cadres, Commanders, and Commissars: The Training of the Chinese Communist Leadership, 1920-45, Jane L. Price

The People's Republic of China: Mineral Resources and Basic Industries, K. P. Wang

The Chinese Military System, Harvey Nelsen

The Problems and Prospects
of
American–East Asian Relations

Edited by John Chay

With the assistance of
Chang-Hyun Cho

Westview Press
Boulder, Colorado

Westview Special Studies on China and East Asia

Copyright © 1977 by Westview Press, Inc.

Published 1977 in the United States of America by
  Westview Press, Inc.
  1898 Flatiron Court
  Boulder, Colorado 80301
  Frederick A. Praeger, Publisher and Editorial Director

Library of Congress Cataloging in Publication Data

Main entry under title:
The Problems and prospects of American–East Asian relations.
    (Westview special studies on China and East Asia)
    Revised papers from a symposium held at Pembroke State University in the spring of 1973.
    1. East (Far East)—Foreign relations—United States—Congresses.
2. United States—Foreign relations—East (Far East)—Congresses.
I. Chay, John. II. Cho, Chang-Hyun.
DS518.8.P7   327.5'073   76-27694
ISBN 0-89158-113-8

Printed and bound in the United States of America

Contents

Preface

Because of the enhanced importance of the Pacific region after the turn of the century, and, in particular, because of the agonizing experience of the Vietnam War, American–East Asian relations have become increasingly significant in the American scholarly world as well as in the arena of foreign policy–making. During the past decade or so, centers of international and area studies in the United States have paid special attention to this subject; most significantly, the establishment in 1968 of the Committee on American–East Asian Relations of the American Historical Association, under the leadership of Ernest R. May, was an important step toward achieving a greater understanding. The publication in 1972 of *American–East Asian Relations: A Survey*, a chronological historiographical survey of the subject from its beginning to the end of the 1960s, represented a challenge to serious students as well as an important groundwork. The present volume is, in a sense, a response to that challenge: it is an issue-oriented, multidisciplinary analysis.

In the spring of 1973, a symposium was held at Pembroke State University in North Carolina. Seventeen specialists in the field of American–East Asian relations met to examine problems and prospects in the field. The symposium was organized into three divisions—American-Chinese, American-Japanese, and American-Korean relations—and three papers were presented in each of these subfields. Eventually, six of the symposium papers were revised and edited for this volume: those presented by Norman A. Graebner, James W. White, Kazuo Sato, John P. Lovell, Ishwer C. Ojha, and myself. Later, four other active scholars in the field of American–East Asian relations—Tong-Whan Park, Akira Iriye, Pong S. Lee, and Douglas H. Mendel—consented to write chapters for this volume.

Following the format used for the symposium, the book includes an introduction and nine chapters in three divisions. Akira Iriye in the introduction presents a fresh examination of the cold war in Asia. Ishwer C. Ojha then gives an overall analysis of American-Chinese relations in the three decades after World War II. Norman A. Graebner's views of the American image of China and Douglas H. Mendel's analysis of American-Formosan relations follow. A general survey of American-Japanese relations is provided by James W. White, followed by Kazuo Sato's study of economic relations and Tong-Whan Park's analysis of energy relations. In the last section, the editor of this volume provides a sweeping survey of the entire period of American-Korean relations, while John P. Lovell and Pong S. Lee concentrate on the security and economic aspects.

These chapters are based on serious research and solid scholarship, but some of them are purposely speculative; it is hoped that both of these aspects will be useful for an understanding of the subject.

Among the many people who made the symposium and book possible, Dr. Carl M. Fisher was most important. The vice-chancellor for academic affairs at Pembroke State University at the time of the symposium, Dr. Fisher provided strong leadership for the intellectual enterprise. The assistance of Chang-Hyun Cho of Pembroke State University was valuable to both the symposium and the publication of this volume. The approval and support of Chancellor English E. Jones of Pembroke State University were very important, as were the interest and support of Vice-Chancellor W. Howard Dean and Dean Richard C. Pisano. The symposium benefited greatly from the participation of Ernest R. May, Robert A. Scalapino, Young Chin Kim, Soon-Sung Cho, and James C. Hsiung. Hungdah Chiu of the University of

Maryland Law School, Grace E. Gibson, Raymond J. Rundus, Thomas J. Leach, Richard R. Vela, David K. Eliades, and Jeffery A. Mirus—colleagues at Pembroke State University— were all extremely generous in providing editorial assistance. My personal thanks go to Shirley Deese for her devoted service in typing the entire manuscript. Last, because no book is written in a vacuum, the editor wishes to thank the readers of this volume for their interest and encouragement.

John Chay
October 1976

Introduction

1

WAS THERE A COLD WAR IN ASIA?
Akira Iriye

Professor of History, University of Chicago

American–East Asian relations since World War II provide one of the most exciting fields of study for historians. More than thirty years have passed since that war, and more than twenty years since the Korean War. America's military involvement in Indochina has come to an end, and the Soviet Union has replaced the United States as the chief target of China's propaganda attacks. All these changes compel us to raise fresh questions about postwar U.S.–Asian relations and to arrive at a new synthesis. Fortunately, more and more material is being opened up to research. The United States has taken a lead in releasing postwar documents to researchers, and Japan has also adopted in principle a thirty-year rule. While most Chinese documents are still closed, there have been several recent compilations of speeches and writings by Peking's leaders.

Despite such favorable circumstances, there are still distressingly few monographs dealing specifically with postwar U.S.–Asian relations. In contrast to the prewar period, about which several impressive works have been published since the appearance of the May-Thomson volume, few studies of the postwar period go beyond journalistic statements or are multilingual in approach.[1] Much of the literature is polemical and tells more about the authors' preconceptions and prejudices than about anything else.

This situation is in sharp contrast to the state of general cold war historiography, which has made vast strides in recent years. Excellent monographs deal with American-Russian relations in Europe during and after the war. For instance, Martin Sherwin, in *A World Destroyed* (1975), traces wartime United States policy toward atomic weapons and establishes the fact that President Franklin D. Roosevelt was determined not to share nuclear secrets with the Soviet Union. Lynn Davis, in *The Cold War Begins* (1975), gives a full analysis of American approaches to the East European question, while Tony Sharp, in *The Wartime Alliance and the Zonal Division of Germany* (1975), discusses the German partition issue in detail. More generalized histories, such as John Lewis Gaddis' *The United States and the Origins of the Cold War* (1972) and Walter LaFeber's *America, Russia, and the Cold War* (3rd ed., 1976), have raised the scholarly level of the cold war studies so that the subject can be discussed in a dispassionate manner. It is to be hoped that in time that same level will be reached by writings about U.S.–Asian relations.

This essay seeks to delineate the characteristics of postwar U.S.–Asian relations by asking the question: How different was the cold war in Asia from that in Europe and the Middle East? Was it the same war, or was the situation in Asia sufficiently different from elsewhere that it cannot be fitted into the conceptual framework of the cold war—which, after all, has a European connotation? The answers to this question would serve to put postwar American-Asian relations in comparative perspective and enable us to raise additional questions about the foreign policies of the countries involved.

Recently declassified documents of the United States government make it clear that one must at least distinguish between cold war perceptions and cold war policies. The cold war in one respect was a perception held by policymakers, opinion elites, and the public about the international situation; it provided the conceptual framework in which they viewed the world. In another respect the cold war connoted a policy or strategy; it defined the foreign policy or military strategy of a country as it dealt with other countries. The cold war in the first sense was mainly rhetorical and ideological, whereas the cold war in the second sense referred to the totality of specific policy decisions and military plans.

That the cold war was a reality as perceived by American policymakers after the war can be fully documented. As they looked at the emerging postwar world, they were immensely impressed with the power and ambitions of the Soviet Union. Such a perception, of course, can be traced to 1917 or even earlier; but in the context of postwar United States policy, it is sufficient to note that as early as October 1945 the joint intelligence committee of the Joint Chiefs of Staff was making a detailed study of Soviet postwar foreign policy and concluding, "The long-term objective of Soviet foreign policy appears to be the establishment of control over the Eurasian land mass and the strategic approaches thereto."[2] In a famous memorandum a year later, Clark Clifford, special counsel to President Harry S. Truman, presented a view of the international situation as an arena of struggle between the Soviet Union and the United States on a global scale. The Soviet Union, Clifford pointed out, was "jeopardizing the security of the United States by her efforts to weaken the military position and to destroy the prestige of the United States in Europe, Asia, and South America."[3] When the National Security Act of 1947 created the National Security Council as the focal organ for developing strategy for the new era, one of the first papers it considered was NSC 7, prepared by its staff in March 1948. That paper offered a clear definition of the existing world situation: "The Soviet Union is the source of power from which international communism chiefly derives its capability to threaten the existence of free nations. The United States is the only source of power capable of mobilizing successful opposition to the Communist goal of world conquest. . . . In these circumstances the USSR has engaged the United States in a struggle for power, or 'cold war,' in which our national security is at stake and from which we cannot withdraw short of eventual suicide."[4]

Similar phrases were used again and again in key official documents. For instance, NSC 20/4, which Truman approved on November 24, 1948, stated, "Communist ideology and Soviet behavior clearly demonstrate that the ultimate objective of the leaders of the USSR is the domination of the world." Consequently, "[the] gravest threat to the security of the United States within the foreseeable future stems from the hostile designs and formidable power of the USSR, and from the nature of the Soviet system."[5]

These statements are sufficient to indicate the existence of a generally accepted world view within the United States government. That view represented the world as perceived by the American leaders. It was a world in which the forces of international communism, led by Russia, and of anticommunism, led by America, were struggling for survival. This was the cold war as defined by the United States. Such a war called for a response, a strategy to deal with the perceived threat of the Soviet Union. Already, in November 1945, the joint intelligence staff had specified twenty targets within Russian territory which were to be destroyed by atomic bombs in case of war.[6] The Clifford memorandum asserted that "in order to maintain our strength at a level which will be effective in restraining the Soviet Union, the United States must be prepared to wage atomic and biological warfare." War plans began to be formulated within the Joint Chiefs of Staff in 1947, and in 1948 Secretary of Defense James Forrestal proposed that the National Security Council undertake a comprehensive study of Soviet intentions and capabilities in order to establish the minimum requirements for American and allied military strength. The result was a series of papers which culminated in the drafting of NSC 20/4. According to that document, the United States was to concentrate on the economic recovery, political stability, and military defense of the Western European countries, since these were considered to be the primary targets of Soviet expansionism. Once Western Europe showed "a will to resist" Russian aggression, it was felt, the threat of war would diminish, and the Soviet leaders might desist from overt acts of war to spread communism. In time Soviet behavior might become sufficiently modified so that there could be an evolution of peaceful, co-operative relations between America and Russia.

Insofar as the cold war concerned American-Russian rivalries in Europe, therefore, there was a basic unity of perception and policy. The United States perceived a threat from the Soviet Union and adopted a strategy to cope with it. By the end of 1948 there was a well-defined approach to the problem, as the United States sought to assist European economic recovery and encourage collective action for long-range military preparedness. Although there were to be further crises and developments in Europe, the basic pattern of American-European cooperation to check Russian expansionism had been established. The United States was to be firmly involved in European affairs to maintain a balance of power. "Winning the cold war" in such a contest means the reestablishment of a status quo, and in that sense this phase of the cold war could be said to have ended with the summit conference of 1955, when the major powers showed willingness to meet and discuss general problems of peace and arms limitation.

If the cold war in Europe thus had a fairly comprehensible history during 1945–55, the situation was far different in Asia. Here the United States had no cold war strategy until at least 1949–50. This is not to say that the situation in Asia was not perceived in the framework of the cold war. American officials were no less inclined in Asia than elsewhere to view developing events after the war in terms of the spread of Soviet communism. The Clifford memorandum, for instance, sounded the alarm over the apparent Soviet intentions to extend Russia's influence to China and Korea. Japan, on the other hand, seemed to have "afforded the USSR no opportunity to establish the influence it desires."

In the first full-scale analysis of the Chinese civil war by the National Security Council, an interim report issued in March 1948 noted that China possessed politico-military significance for both America and Russia "because of its (a) geographical position and (b) tremendous manpower." Moreover, "China's propinquity to Southeast Asia means that if the Chinese Communists take over all China, they would in

time probably strengthen Communist movements in Indochina, Burma, and areas further south." Although the Soviet
Union was refraining from overt assistance to the Communists, the report noted, it was apparent that "Soviet sympa-
thies lie with the Chinese Communists, who are in effect an
instrument for the extension of Soviet influence." Similarly,
in November 1948 the Joint Chiefs of Staff warned, "Unless
Formosa can be denied to Kremlin-directed exploitation, we
must expect . . . enemy capability of dominating to his advantage and our disadvantage the sea routes between Japan
and the Malay area, together with a greatly improved enemy
capability of extending his control to the Ryukyus and the
Philippines, either of which could produce strategic consequences very seriously detrimental to our national security."[7]

As for Japan, the joint strategy survey committee pointed
out as early as April 1947 that "Japan is the one nation
which could contain large armed forces of our ideological
opponents in the Far East."[8] A year later the National Security Council undertook a study of alternative policies toward
Japan "in view of the serious international situation created
by the Soviet Union's policy of aggressive Communist expansion."[9] Even Southeast Asia came gradually to be seen in the
context of the cold war. There could be little doubt, the
State Department pointed out in July 1949, that "the Kremlin seeks ultimate control over SEA as a pawn in the struggle
between the Soviet World and the Free World." Not that a
Communist victory in China, "a grievous political defeat for
us," was in sight, "if SEA is also swept away by communism
we shall have suffered a major political rout the repercussions
of which will be felt throughout the rest of the world, especially in the Middle East and in a then critically exposed
Australia."[10]

These excerpts sufficiently demonstrate that American
leaders were applying the cold war framework to postwar
developments in Asian countries. At the same time, such a
perception did not automatically result in an assertive policy
or a specific strategy, as was the case in Europe. To the extent that there was an Asian policy/strategy of the United
States, it was to place the region at the bottom of defense

priorities. War plans, to be sure, visualized the use of American forces in China, Okinawa, and elsewhere against Soviet territory in the event of war with Russia. But these were isolated plans which were not incorporated into an integrated strategy for coping with the Soviet Union's perceived global menace. Rather, United States policy, as developed by the White House, the State Department, the National Security Council, the Joint Chiefs of Staff, and other agencies during 1945–59, tended to minimize chances of war with Russia in Asia. There was the basic principle, as stated by the joint strategic survey committee in 1947, that "[the] area of primary strategic importance to the United States in the event of ideological warfare is Western Europe, including Great Britain." Next came the Middle East, then Northwest Africa, then Latin America, and finally the Far East.[11] This was the order of priority from which United States strategy did not deviate for several years, and it amounted to a general policy of passivity in Asia even in the face of apparent growth of Communist influence in the region.

Space does not permit a detailed discussion of American policy toward China, Japan, Korea, and other regions of Asia during this period. Suffice it to say that until the end of 1949 the United States dealt with each country separately, in terms of its relevance to American security and America's capacity to affect the course of events within the country. Regarding China, for instance, the National Security Council reported in March 1948 that the "basic long-range objective of the United States in China is the furtherance of a stable, representative government over an independent and unified China which is friendly to the United States and capable of becoming an effective barrier to possible Soviet aggression in the Far East." However, the chaos in that country and America's commitments elsewhere made it impossible for America to seek to realize such an objective. The United States, if it were to give full-scale support to the Nationalists, "would have to be prepared virtually to take over the Chinese government and administer its economic, political and governmental affairs." Such assistance would invite similar Soviet assistance to the Chinese Communists. In the resulting crisis, "the advantage would be with the USSR, because of its favorable geographical position and the vitality of the Chinese Communist movement." Under the circumstances, the only feasible alternatives open to America would be to either furnish limited economic assistance to China or give it limited aid in the form of both military and economic assistance.[12]

The aforementioned document is interesting in a number of respects. First, it reflected the prevailing notion that the Soviet Union was behind the Chinese Communists; consequently, policymakers assumed that it would be impractical to try to keep these two countries apart by approaching the latter. The alternatives discussed were all within the framework of possible American aid to the Nationalists. Second, there was no mention of Great Britain in the memorandum. This was in sharp contrast to the situation in Europe, where cold war diplomacy was usually defined as an Anglo-American policy of containing Russian communism. No such cooperation with Britain was envisaged in regard to China; the United States continued to view policy in China as its exclusive business. Third, the memorandum reflected the awareness that support of Britain in Europe was the major goal of United States foreign policy, and that this policy did not have to be carried out in Asia. Thus, in a clearly stated memorandum, the staff of the National Security Council insisted in January 1949 that the United States should "[regard] efforts with respect to China as of lower priority than efforts in other areas where the benefits to U.S. security are more immediately commensurate with the expenditure of U.S. resources."[13] For all these reasons, the basic orientation of American policy toward China belied the general cold war perception. The United States furnished limited assistance to the Nationalists after the failure of the Marshal mission in early 1947, but refrained from overt intervention in the Chinese civil war. Although the Communist victory was clearly perceived as a gain for the Russians in the zero-sum game of the cold war, the United States in effect chose not to wage a cold war with Russia in China.

Formosa was perceived to be somewhat different from mainland China, insofar as the island was of "potential value to the United States . . . as a wartime base," as Admiral William D. Leahy noted in November 1948.[14] There was general agreement in Washington that Communist takeover of the island would be unfortunate both militarily and politically. However, no effective strategy to cope with the situation was devised. The Joint Chiefs of Staff recognized that, despite Formosa's strategic importance, "the current disparity between our military strength and our many global obligations makes it inadvisable to undertake the employment of armed force in Formosa."[15] Under the circumstances, the most the United States could do was to employ diplomatic and economic means to try to deny the island to the Communists. The State Department at one point went so far as to suggest a policy of maintaining contact "with potential native Formosan leaders with a view at some future date to being able to make use of a Formosan autonomous movement should it appear to be in the U.S. national interest to do so."[16] No specific policy, however, had been established by the end of 1949. Moreover, none of the alternatives contemplated for United States action in Formosa envisaged joint action with Great Britain—another indication that the United States was trying to cope with Asian affairs unilaterally rather than, as was the case in Europe, cooperatively with Britain.

In Korea, America's passivity was even more notable. While United States forces occupied southern Korea and administered the territory through military government, there was no idea of maintaining a permanent presence in the peninsula. When a scheme for holding a United Nations-sponsored election prior to the establishment of a unified government came to nothing (due to the opposition of the Soviet Union), and Korea had become virtually divided into two separate entities, the United States concluded, as the National Security Council put it in April 1948, that "the permanent aim of Soviet policy in Korea is to achieve eventual Soviet domination of the entire country." Under the circumstances, America faced three alternatives: "to abandon" the South Korean regime, "to guarantee the political independence and territorial integrity" of the country by force of arms if necessary, or "to establish within practicable and feasible limits conditions of support . . . as a means of facilitating the liquidation of the U.S. commitment of men and money in Korea with the minimum of bad effects." The third alternative appeared the most feasible, and plans were put into motion for the evacuation of American troops from Korea.[17]

The United States continued to be deeply involved in Japan, but this was a consequence of wartime decisions which had assigned the primary role in the occupation of that country to America. Before 1949-50, there was as yet no firm policy beyond the implementation of the broadly defined occupation objectives. Here too, it is true, cold war perceptions were affecting American attitudes. The Joint Chiefs were eager for a major shift in occupation policy so as to deny the country's use to the Soviet Union in the event of war. As they put it in a memorandum of June 1949, "[the] ability of the United States to derive full strategic advantage from the potentialities of Japan and to deny Japan's ultimate exploitation by the USSR will depend largely on the course we follow from now on with respect to Japan." The Joint Chiefs would recommend that Japan's capacity for self-defense be developed and that the United States retain rights to have bases in Japan for the indefinite future. Moreover, they considered that a peace treaty with Japan would be premature, since "the continuing Soviet policy of aggressive Communist expansion makes it essential that Japan's democracy and Western orientation first be established beyond all question, since global developments are still in such a state of flux that measures leading to the risk of loss of control of any area might seriously affect our national security."[18] Here again there was no mention of cooperative action with Britain. The United States should act unilaterally, in this view, in order to ensure its security and interests in that part of the world. The Department of State disagreed with the military and argued that "the achievement of our objectives with respect to Japan is now less likely to be thwarted by proceeding promptly to a peace treaty than by continuance of the occupation regime, provided that essential U.S. military needs in Japan are assured in the treaty or other concurrent

arrangements."[19] The debate on the desirability of an early
peace treaty with Japan was not settled at this time—an indication that there was no radical shift in American policy
toward Japan despite the cold war perceptions.

Finally, the general framework of cold war diplomacy did
not produce a specifically cold war–type policy with respect
to the countries of Southeast Asia. As Britain, France, and
the Netherlands formulated their respective approaches to
their colonies in the region, the United States more or less
stood by, without trying to integrate these countries into an
overall strategy of anticommunism. In one area where American action made some difference—Indonesia—the thrust of
United States policy was to support the local movement for
autonomy even at the risk of alienating the Netherlands.
There was obviously a conflict between supporting Asian
nationalism and appeasing the Atlantic community. As a
State Department memorandum noted in mid-1949, "[if] an
effective counterforce to communism is to be developed in
the Orient, it is essential that relations between SEA and
the Atlantic community be rationalized." But this was much
easier said than done. The United States, in danger of being
caught in the middle of the struggle of "colonial imperialism
versus militant nationalism," could only hope that Asians
would cooperate with the Western powers against "Red imperialism." Yet it was far from clear whether the Atlantic
nations were prepared to meet the demands of Asian nationalism, or whether the United States was prepared to alienate
the Atlantic community for the sake of so abstract an objective as "the development of an effective counterforce to
communism in the Far East, leading eventually to the emergence of SEA as an integral part of the free world."[20]

Thus, there was a notable gap between perception and
policy in America's cold war diplomacy in Asia. The generally shared perception of a global conflict with the Soviet
Union was applied to Asia, but it did not produce specific
policies or strategies. In contrast to American involvement in
Europe and the Middle East, it may even be said that the
years 1945–49 were a period of comparative retrenchment of
American power from Asia. Despite the view, as the State

Department's aforementioned memo on Southeast Asia put
it, that America's "predominant power and influence do not
permit us to be inconspicuous," this was in fact the situation
at this time. The United States was losing its influence and
power in China and Korea, caught between divergent forces
in Southeast Asia, and still debating its next course of action
in Japan. If this was the cold war in Asia, it was surely one
that America was losing. It would be more correct to say,
however, that the United States chose not to engage the
Soviet Union in a cold war in this region during these years.
There was a cold war perception, but no cold war.

Does it follow, then, that the United States had no overall
policy or strategy toward Asia at that time? To reach such a
conclusion would ignore the fact that during World War II
the United States had developed plans for parts of Asia and
the Pacific, and was ready, upon Japan's defeat, to implement them. It was these wartime (and therefore pre-cold war)
plans which provided guidelines for American policy in postwar Asia. It was no accident that, toward countries where no
definitive plans were made during the war, the United States
failed to act affirmatively after the war.

Put very simply, United States government and military
planners had succeeded by early 1944 in developing rough
outlines of postwar Asian policy. According to these plans,
the United States would control the Japanese islands in the
Pacific Ocean and convert some of them to bases. American
forces would be stationed in the Philippines and the Ryukyus. Japan would be occupied but not divided into zones of
occupation. Occupation forces would be multinational, but
allied participation would not "be so large as to prejudice
the dominantly American character" of the military government which would be set up under the American field commander. The occupation regime would undertake liberal
reform measures so as to reorient the Japanese people toward
democratic and peaceful pursuits of their country's welfare.
The armament and munitions industry would be forbidden,
but the Japanese would be permitted to trade with other
countries so that their economy would be reintegrated into
the multilateral world economy. Moreover, the Japanese

emperor system would not be abolished outright but would be utilized for the carrying out of reform measures. Occupation authorities would seek out liberal, cooperative Japanese with whom they would work for the country's peaceful transformation.[21]

In contrast to such a fairly specific program for postwar Japan, wartime planning for American relations with China, the Soviet Union, and Britain was rather vague. Territorially, to be sure, there was a definite goal. Japan would be deprived of all but the home islands and the Ryukyus; thus, China would regain Formosa and Manchuria. In addition, China would become one of the trustee powers in the event that some sort of trusteeship arrangement was established over Korea and possibly Indochina. These steps amounted to the idea that China was to be a "great power" after the war, but it was an extremely vague concept, and there was no concise formulation of how the United States and China might work together in postwar Asia.

Some officials, to be sure, were advocates of close cooperation with China as the key to postwar Asian policy. Stanley K. Hornbeck wrote in 1943, "The powers that can help or can hinder us most in connection with what we believe in and what we will want to do in regard to the Far East are Japan, the Soviet Union, China, and Great Britain. Query: What of those powers is capable of giving in greatest degree the kind of cooperation and assistance which we still need and desire? Answer: China."[22] Hornbeck was visualizing the formation of a firm partnership between China and the United States, but his "China" usually meant the Nationalist leadership of Chiang Kai-shek.

This view was challenged by others, notably by John P. Davies, who argued that close ties between Chiang and America would be dangerous, as they would alienate the Chinese Communists and drive them to seeking Soviet support. The result would be Russian penetration of China, thus defeating the very purpose of establishing a Sino-American entente. Davies advocated, therefore, that the United States give support to the Communists in order to prevent the growth of Soviet influence in Chinese affairs.

Hornbeck and Davies were in agreement of the desirability
of forming friendly ties with China, but their disagreement as
to Chinese domestic politics symbolized the difficulties the
United States government encountered whenever it tried to
map out a coherent strategy for postwar policy toward
China. The result was that at the war's end no workable policy had been developed in Washington. Unlike Japan, China,
in American official thinking, was left more or less alone to
work out its own destiny. There was no idea that the United
States would form an alliance with China against a third
power or would cooperate with it in managing Asian affairs
in the wake of Japan's defeat.

This was also the case with American-Russian relations. At
Teheran and Yalta, to be sure, the United States conceded
Soviet terms for ending the war. Russia would regain Sakhalin, the Kuriles, and some of the rights Japan had enjoyed
in Manchuria. The "Yalta system"—the system of postwar
Asian international relations which was embodied in the
secret agreements made at Yalta—codified Soviet preponderance in these areas, and the United States was willing to live
with the new reality. Neither then nor later, however, was
there a thought that the two countries would cooperate in
the occupation and governing of Japan or in promoting a unified China. It was foreseen that American and Russian
troops would come to contact in the Korean peninsula, and
that the United States and the Soviet Union would be two of
the trustees over Korea. But it was symbolic that American
and Russian forces ended up dividing the peninsula as soon
as they reached it after Japan's surrender. Despite much talk
of the two countries' strategic cooperation against Japan,
by the spring of 1945 all efforts at coordinating their military
action had been abandoned by the Joint Chiefs in Washington, and each went its own way in trying to bring Japan to
its knees.

The same was true of American-British relations. Wartime
American plans for postwar Asia were very vague about the
future of the colonial empires, although the State Department early came to the conclusion that the European colonies should be restored after Japan's defeat.[23] Beyond such a

passive stand, it was extremely difficult to visualize cooperative action with Great Britain in postwar Asia. Too close a
relationship with Britain would alienate China, just as too-
intimate ties with the latter would impress the former as an
anti-colonialist conspiracy.

For a time, State Department planners toyed with a
scheme for establishing a regional council in Southeast Asia.
Such a body, it was hoped, could be made to supervise colonial development so as to safeguard security and to ensure
the welfare of the native populations. A regional council, in
which the United States would participate, would "assume
responsibility for promoting economic development, while
providing equal opportunity to all countries for investment
and safeguarding native interests."[24] The scheme reflected
America's concern with maintaining a harmonious relationship with industrial countries while at the same time inte-
grating the less-developed areas more closely into the world
economic system. Nothing came of the idea, however, as
Washington and London were never able to come together on
the character and composition of the regional council.

American-British relations in Southeast Asia became less
and less cooperative toward the end of the war, and there was
even less coordination in China and Japan. As the United
States proceeded to plan more or less unilaterally for the defeat and occupation of Japan, the British complained of
America's "most uncooperative spirit," while in China they
tried desperately to regain their once-predominant economic
position, which had been taken over by Americans.[25] All in
all, the two countries went about preparing for postwar Asia
quite independent of each other, and there was no concrete
idea on either side as to establishing the kind of cooperation
they were carrying out in Europe.

It is clear, then, that the United States had developed, during the war, a framework for postwar Asian affairs which was
characterized by unilateralism, control over the Pacific islands, and close supervision of postwar Japan. It was this
framework that survived the defeat of Japan and provided
the basis for United States policy for a few years after 1945.
The American occupation and reform of Japan with little

interference from other countries, the attempt at establishing a trusteeship scheme for Korea, the minimum of involvement but absence of large-scale interference in the Chinese civil war, the lack of interest in working with Britain in Southeast Asia and elsewhere, the determination to safeguard the security of the island chain extending from the Aleutians through Hawaii, the former Japanese mandates, and the Philippines— all these were objectives that had been adopted in Washington before 1945 and became implemented after the war. It may be noted parenthetically that the recently declassified war plans of 1947–49 against the Soviet Union tend to confirm this framework, in that they all visualized the defense of the Pacific islands and Japan as the primary objective in that theater of the hypothetical war. The famous speech by Dean Acheson in January 1950, defining America's defense perimeter as excluding the Asia mainland, echoed this strategy, which was not so much a cold war as a pre–cold war strategy.

Possibly Japan was the only Asian country where these two strategies coincided, as far as the United States was concerned. Wartime planning had stressed the reform of Japan's institutions and ideas along liberal, democratic lines; this was tantamount to making Japan a Westernized (that is, politically liberal and moderately industrialized) nation—in essence the same thing as ensuring "Japan's orientation toward the Western powers," the cardinal goal of United States policy in 1949. With respect to Japan, in other words, the United States did not have to adopt a new policy in view of the developing cold war. Wartime ideas and objectives sufficed, and the close bilateral relationship between Japan and the United States provided the one continuous link between these ideas and the policies of the cold war.

Although we know much less about the foreign policies of the Soviet Union, China, and Great Britain after 1945, it may be noted that they too pursued Asian objectives that were little related to the cold war in Europe. Russia was determined to control North Korea, but this had been evident even during (and indeed, long before) the war. On the other hand, the Soviet Union was not really interested in Japanese affairs once it regained Sakhalin and the Kuriles. Nor was the

USSR very enthusiastic about the civil war in China; it continued to deal with the Nationalist regime as the government of that country. While Chinese Communists, on the other hand, did adopt the ideology of "leaning to one side" during this period, it seems plausible to argue that this was more a tactical move than a reflection of an ideological commitment; they did not want to become involved in a U.S.-Soviet confrontation in Asia which could develop into armed hostilities at the expense of Chinese interests. The Chinese Communists thus stressed the theme of self-help as the best way of unifying the country and maintaining its independence. As for Britain, its overall view of Asia as lying within America's sphere of influence, together with its unilateral initiatives in the colonial areas, had little to do with the cold war. London was no more prepared than Washington at this time to extend to this region the kind of cold war cooperation that was being implemented in Europe.

It was only at the end of 1949 that the United States began to develop a cold war strategy for Asia that corresponded with its cold war perceptions. By then the People's Republic of China had been established, and the Soviet Union had successfully exploded its first atomic devices. The situation in Europe, on the other hand, had become stabilized, and a new status quo was being consolidated.

It was not surprising, then, that the United States should have begun to reformulate its cold war strategy to take account of Asia far more seriously than before. Discussions and exchanges of ideas were carried on with great intensity within the National Security Council and between State and War Department officials. One product of their deliberations was NSC 48/2, a document entitled "The Position of the United States with Respect to China," which was approved by President Truman on December 30, 1949. This was the first comprehensive statement of United States policy toward the whole of Asia, and it was characterized by an awareness of interrelatedness among different parts of this region. Now that China had fallen to the Communists, it was clearly imperative for the United States to formulate a new Asian policy so as to bring about the "[development] of the nations and peoples of Asia on a stable and self-sustaining basis in conformity with the purposes and principles of the United Nations Charter," as the document stated. More specifically, the United States should "[support] non-Communist forces in taking the initiative in Asia," "[exert] an influence to advance its own interest," and "[initiate] action in such a manner as will appeal to the Asiatic nations as being compatible with their national interests and worthy of their support." In Korea, in particular, the United States should "continue to accord political support to the Republic of Korea, both within and without the framework of the United Nations," while in China there should be no recognition of the Communist government "until it is clearly in the United States' interest to do so."

The document, however, left open the possibility that the United States might try to approach the Peking regime to detach it from Soviet influence. America, it was stated, "should exploit . . . any rifts between the Chinese Communists and the USSR and between the Stalinists and other elements in China." Most important was the statement that "it would be inappropriate for the United States to adopt a posture more hostile or policies more harsh towards a Communist China than towards the USSR itself." In other words, the Soviet Union was the main antagonist in Asia as well as elsewhere; and, while China under the Communists would be treated as a hostile country to which economic sanctions should be applied, it should not be entirely given up as lost to the Communist camp.

NSC 48/2 also covered the colonial areas, pointing out the need to "satisfy the fundamental demands of the nationalist movement while at the same time minimizing the strain on the colonial powers who are our Western allies." For this reason it was important to induce the members of the British Commonwealth "to play a more active role in collaboration with the United States in Asia." French Indochina seemed particularly vulnerable to Communist attacks, and from this time on, the Joint Chiefs of Staff grew increasingly concerned over the situation on that peninsula. As they reported in April 1950, "In case of global war with the USSR, United

States forces in Japan and in the Western Pacific now are sufficient to withstand initial enemy attacks." However, the
United States would have to strengthen its position in Japan
and Okinawa if Indochina fell to the Communists. Such a
situation "would have serious consequences throughout
Southeast and southern Asia and Japan."[26]

In view of the new assertiveness of American policy in
Asia, it would seem that the Acheson speech of January 12,
1950—which practically wrote off Korea, Formosa, Southeast Asia and the rest of Asia as indefensible—was not in accordance with the spirit of NSC 48/2 in that it echoed an
earlier attitude rather than the evolving cold war strategy for
the whole of Asia. Be that as it may, there is little doubt that
the United States now began framing its approach to the
Asia-Pacific region along the lines of the new policy. The famous NSC 68, adopted by the National Security Council in
April 1950, was evidence that the cold war strategy now embraced the whole world, not just Europe and the Middle East.
That document was a call to action on the part of all countries interested in resisting the Soviet challenge. Whereas earlier priority had explicitly been assigned to Western Europe,
now the need was for a worldwide system of non-Communist
nations so as to "organize and enlist the energies and resources of the free world in a positive program for peace
which will frustrate the Kremlin in its design for world domination." Given such a perspective, America's decision to re-
act instantaneously to the North Korean invasion of South
Korea two months later was the only plausible response. Not
only was the attack perceived as part of the global cold war,
but it was the first open confrontation in Asia after the adoption of the new assertive policy. Thus Asia became a theater
of the cold war.

At the same time, it should be noted, America's cold war
diplomacy had sought to employ "all means short of war" to
contain Soviet communism, as numerous policy papers
pointed out. While war could not be ruled out, the emphasis
had been to prevent it through such methods as atomic deter-
rence, economic recovery of Western Europe, and suppression of subversive activities. In that sense, the cold war had

been a device to restrain the Soviet Union without actually fighting that country. The Korean War was thus as much a failure of cold war diplomacy as an Asian phase of it. From June 1950 onward, the cold war in Asia came to mean America's military involvement, not simply a nonmilitary response to the Soviet challenge. It was war, no longer a cold war. Moreover, even if the outbreak of the Korean War and America's initial intervention were to be considered aspects of the cold war, the story entered a new phase after October 1950, when China intervened in the conflict by force. Gradually China came to replace the Soviet Union as the principal target of American strategy in Asia. This too was an unforeseen development, insofar as the cold war had originated as a confrontation between America and Russia; henceforth the former's growing involvement in Asia freed the latter to pursue its interests and ambitions elsewhere.

The U.S.–Chinese confrontation in Korea was at first a subtheme of the cold war, but steadily it began to acquire a momentum of its own. While the original cold war had culminated in the summit conference of 1955, after which the two principal antagonists entered a period of peaceful coexistence, the United States and China intensified their conflict in Asia. In that process the cold war became something else: From the American standpoint, it was a struggle to prevent Chinese domination of the whole of Asia, whereas for the People's Republic of China it came to be seen as a conflict between American imperialism and Chinese nationalism. The Bandung Conference of 1955 was, in a sense, China's answer to the developing U.S.–Soviet understanding on the basis of the global status quo. As Mao Tse-tung said in 1958, there were three forces in the world: imperialism, nationalism, and communism. The latter two were potential allies against the first, but China's emphasis was clearly on encouraging the nationalism of small countries against big-power imperialism.

In time China's opposition to *ta-kuo chu-i* (big-powerism) came to involve resistance not only to America but also to Russia. It was but a step from here to the new doctrine of the "intermediate zone," which included not only Afro-Asian and Latin American countries but also all industrial countries except for the United States and the Soviet Union. Eventually, in the late 1960s, a point was reached in U.S.-Chinese relations which necessitated a fundamental reorientation. China had to cope with "socialist imperialism" even by resorting to rapprochement with imperialist America, while the United States reversed its containment policy toward China in order to take advantage of the Sino-Soviet rift and to put an end to a long period of military involvement in Asia.

Obviously, the story of American-Asian relations after the outbreak of the Korean War is a complex one, and no simplistic conceptual scheme suffices to deal with this phenomenon. At the very least, it must be recognized that the cold war in Asia went through several distinctive stages. The cold war in the sense of American-Russian confrontation was of very short duration in Asia, whereas in the sense of American-Chinese confrontation it had many different characteristics. It pitted China—an Asian, underdeveloped, Communist state espousing the cause of other underdeveloped countries— against the United States, the most powerful and richest country in the world. The main theater of this conflict was Asia, which had had no tradition of international relations comparable to that of Europe, where spheres of influence, balances of power, and the like had fairly clear meanings. The United States was far more willing to act unilaterally in Asia, and it was far less restrained in the use of force in this region than in Europe. The European countries were usually not involved in the U.S.-Chinese struggle in Asia, and in time the United States became isolated in its dealings with the People's Republic of China. By undertaking rapprochement with China, America was in effect harking back to the views of John P. Davies, who during World War II had suggested that bilateral friendship was the key to peace in Asia. In the 1970s, however, Asia was not quite what it had been thirty years earlier. Even if a solid framework of U.S.-Chinese cooperation were to develop, this alone would not be sufficient to ensure peace and stability. The roles of Russia, Japan, the two Koreas, and other countries would be crucial. All in all, the future would be filled with uncertainties.

America has traditionally been an Asian power. This

reflects not only its geographical location between Europe and Asia, but also its position between the advanced industrial countries of Europe and the less-developed areas of the globe. Generation after generation, Americans have tried to cope with these two worlds in some systematic fashion. One of their key strategies has been to bridge the gap between advanced and underdeveloped countries through technology, enterprise, and democratic ideals. This endeavor would have continued after 1945 but for the intrusion of the cold war, which compelled the adoption of a rigid policy after 1950. That long interlude came to an end in the early 1970s, but simultaneously there arose serious problems of natural resources, exchange instability, and environmental disequilibria. American-Asian relations in the future are likely to be a drama played out in the context of economic and energy issues superimposed on the old problems of security and peace.

It is evident that a fresh look at post–World War II American-Asian relations is long overdue. Even this brief essay, focusing on the 1945–50 period, has raised more questions than it has answered. At least it indicates that we need more monographs on America-Asian relations which transcend the usual clichés and textbook generalizations. Standard generalizations about the cold war ought to be reformulated, if not discarded, and rigorous analysis should be made of available documents in various languages. Speculation about the future should not be a mere compendium of contemporary issues, as is so often the case, but should ask new, even disturbing questions about the role of America in Asia and about the role of Asia in American policy, both political and economic. It is to be hoped that each of the following essays will contribute to broadening the horizon of understanding and challenge other students of American-Asian relations to produce similar works. Only through such a collective effort of specialists dealing in different languages will it ever be possible to liberate this field of inquiry from narrowly parochial outlooks and simpleminded dogmas.

Part 1
American-Chinese Relations

2

NEW PERSPECTIVES ON
SINO-AMERICAN RELATIONS
Ishwer C. Ohja
Professor of Political Science, Boston University

It is now common practice to state that until 1972 Sino-American relations had been frozen for twenty-three years. Commentators are fond of citing Sino-American rapprochement as being a great departure from the preceding period, a period they view as having been characterized by the intransigent attitudes of consecutive American administrations which refused to reevaluate their positions. The great departure of 1972 is seen as being in contrast to more than two decades of fixed or unchanging attitudes, beliefs, and policies. China's policy toward the United States is seen in similar terms; the year 1972 represented a great departure from the previous Chinese position, which, dictated by ideological commitments, had prevented a pragmatic consideration of strategic, political, or economic issues in foreign affairs.

While a great change has undoubtedly come about in America's relations with the People's Republic of China (PRC), an in-depth analysis will show that this transformation was not sudden. Careful scrutiny reveals that the attitude of the United States toward China was marked by slow and gradual change over the years, a change that did, in fact,

move into high gear as early as 1966. Our "new" China policy is not merely the result of the efforts of a clever and
perceptive presidential assistant, but is, rather, the natural
outcome of a fundamental and ongoing reevaluation of attitudes toward communism in particular and the international
system in general.

On China's part, similarly, the newest phase in relations
with the United States must be looked at, not as a radical
departure from her past, but rather as the logical policy to be
adopted in the context of her national revolutionary process
and growing differences with the Soviet Union. Seen in this
light, Sino-American rapprochement was predictable, for it
marks the gradual transformation which both countries have
undergone in their roles in the international system.

In a general sense, the basic objectives of both American
and Chinese foreign policies were formulated in terms of
their universalized conception of the international system.
For the Americans, abstract hatred of communism became
the underlying and motivating factor in determination of foreign policy priorities. This factor was underscored by the
view that American involvement in foreign affairs was justified only when some morally perverse enemy could be located. These tendencies were concretized in the form of considering the Soviet Union as the principal enemy, thereby
preventing the recognition of China as an independent actor
in the international system.

The transformation of American foreign policy toward
China partly resulted from a series of direct or indirect Sino-
American confrontations over Korea, Taiwan, and Vietnam.
Such confrontations forced American policymakers to move
to a more strategic view of the international system—one
which necessitated paying attention to regional political realities, independent of projected Soviet reactions and policies.

It is in this context that American initiatives toward rapprochement with China since 1969 should be considered, as
part and parcel of the changing conception of the nature of
the international system. This change facilitated the capacity
on the part of American policymakers to apply diplomatic
rather than military solutions of international conflicts. With

help from the realms of scholarship, Americans were also able to distinguish Soviet from Chinese communism, a development that began to have a marked impact on American foreign policy once it became operative common sense among policymakers.

Similarly, on the Chinese side, the transformation from the universalized conception of China's revolutionary model to growing skepticism about that model's international applicability altered China's orientation to the world order. Whereas China's political leaders in the first years of the PRC entertained a commitment to alliances based on the internationalization of the revolution, they have come to consider the uniqueness of their revolutionary experiment as being more significant. The problems of continuing the revolution in China and securing territorial boundaries have added a greater significance to the national characteristics of its revolutionary model; hence the latter has become of less importance in providing the guiding principles for China's foreign policy. With this trend has come increasing emphasis on regional, inter-regional and state-to-state relations, for strategic reasons. This transformation may be regarded, not as a simple de-ideologization of China's foreign policy, but rather as the gradual emergence of a true foreign policy—i.e., one based on a conception of China's position in the international system and informed by a practical ideology appropriate to that conception, rather than by a projection of the ideology of generating domestic revolutions. This transformation, in conjunction with China's consistent willingness to negotiate international conflicts in diplomatic settings, renders the recent Sino-American rapprochement as a crystallization in one setting of a much more general and long-term trend.

In tracing the history of Sino-American relations, one can say that until 1945 America had no China policy at all. Under the Roosevelt administration, the United States was interested not so much in aiding the Nationalists as in controlling the Japanese. And even then, while Soviet military aid was directed at the Nationalists and totally denied to the Communists, Americans were more interested in restraining Japan through international agreements or pronouncements such as

the Stimson Doctrine or the London Naval Agreement of
1935. In the early 1940s, the United States maintained that
the assistance provided the Nationalists was for fighting
Japan, and that a part of this aid must, therefore, go to Communist forces. The United States even gave to the Communists the status of tacit ally by stationing a liaison mission in
Yenan. In contrast, the Soviets never gave the Chinese Communists any such recognition.

It is, therefore, incorrect to assume that the United States
and the Chinese Communists have a history of serious points
of contention. Generally, between 1936 and 1945 the
Chinese Communists enjoyed a very favorable and even sym-
pathetic public opinion and press in the United States. While
this reaction was partly due to the effort of journalists and
reporters such as Edgar Snow, it was also the result of a growing number of discerning Americans' coming into contact
with the Nationalists and realizing how corrupt and weak
that government was. It was the disenchantment with the
Nationalists and the growing belief that, pragmatically, it
would be impossible for them to really unite and modernize
China which were responsible for turning the tide toward the
only other model—the Communists.

Until 1946, American foreign policy did not suffer from
the paralysis that ideology can inflict. Communism was not
the guiding factor of American foreign policy in the 1920s,
1930s, or early 1940s. Whatever foreign policy initiatives the
United States undertook were concerned with the rising
power of Germany and, particularly, Japan; yet even this
concern had not crystallized into a national obsession. It was
thus very hard for Roosevelt to enter World War II. If Japan
had not attacked its soil, the United States would have found
it extremely difficult to declare war.

For their part, Chinese Communist leaders matured with
the ideology of the Seventh Comintern Congress. This ideology insisted that the danger from fascism was greater than
that from democratic capitalistic countries, and that the
danger from the militaristic adventurism of Japan was far
more potent than the warlordism of the Nationalists. It was
on the basis of this type of analysis that the Communists

entered a united front with the Nationalists after 1937 and even tried to maintain a managed conflict situation with them until 1946.

But by the end of World War II, the ideology of the Seventh Comintern Congress was no longer applicable; the danger from fascism had ceased, while the danger from the United States had not yet become apparent. The Soviets were genuinely surprised at the extent of the buffer areas they acquired in both Europe and Asia. Rather than turning their attention to the Chinese civil war, they adopted a foreign policy whose main aim was security through consolidation of the buffer states. Fearing that a new conflict emerging in China might somehow cause them to lose their newly acquired territories, the Soviets denuded Manchuria, denied assistance to the Chinese Communists, and advised them to seek a coalition government with the Nationalists. In 1945, the Soviets made it clear that they accepted the permanency of the Nationalists when they negotiated the Sino-Soviet Treaty of 1945 with the representatives of Chiang Kai-shek.

The Chinese Communists found themselves in the same position that the Vietnamese would later find themselves in 1954, 1961, and 1973. The pressure to compromise in order to keep what they had achieved and avoid upsetting the international system was clear in both cases. In 1946 the Chinese Communists accepted American guarantees of safety and went to Chungking to negotiate the possibility of a coalition government with the Nationalists. If the Chinese Communists resented the pressure to compromise, that resentment was aimed more at the Soviets than at the Americans. The Soviets had made it clear that they had no faith in the Communists' ability to attain power over any significant portion of the Chinese people or territory in the foreseeable future.

If the Soviets were surprised at the extent of their buffer areas, so were the Americans, who had naively assumed that after the war was over the international system would be composed only of states that could no longer pose a serious threat through a preponderance of power. The year 1945 was supposed to spell the end of an international system based on

Bismarckian principles. But after the war America, as the sole nuclear power, did have a preponderance of power, at least in a symbolic sense. The American military-industrial complex had arisen because America was the sole supplier of arms and military assistance to the rest of the world. A powerful new interest group was in the process of consolidating itself; survival of this interest group depended upon maintaining a preponderance of power, assuming that preserving that dominance was the only means of ensuring peace, portraying the Soviet Union's cautious and consolidatory policy of establishing buffer areas as one of rampant aggression and expansion, and reactivating the latent abstract hatred of communism into a national obsession.

This national obsession led United States foreign policy to a strategy of resistance to communism, any brand of communism, and to alliance with all anti-Communists—even weak, inefficient Fascist regimes and antimodernizing elites all over the globe. It was not that such antidemocratic regimes were America's first choice for allies, but that they became the only choice as the hysteria over communism foreclosed the options of American foreign policymakers to take any kind of risk for social change through conflict, particularly violent conflict. Maintenance of peace, therefore, became an end in itself and not a means for change.

In the light of these developments, any eyewitness observers who maintained a discriminatory posture based on the concrete reality of Chinese communism and who did not maintain an obsessive hatred of communism had to be silenced. Thus men who, like General Joseph Stilwell, considered the Chinese Communists more militarily efficient than the Nationalists or who, like Owen Lattimore and John Service, considered the Chinese Communists socially progressive could not be tolerated in the McCarthy era. Senator Joseph McCarthy was not really hunting for Communist sympathizers or agents. His efforts were, rather, aimed at—and succeeded in—stamping out all distinction among various Communist regimes and types of communism. He managed to institute as a guide to action, for over a generation, a blind, obsessive hatred toward the abstract concept of communism.

By 1946, the idea that communism was inherently expansive and aggressive had emerged and was being propagated by a new interest group that had allies in both business and the military. Four successive cases were used to justify the crystallization of this idea. These cases were Czechoslovakia, Greece, Vietnam, and Korea, where American analysts failed even to consider either the desire to consolidate buffer areas or the possibility of a genuine nationalist movement. American literature of the late 1940s and the 1950s was obsessed with the idea of invoking an international quarantine against communism or anything that remotely looked like communism.

Thus, the period from 1945 to 1948 was a time of transition. American foreign policy during this period shifted from antiimperialism to tolerance of neocolonialism and imperialism as being lesser evils than communism. During this period, the United States became so determined to contain the Soviet Union that it was to formulate all its foreign policy for the next two decades only in terms of that goal. In a very real sense, American foreign policy from 1948 to the mid-1960s was a Soviet policy and nothing else. Whereas in the pre-1945 period America's China policy was really a Japan policy, after 1945 America's China policy became a Soviet policy. There was no Chinese or Asian policy at all. Furthermore, anyone trying to initiate or develop a China policy was quickly silenced.

In view of this background, it is easy to understand the rise in the influence of the so-called China lobby in the United States. The success of the China lobby was due, not to the efficiency or virtues of the Nationalists, but rather to the American environment in the late 1940s. Conditions were ripe for any government that claimed to share the abstract and indiscriminate hatred of communism which Americans were rapidly developing. Support for the Nationalists was thus as irrational as evolving American foreign policy. Vague and overwhelming fears of uncertainty caused more and more Americans to adopt and hold on to causes that were doomed. This was most apparent in the case of the United States' support of the French in Vietnam and of the

Chinese Nationalists, first on the mainland and later in Taiwan.

Since China was considered an extension of Soviet communism and an instrument of Soviet foreign policy, the Korean War was fought not against China or even North Korea, but rather as a test case against the Soviet Union. The stalemate that ensued was to have a profound effect on America's attitude, not only toward China but toward the entire international system. The desire to avenge Korea became a very strong motivation in American foreign policy. More and more popular and widespread became the viewpoint that America must have a preponderance of power, not only in relation to the Soviet Union but in the entire world. It was argued that the United States should have the capacity to fight two-and-a-half wars simultaneously, should maintain strategic and nuclear superiority over the Soviet Union, should maintain unquestioned superiority over all oceans, and should do everything possible to stop others, including allies, from becoming nuclear powers.

It was while pursuing these goals in the 1950s that the American defense establishment was expanded, the military-industrial complex crystallized, and American intervention, either covert or overt, in the domestic affairs of every nation became commonplace. While Americans aspired to become the "policemen" of the world, the role their foreign policy actually assumed was quite estranged from law enforcement. Whereas a policeman strives to maintain law and order, the role of American foreign policy in the 1950s was to maintain pro-American governments in power by whatever means possible. In fact, most of these means would not have borne the scrutiny of any kind of natural or international law.

Even during the Kennedy administration, the shadow of Korea loomed large. It was for this reason that the airlift to Berlin and the Soviet backdown during the Cuban missile crisis became so important. Once he came out ahead in his "eyeball to eyeball" confrontation with the Soviets, Kennedy was praised for having "avenged Korea."

At the same time, Kennedy's Cuba policy demonstrated the same inability to discriminate among Communist countries

as had previously been shown toward China. Given this lack
of discrimination, it is understandable why Kennedy was to
escalate American involvement in Vietnam.

Concomitantly, Americans began to prepare, at first psy-
chologically and then technologically, for a modern version
of the Hundred Years' War. A substantial number of writings
were published dealing with guerrillas and how to fight them.
The general theme of these works seemed to have been an
effort to build in Americans a psychological and political
determination to meet the challenge of protracted war by
initiating and fighting a protracted war themselves. The policy of the 1960s was thus to fight a protracted war by waging
protracted war. Even in this decision, the lesson of Korea
played a large part. It was taken for granted that, had Americans continued their effort in Korea, they would have won.
Policymakers reasoned that the stalemate occurred, not so
much because of a lack of resources or ability, but because of
a lack of psychological preparation and the will to fight a
protracted war.

It took twenty years of involvement in Vietnam to get
American policymakers to reevaluate their long-held political
beliefs. It was only when the Vietnam War divided the nation, when the psychological will to wage protracted wars
was found wanting, and when the resources for simultaneously maintaining strategic and nuclear superiority were no
longer available that American foreign policy finally came to *Nixon*
terms with its obsession with indiscriminate, abstract anticommunism.

It is, therefore, not a matter of coincidence that the policy
of resolving conflicts by diplomacy rather than by military
means was simultaneously applied by the United States to
both Vietnam and China. By the same token, it is interesting
to observe that Sino-American negotiations have begun after
each of the major conflicts or tests of will between the two—
after Korea, when Sino-American talks started on a regular
basis; after the Taiwan Straits crisis of 1958, when talks were
resumed after a hiatus; and in 1969, when the military aspects of the Vietnam conflict had been substantially deescalated. In retrospect, it is clear that the Chinese correctly

estimated in 1969 that the defensive counterescalation strategy of the North Vietnamese and the NFL had successfully
stymied the Americans, forcing them to give up the goal of
achieving a political solution through military means. By
their willingness to go to the conference table when it seemed
a viable alternative, the Chinese have shown themselves to be
remarkably flexible over the last quarter of a century.

While the national obsession with communism was in full
bloom, Taiwan was used as an excuse and a rationale for
maintaining the United States' posture of not having any
serious detente with China. From 1954 to 1969 no American
administration seriously believed in the potential or actual
capability of the Nationalists in Taiwan to reconquer the
Chinese mainland and reestablish themselves as its leaders.
Until 1957, the Eisenhower administration contented itself
with the specious hope that the Chinese Communists might
not have the ability to lead a peasant-modernizing revolution
and might, therefore, collapse as a result of their own ineffi-
ciency; but even this hope could not be maintained after
1957. Although Eisenhower did support the Nationalists in
their military venture against the offshore islands of Quemoy
and Matsu in 1958, his motive was to keep the morale of the
Nationalists high enough to avoid a total collapse of the rem-
nants of the Nationalist forces in Taiwan. For their part, the
Chinese were not out to actually take the islands by force,
but rather to test the extent of the Sino-Soviet alliance. The
lesson they learned—that they could not count on the Soviets
in a conflict with the United States—was not to be forgotten.

While negotiations between China and the United States
continued on a pro forma basis between 1955 and 1969, the
assumptions behind these negotiations made it impossible for
any real breakthrough to occur. Americans assumed, under
Eisenhower, that China was not an independent actor in the
international system. United States policymakers held a
rigidly bipolar view of the world. As long as coexistence was
not possible with the Soviet Union, negotiations toward a
rapprochement with China were considered an exercise in
futility. Both sides, however, used Taiwan to account for the
stalemate.

From the Chinese point of view, Taiwan did pose a serious problem. The issue was not so much a question of territory as one of legitimacy in the international system. The Chinese Communists had in the past given up territory when they accepted the existence of the Mongolian People's Republic in 1950 and formalized a boundary settlement with that state in 1962. Thus, if Taiwan had meant simply giving up territory, the Chinese might have considered some formula of diplomatic accommodation with the United States. But as long as the Nationalists technically represented China in the United Nations, including the Security Council, the People's Republic saw itself relegated to the position of a rebel, de facto government. In its eyes, the United States was the sole protector and perpetrator of the legitimacy of the Nationalists as the government of China.

During the 1950s, the Chinese, therefore, resisted attempts by the United States to transform their relationship with Taiwan from a domestic conflict to an international one. In so doing, the United States was trying to create a two-China policy that would have improved the PRC's position of legitimacy but which would not have totally restored it. The United States maintained that China must not only renounce the use of force in the solution of international conflicts but also must apply the same principle to the question of Taiwan. This, of course, would have amounted to accepting the legitimacy of the Nationalists on Taiwan as an independent international entity.

Another so-called barrier to normalization of Sino-American relations was the other rationalization used to keep China out of the U.N.; i.e., the resolution of October 1950 that branded China an aggressor against the United Nations. It was argued that China, being the only state that had fought the U.N., would never qualify for its membership because it could not be trusted to implement the provisions of the charter. (The Chinese view consistently has been that United Nations participation in Korea was really intervention by the United States in disguise, and that the resolution to send forces was illegal to begin with.)

Despite what some analysts and scholars have maintained

for years, in retrospect these debates have importance only as they serve to demonstrate the lack of serious obstacles to a possible rapprochement between China and the United States. Such a rapprochement could have occurred as soon as China was recognized as an independent actor in the international system. Being obsessed with an abstract concept of anticommunism, the United States did not recognize China as such until the deep-seated differences between the natures of the Chinese and Russian revolutions became apparent.

By the last months of the Kennedy administration, it was no longer possible to deny the existence of a serious Sino-Soviet rift. The acceptance of this fact radically changed the nature of the international system. In the realm of Sino-American relations, the position of China as an independent actor began to emerge. A new dialogue based on new assumptions was considered a distinct possibility after Kennedy's reelection to a second term. But the second term never materialized. The Kennedy years were short; and China was too low a priority, what with the mythology of the missile gap weighing heavily on American policymakers' minds.

China policy remained constant in the United States, not because there were assumptions which made it constant, but because even as the assumptions changed, inattention to China policy did not. During the Eisenhower, Kennedy, and Johnson administrations, one primary factor influenced America's China policy: there was no domestic or international pressure to change it and, therefore, to put it in the center of executive attention.

In spite of all the emotional commitment to China which caused Americans to be "shocked" at its loss, China never has been a serious issue in any domestic election at any level in the United States. Opinion poll after opinion poll has confirmed this attitude, yet Eisenhower, Kennedy, and Johnson consistently overestimated the influence of the China lobby on American opinion and thus postponed giving China policy serious attention. It was this incorrect estimation of the force of public opinion which caused President Kennedy to decide to delay reappraisal of the United States' China policy until his second term in order to avoid making it a serious election issue. That public opinion was more in favor of change than opposed to it, and that the American leadership for the past twenty years would have enjoyed a greater freedom for changing China policy than it chose to exercise were proven with the elections of 1972. It was not then public opinion, but an ideologically based foreign policy guided by an abstract and indiscriminate hatred of communism, which was significantly responsible for American inaction.

This lack of any movement in Sino-American relations was also reflected in and reinforced by the nature of academic studies. Before 1949, a number of attempts were made to understand and explain the nature of the Chinese revolution. The most notable of these were Edgar Snow's *Red Star over China* and Jack Belden's *China Shakes the World*. There were also partial efforts made by diplomatic personnel to explain the nature of the Chinese revolution as agrarian socialism in the American White Paper issued in 1949. It is unfortunate that no major attempt was made to put the Chinese revolution in the perspective of a comparative history of China and Russia. No methodological or clear-cut distinctions were made in terms of the modification of the Leninist leadership principle, the nature of political action, or the political theories of Maoism versus Leninism. Caught in the McCarthy era, it became difficult for scholars, let alone laymen, to grasp clearly the nature of the differences between these two revolutions. They were unable, therefore, either to conclude that there was no inevitability about the PRC's being a dependent or client state of the Soviet Union or to predict the possibility of a Sino-Soviet dispute. It was only in the 1960s, after the publication of a book by Donald Zagoria documenting the details of the Sino-Soviet dispute, that serious studies on the nature of the Chinese system started to emerge. Yet even Zagoria's type of analysis disproportionately weighted the role of ideology in the dispute, giving too little significance to the divergences in practical ideology which have evolved.

A new scholarship on China started to emerge in the mid-1960s when Franz Schurmann published his book, *Ideology and Organization in Communist China*, which clearly emphasized the role of practical ideology and explained how crucial

differences developed between the Chinese and Russian revolutions. Further elaboration was facilitated by such works as
Richard Solomon's *Mao's Revolution and the Chinese Political Culture* and Ezra Vogel's detailed study of the practice
of the Chinese revolution, *Canton under Communism*. Studies of the historical foundations of the Chinese revolution
were aided to a considerable extent by Mark Selden's account
of how Mao fashioned his practical ideology, *The Yenan Way
in Revolutionary China*, and John Rue's *Mao Tse-tung in
Opposition*. These studies portrayed the Chinese revolution
neither as simple agrarian socialism nor as a carbon copy of
Stalinism; they explained the efforts made by the Chinese to
keep their leadership principle from lapsing into bureaucrat-
ism or bureaucratization.

The unique contribution of the leaders of the Chinese
revolution has been their success in developing a theory of
political action which on the one hand breaks the isolation
and passivity of the peasantry and on the other hand tries to
fashion a new way of exercising authority. Mao developed a
theory of political action among the peasantry in the Kiangsi
Soviet period through emotional mobilization of the historic
resentment and bitterness of the peasantry. He allowed peasants to make mistakes in the interests of participation, and
initiated nation-building in China for the first time in its long
history of cultural homogeneity and centralized state power.
Mao's theory of political action regarding intellectuals was
fashioned during the Yenan period, when he tried to forge
links between the training and skills of the intellectuals and
the problems that the masses faced. Through his theory of
political action, Mao tried to make education and skills func-
tional and to harness them to the efforts of nation-building.
However, the unexpected Communist victory in 1949 and
the establishment of the People's Republic of China left Mao
without a theory of political action in the sphere of political
economy.

It is often asserted that Mao consistently looked back to
the Yenan period for solutions to current problems, and that
he suffered from a "Yenan syndrome." But the history of
China from 1950 to 1958 shows realization on the part of

Mao that the theory of action in the sphere of political economy, as developed in Yenan to meet the needs of a preindustrial society engaged in guerrilla warfare, was not applicable to other areas and other times in China. If Mao looked back to Kiangsi and Yenan, it was only in regard to the successfully proven theory of political action for mobilization of the peasantry and to the leadership principle that has linked the intellectuals and the masses. For a theory of political economy, Mao went to the Soviet Union, and subsequently outdid the principles of Soviet economic planning in the first Five-Year Plan of China. It was only during the course of this experiment that Mao came to realize more and more that his theories of political action regarding the peasantry and intellectuals could not be superimposed on the Russian model of economic development; if the two were superimposed, the result would be not an integration but an erosion of Maoist theories of political action.

Faced with the threat of such an erosion, Mao tried to develop his own theory of political economy during the Great Leap Forward—which, if successful, would have created a totally Chinese model of political and economic modernization and nation-building. But the Great Leap Forward was certainly not an unqualified success; in many ways it was a disaster. Thereafter, Mao came to the conclusion that the failure of a political economy based on the simultaneous development of agricultural and industrial sectors was, not a failure of his innovative vision, but rather one of proper preparation and application of his theories of political action by the peasantry and the intellectuals.

During the 1960s, China continued its search for a theory of political economy which would be in harmony with its theories of political action. The Socialist Education Campaign and the Cultural Revolution were two major attempts at applying Maoist theories of political action in their purest form in preparation for at least a controlled Great Leap Forward during the late 1960s.

In choosing a cadre type of leadership and emphasizing the development of a political community rather than economic growth, China diverged so severely from the Soviet model that it started to pose a grave threat as an alternative model to other Communist, and possibly non-Communist, states. With such fundamental divergences in both the style and the content of the two revolutions, any possibility of China becoming a client state of the Soviet Union should never have been entertained; yet it was only in the 1960s that the realization slowly emerged. As a result of the overt Sino-Soviet dispute and polemics, it was no longer possible to deny to China the status of an independent actor in the international system.

As more analytical studies became available in the fields of comparative politics, sociology, and history concerning the various Communist societies, it became clear that not all revolutionary societies were monolithic, or imitations of each other. A revolution can neither be exported nor successfully implanted over a long period of time; in the cases of both China and Vietnam, it took a long time to understand this fact. But as such understanding became a conscious factor in decision making, foreign policies could no longer be based on an indiscriminate hatred of communism.

The Chinese came very early to the conclusion that a repetition of their revolutionary model would be an extremely difficult venture for other peasant/agrarian societies. The Chinese revolution has no parallel in history; it is unique because it is the first modernizing revolution essentially consummated by peasants. While the Soviets essentially followed a strategy of crushing or disregarding peasant attitudes, the Chinese revolution has made persistent and significant efforts to change peasants through ideological remolding. In this essential sense, the Chinese revolution has been an enormous educational venture, the purpose of which has been to persuade the peasant to eliminate himself by consent. What the Chinese have not been able to totally avoid is the continuous resurgence of elite and bureaucratic attitudes among the intelligentsia and the bureaucracy.

The Chinese revolutionary leadership is cognizant of the enormous difficulties in executing a peasant-modernizing revolution, and it has shown sufficient apprehension about the possibility of an arrested revolution if an intellectual/

bureaucratic elite should take over its direction. It has, therefore, alternated between a strategy of revolutionary mobilization and one of organizational consolidation, reflecting both
concerns. While Communist leaders have tried to undermine
the formation of a bureaucratic elite by applying strategies of
periodic revolutionary mobilization politics, they understand
that a modernizing revolution needs both a leadership principle and an organizational structure.

It is remarkable how few organizational changes have occurred in China since 1958. It is equally remarkable how few
leaders have been consistently able to handle the needs of
both mobilization and authority. (This was one of the principal reasons for the fall of Liu Shao-chi.) The Chinese insistence on an indefinite continuation of this balance between
authority and revolution is sufficient indication of their
awareness that a peasant-modernizing revolution can least
afford bureaucratization of the party, and that any premature bureaucratization would arrest the modernizing revolution for an indeterminate length of time.

A quarter-century of struggle and experience has made the
Chinese leadership more sober and realistic about the possibility of mushrooming peasant revolutions around the globe.
The assertions that the leaders made between 1947 and 1949
about the universality of their model are still being made, but
with less and less frequency and probably with less and less
confidence. Vietnam was a watershed in the history of twen-
tieth-century revolutions, yet no more Vietnams are in sight.
Political and social theory and practice have yet to create a
model for the next modernizing peasant revolution. It is
difficult to say whether the Chinese are totally conscious of
the diminishing options and possibilities, but it is safe to
assert that they do not find much encouragement in the
various attempts at pseudorevolutions going on in isolated
pockets of the world.

As China has deescalated the internationalization of
the revolution, it has become progressively easier for the
United States to deescalate the internationalization of the
counterrevolution. Alliance systems of the 1950s, formulated
on the basis of internationalization of the revolution and

counterrevolution, are starting to fall apart as this deescalation gradually occurs in the post-Vietnam period. The common term for such a state of affairs in the international system is *polycentrism*. But polycentrism generally emphasizes the existence of many poles of national power, while the deescalation or internationalization of revolution and counterrevolution emphasizes the restructuring of reality regarding the international system. Foreign policies in such an international system are not necessarily ideological in character, simply because ideology no longer is the single or most crucial variable in determining a foreign policy and because restructured reality more closely resembles a nationalist ideology than an abstract, internationalized conception of communism or capitalism, democracy or totalitarianism. These changes have also helped to bring about a rapid rapprochement in Sino-American relations.

The Chinese have never denied the element of nationalism in their foreign policy; in fact, they announced the nationalistic content of their foreign policy in clear, unmistakable terms in 1954 through their Five Principles of Peaceful Coexistence. These principles were formulated neither for propaganda purposes nor for the purpose of creating an international united front of "have nots" against "haves"; rather, they clearly and precisely defined the parameters of the nationalistic elements in Chinese foreign policy. The Chinese set three basic nationalistic goals: first, that China, having definitely shifted from culturism to territorial nationalism, would make every effort to transform its frontiers into boundaries; second, that China would maintain a traditional view of sovereignty; and third, that China would demand respect and equality from every nation in the world.

By articulating these five principles, China sent a clear message to the world that it would not tolerate an international system that treated China as a less-than-sovereign state. Therefore it seems almost tragic that countries such as the Soviet Union and the United States, which for the past century had been used to treating China as a less-than-sovereign state, could not correctly gauge the nationalistic sentiment behind the Five Principles of Peaceful Coexistence. Even if these nations could have read the message correctly, histori-cal and psychological barriers made it impossible for them to treat China as an equal until such time as the Chinese could "prove themselves," as the Japanese had, by means of the crudest possible indicators of national power. Even countries that had suffered more than China in the era of imperialism, even to the total eclipse of their sovereignty, could not understand the enormous sensitivity of the Chinese on this issue. Therein lay the seeds of the Sino-Indian conflict, the escalation of the Vietnam War, the atomization of Asia, and the disintegration of the Asian international system during the Bandung era in the early 1960s.

It was this nationalistic content in Chinese foreign policy which created and which still sustains the Sino-Soviet dis-pute. If nationalism is to be defined as the desire to discover and implement a specific strategy of change in order to build a national society, then the divergence in the natures of the Chinese and Soviet revolutions has made the Sino-Soviet con-flict as nationalistic as it is ideological. Yet even the Soviets have failed to comprehend this situation. The rift has been exacerbated by the Soviets' underestimating the need of China to transform its frontiers into boundaries through re-negotiation of nineteenth-century treaties and agreements. It is not simply territorial gains that the Chinese seek, nor ex-clusively treatment as an equal, although that is a large part of it. In their struggle to build a nation, the Chinese are ex-tremely concerned with the need to integrate human and material resources from the frontier areas into the national society. This very important factor has been overlooked by the Soviets.

The dispute may be considered on another level. Having had some measure of success in the process of nation-building, the Chinese have managed to change the nature of the distribution of power in the Asian international system during the last two decades. Peking represents serious compe-tition to Moscow in peripheral areas and is striving to com-pete with the Soviets in the entire international system to the extent that its capacities and resources will allow.

The last twenty-five years have seen the rise and fall of the

American preponderance of power. The American monopoly on nuclear power lasted less than a decade; by the early 1960s, even its superiority in that field had vanished. The Vietnam War depleted American resources and capabilities in conventional warfare, doing to the American armed forces what Algeria had done to the French. The American military establishment had become not only lethargic and bureaucratic but ineffective as well. The Soviets, by following a more cautious strategy of conserving their military resources and placing equal emphasis on conventional and nuclear weapons systems, have achieved parity in nuclear weapons and a possible edge in conventional weapons. While the American armed forces overseas in Europe and Asia have progressively found themselves serving as political hostages rather than as effective military deterrents, the Soviet armed forces have remained free and highly mobile. The Cuban missile crisis demonstrated to the Soviets the need to develop a worldwide naval capability; by the early 1970s, the Soviet navy had ended America's monopoly of the seas.

Far from being an extension of the Truman Doctrine, the much-heralded Nixon Doctrine of February 18, 1970, shows cognizance of this imbalance between power and policy. The Vietnam War pointed out the limits of power in no uncertain terms and therefore made it necessary to change policies. On one level, Nixon's strategy of one-and-a-half wars greatly reduced the nuclear threshold; for as long as American forces overseas continue to remain political hostages of their allies, the chances of American involvement in serious international conflicts remain high. The only ways to reduce this contingent threat are to develop a very sophisticated division of labor between the United States and its allies in Asia and Europe and to withdraw from untenable positions. The possibility of the development and maintenance of such a sophisticated division of labor over a long period of time is not very great. And even if such a division of labor were possible, none of America's allies could by itself face another superpower without the protection of America's nuclear umbrella.

At another level, the Nixon Doctrine could be quite effective if it succeeds in its goal of changing the United States'

role in the international system. It aims at creating for the
United States the role of balancer rather than active participant in the international system. While both scholars and
policymakers debated whether to adopt the type of isolation-
ism which preceded World War II or the internationalism that
followed it, the Nixon Doctrine has recommended a policy
that should be followed in an era in which the United States
has neither the capability nor the resources to maintain a preponderance of power over other major actors in the system.

The Nixon Doctrine has, therefore, aimed at rapprochement with the great powers (the Soviet Union and China)
while employing diplomatic determinism to solve minor conflicts, as in the Middle East. This doctrine has already begun
to cast America's role in a light significantly different from
that of the pre-Nixon era. American foreign policy is no
longer ideological in the sense that it is guided by hatred of
communism as an abstract concept; it no longer seeks solutions to international problems through a preponderance of
power and strategy of denial. Rather, it seeks solutions by
providing diplomatic media and by acting as a balancer in
such situations.

Both the Soviets and the Chinese have become increasingly
aware of America's capacity as a balancer, and both have
actively sought to promote such a role for the United States.
In all likelihood, they reason that a detente with the West
would allow them to devote their full power and capabilities
to competing with one another. On its part, as the United
States transforms its weakness into strength in adopting the
role of a balancer between the various competing forces in
the world, a detente with both China and the Soviet Union
becomes of crucial importance.

Certainly new assumptions were required before this new
outlook could be adopted. While it seems that United States
policymakers have finally shed their beliefs in monolithic
communism, they run the risk of falling into an opposite but
equally dangerous pitfall. In accepting the role of balancer,
the United States has shown cognizance of the Sino-Soviet
dispute. But certainly this dispute is not to be interpreted as
the "disintegration of communism." Rather, it could be

argued that the Sino-Soviet dispute has strengthened the dynamism and vitality of communism as an international force. By providing independence to the various actors in the Communist bloc, it has also provided opportunities for the innovation and experimentation so necessary for survival. This process has, therefore, stopped the routinization and decay of the concept of communism by introducing motivation, in the form of competition, for coming up with a more viable system. American foreign policy should, therefore, be based no more on disintegrating communism than on monolithic communism.

Since 1969, scholars studying Sino-American relations have debated whether to give China or the United States credit for initiating the thaw. Broadly speaking, three possible explanations of China's desire for rapprochement are usually put forth: first, that China needed detente with the United States as a counterweight to the Soviet Union; second, that the new relationship allowed China direct access to United States leaders, as well as international bodies such as the United Nations—no longer would the Chinese have to depend on having their positions interpreted by the Soviets or the Albanians; and third, that China's growing economic needs could only be fulfilled by the United States.

Those who have maintained that the United States initiated the change in policy offer two explanations: first, that American withdrawal from Asia was not possible without normalization of Sino-American relations; and second, that the U.S., not having the resources to commit simultaneously to both Europe and Asia, opted for rapprochement with China to allow for maximum security against the Soviet Union.

Actually, it is of little importance who initiated the change in Sino-American relations. What matters is simply that the needs of both sides were served by rapprochement. The questions we should seek to answer are these: How do the superpowers now view their roles in the international system? What new assumptions and perceptions do they have?

Both China and the United States continue to consider the Soviet Union as a major threat. By the same token, the

Soviets consider the United States and China as major threats, although the United States poses a different kind of threat from China. The Soviets view the United States threat as immediate and short range, and the Chinese threat as potential and long range. The United States threat is easier to match because it is principally of a military nature, while the Chinese threat is difficult to evaluate and requires a very complex political response. The heart of the competition between the Soviet Union and China concerns the success or failure of the revolutionary practical ideology of each, and, as such, cannot be judged for decades to come.

Chinese scars, left by the era of imperialism, have healed. Having clearly evaluated their competition with the Soviet Union and fully realizing their potential role in the international system, Chinese leaders are concentrating on making a highly successful revolutionary model at home. Their twenty-year-old goal—to assume leadership of the Third World—is bound to fail in the short run. They do not have the resources to compete with the Soviets or the Americans. But in the long run, China hopes to provide not so much a model for capturing power as a model for social reconstruction.

In order to complete their model, the Chinese, for the time being, are interested in securing a stalemate in the Sino-Soviet power relationship by encouraging America's role as a balancer. The Soviets are aware of China's perception of its new role, but have been unable to successfully structure their political and economic policies to compete with China for long-range leadership of the Third World. Concentrating instead on short-term victories, they have taken certain concrete steps in the Middle East and South Asia. In 1969, as Sino-American rapprochement began, Soviet involvement in the Middle East escalated, relationships with countries such as Iran and Turkey were improved, and Soviet-Indian security arrangements were negotiated. Soviet policy thus seems to be to nullify any advantages to China which have arisen from Sino-American rapprochement.

It has been pointed out that Henry Kissinger's influence on American foreign policy primarily lies in providing a transition from cold war to detente, and that new principles of

American foreign policy have yet to emerge. Such a view also provides an explanation about the stalled Sino-American rapprochement. Neither the present administration nor, as far as can be foreseen, its possible successors have any clear-cut notion about transformation of detente from an instrument of foreign policy to a vehicle for a new international system.

The Chinese, correctly utilizing the American role as balancer, have begun to benefit from the changes in American foreign policy. They have deepened and extended their rapprochement to other areas, such as India, Egypt, and Yugoslavia. There is every indication that a limited Sino-Soviet rapprochement may be in the offing.

Both the international system as a whole and the respective foreign policies of its three major actors—China, the Soviet Union, and the United States—are now in the process of reformulation. The way in which these policies crystallize will determine the future of the international state system, as well as the interrelationships among the states. Finally, the two areas in which new studies are necessary are: (1) the changing nature of the Soviet and Chinese revolutionary experiments and their impact on each other, as well as on the rest of the world, and (2) the changing assumptions behind the foreign policies of the three superpowers. Only such studies will provide new perspectives on the international system in general and on Sino-American relations in particular.

3

CHANGING PERCEPTIONS OF
CHINA SINCE MIDCENTURY

Norman A. Graebner

*Edward R. Stettinius Professor of History,
University of Virginia*

Almost from its inception, Mao Tse-tung's rise to power in China separated American officials, politicians, writers, and scholars on matters of causation and significance as had no previous external episode in the United States history. Initially, even as Chiang Kai-shek gave way to Chinese Communist leadership in 1949, neither the government of the United States nor the American people generally recognized, in this grinding transferral of power, any danger to the United States. Indeed, until 1949 Washington did not reject the possibility of establishing normal and satisfactory relations with the new regime. The United States had not withdrawn its officers from their posts. What determined official attitudes toward the Chinese civil war was the conviction that the Communist success manifested a clear expression of self-determination, that nationalism—and not communism—was the driving force behind the Chinese revolution.

Nothing better illustrated the tendency to view the Communist victory as the legitimate expression of popular demand—and thus no real challenge to American interests or Asian stability—than the noted State Department White

Paper published in August 1949. In his letter of transmittal, which prefaced the White Paper, Secretary of State Dean Acheson assigned the responsibility for the Nationalist collapse to the failures of that regime. "The Nationalist armies," wrote Acheson, "did not have to be defeated; they disintegrated." The United States, he continued, could have saved Chiang only by a "full-scale intervention in behalf of a government which had lost the confidence of its own troops and its own people."[1] In eschewing any attempt to control the internal affairs of China, Washington denied that the U.S. had any special security interest in the continuation of Nationalist control of China. Had this not been true, official American reaction to the Nationalist collapse would have been far less passive. It was not clear, moreover, how the United States could build a stable Orient through cooperation with a disunited and warring China. More essential to American purpose after 1948 was the restructuring of postwar Japan.

To the extent that a powerful minority of potential critics within the United States anticipated the Communist victory in China with deep regret, they regarded the new Chinese leaders as dangerous to Chinese traditions and to China's historical relations with the United States. They feared above all that Mao might slam shut the Open Door and thus deprive American scholars, missionaries, travelers, officials, and merchants of their access to a country which had become, for them, a region of immense charm. But even for the friends of China and Chiang Kai-shek, the closing of the Open Door, and the subsequent mistreatment of American officials in China, was not necessarily evidence of Mao's aggressive intent toward China's neighbors. Communist influence and behavior in China might be tragic, but it did not necessarily comprise a threat to American interests in Asia.

Still, there existed in 1949 a marked ambivalence in American attitudes toward the impending retreat of Chiang to the island of Formosa. Some Americans detected trouble in Mao's prediction in June 1949 that his regime had no choice but to ally China with the USSR. "Not only in China but throughout the world," Mao said, "one must lean either to imperialism or socialism. There is no exception. Neutrality is

merely a camouflage; a third road does not exist." In an era
of continuing imperialism, Mao continued, "it is impossible
for a genuine people's revolution in any country to achieve
victory without various forms of help from the international
revolutionary forces."[2] Washington, moreover, could scarcely
ignore the fact that before long 900 million people would be
living under Communist-led governments. Indeed, with the
fall of Chiang Kai-shek the nation entered a period of deep
intellectual crisis. What mattered during those critical months
of decision was the role which American officials, editors,
and political leaders—the creators of public opinion—chose to
assign to the USSR in the triumph of Communist power in
China. Was Asian communism at midcentury a vertical or a
horizontal movement? Was it lodged essentially in indigenous
conditions, reflecting national hopes and ambitions? Or was
it an international movement, directed from Moscow, skim-
ming the Asian landscape in search of nations to conquer and
add to the international Communist bloc? Washington's official answers to these critical questions became increasingly
clear. What had so recently appeared indigenous suddenly
appeared as possibly the initial triumph of Soviet aggression
in Asia.

During July 1949, Acheson dispatched Ambassador-at-
Large Philip C. Jessup to Asia to conduct an objective appraisal of Far Eastern problems and make recommendations
for the formulation of an American strategy. Whereas it was
quite clear that the administration would do nothing to save
the Nationalist government, Acheson, in a top-secret memorandum, instructed Jessup as follows: "You will please take
as your assumption that it is a fundamental decision of American policy that the United States does not intend to permit
further extension of Communist domination on the continent of Asia or in the southeast Asia area."[3] Even in the
White Paper, issued in August, Acheson called attention to
the danger of Soviet imperialism in the Far East and reaffirmed United States opposition "to the subjugation of
China by any foreign power, to any regime acting in the interest of a foreign power, and to the dismemberment of
China by any foreign power, whether by open or clandestine

means.''[4] Later that month George F. Kennan publicly declared that the new Chinese leadership, whether sincere or not, was committed to unrealistic doctrines which had induced the Chinese people "to accept a disguised form of foreign rule."[5]

Such perceptions of Soviet expansion into Asia quickly drifted into Congress. Senator Kenneth Wherry of Nebraska and other Republicans charged that the State Department's White Paper was "to a large extent a 1,054-page whitewash of a wishful, do-nothing policy which has succeeded only in placing Asia in danger of Soviet conquest with its ultimate threat to the peace of the world and our own national security."[6] Similarly, Senator William F. Knowland of California declared in September that, since communism was global in character, it did not make sense "to try to keep 240 million Europeans from being taken behind the Iron Curtain while we are complacent and unconcerned about 450 million Chinese going the same way, when, if they should go that way, it would probably start an avalanche which would mean that a billion Asiatics would be lined up on the side of Soviet Russia and in the orbit of international communism."[7]

Throughout the autumn months of 1949 the Truman administration continued to search for a definition of the Asian problem. In part the discussions of the Washington Roundtable Conference in October revolved around the question of Soviet ambitions in Asia. In November George C. McGhee, the assistant secretary for Middle Eastern, South Asian, and African Affairs, acknowledged again the official fear of Communist aggression in Asia when he declared at Chattanooga, Tennessee, that the rapidity of the Communist advance in China compelled the Soviet Union "to define the nature and extent of its influence over the Chinese Communists, and then to consolidate this vast area within the Soviet orbit."[8] That month foreign service officer Karl Lott Rankin warned from Hong Kong that Communist China, under Soviet influence, would attempt to extend its influence throughout South and Southeast Asia. "Now that Communist control of China proper is all but assured," wrote Rankin, "it may be taken for granted that efforts will be redoubled to place

Communist regimes in power elsewhere in Asia. . . . China may be considered weak and backward by Western standards, but . . . in Eastern terms, Communist China is a great power, economically, militarily, and politically. Supported by Communist dynamism, China might well be able to dominate not only Indochina, Siam, and Burma, but eventually the Philippines, Indonesia, Pakistan, and India itself."[9] To undermine the independence of the minor countries of Southeast Asia, Rankin warned, China would employ the techniques of infiltration, sabotage, propaganda, and support of guerrilla movements.

These two tendencies in official American thought—one accepting the indigenous, non-Soviet nature of the Chinese revolution, another assuming Moscow's burgeoning influence in Chinese affairs—collided in Acheson's noted speech before the National Press Club on January 12, 1950. Acheson explained the fall of Chiang Kai-shek in terms of an indigenous revolution. "What has happened," he said, ". . . is that the almost inexhaustible patience of the Chinese people in their misery ended. They did not bother to overthrow this government. There was really nothing to overthrow. They simply ignored it. . . . They completely withdrew their support from this government, and when that support was withdrawn, the whole military establishment disintegrated." Within that context, the secretary argued logically against any American effort to control the affairs of the new Asia, especially by military force.[10]

But Acheson recognized the danger of Soviet expansion through the Chinese revolution. "Communism," he said, "is the most subtle instrument of Soviet foreign policy that has ever been devised, and it is really the spearhead of Russian imperialism which would, if it could, take from these people what they have won." Russian ambition toward north China long antedated communism. "But," Acheson continued, "the Communist regime has added new methods, new skills, and new concepts to the thrust of Russian imperialism. These Communist concepts and techniques have armed Russian

imperialism with a new and most insidious weapon of penetration." Through these techniques the Soviets possibly had
detached Manchuria, inner and outer Mongolia, and Sinkiang
and added them to the USSR. "The consequences of this
Russian . . . action in China," Acheson warned, "are perfectly
enormous. They are saddling all those in China who are pro-
claiming their loyalty to Moscow, with the most awful responsibility which they must pay for. Furthermore, these
actions of the Russians are making plainer than any speech
. . . or any legislation can make throughout all of Asia, what
the true purposes of the Soviet Union are and what the true
function of communism as an agent of Russian imperialism
is."[11]

That the Chinese had indeed become puppets of the Moscow Politburo appeared to pass beyond any doubt when, in
February 1950, the world read the terms of the new Sino-
Soviet Treaty of Friendship, Alliance, and Mutual Assistance.
By its terms the Soviets promised China considerable financial and technical aid. Acheson admitted that the Chinese
people might welcome such promises, but, he added, "they
will not fail, in time, to see where they fall short of China's
real needs and desires. And they will wonder about the points
upon which the agreements remain silent."[12] The secretary
warned the Chinese that, whatever China's internal development, they would bring grave trouble on themselves and the
rest of Asia "if they are led by their new rulers into aggressive
or subversive adventures beyond their borders."

This burgeoning concept of a single conspiracy, global in
its pretensions and centering in Moscow, had not won universal acceptance. Indeed, many American scholars at midcentury rejected the notion completely. Walter Lippmann,
speaking before the Chicago Council on Foreign Relations on
February 22, 1950, reminded his audience: "While it is true
that we have lost our power and for the time being most of
our influence in China, it by no means follows that Russia
has won control of China or has achieved an enduring alliance
with China." Some observers could detect little evidence of
Russian dominance in the Sino-Soviet Pact.[13] American
writers on Far Eastern subjects agreed generally that the

United States should not introduce military force into Asia. But the final Communist victory in China, added to the official interpretation of the Sino-Soviet Pact, propelled the administration logically toward the extension of the containment principle to the Far East. By March 1950, the Chinese revolution itself seemed sufficient to demonstrate Soviet expansionist power in Asia.

Acheson took the lead in defining the new challenge and in formulating the requirements of American policy. When China appeared to be achieving true national independence, he told the Commonwealth Club of California in March, its leaders were forcing it into the Soviet orbit. "We now face the prospect," he admitted, "that the Communists may attempt to apply another familiar tactic to use China as a base for probing for other weak spots which they can move into and exploit."[14] He warned the people of Asia that they "must face the fact that today the major threat to their freedom and to their social and economic progress is the attempted penetration of Asia by Soviet-Communist imperialism and by the colonialism which it contains." Asia, unfortunately, lay "in the path of the main thrust of Soviet subversion and expansionism." The United States, the secretary promised, would oppose the spread of communism because it comprised the means whereby the Kremlin attempted "to extend its absolute domination over the widest possible areas of the world."

United States officials in Asia joined the secretary in giving form to this concept of global danger. Ambassador Loy W. Henderson admitted before the Indian Council of World Affairs at New Delhi on March 27 that the United States, with its long tradition of involvement in the Atlantic world, understood better the culture of Europe than that of Asia. Recent events in the Orient, however, had given the American people a new and enlarging interest in the region. "It should be borne in mind, in considering various policies of the United States in respect to Asia," he said, "that the United States does not pursue one set of policies with regard to the Americas or Europe and another with regard to Asia. The foreign policies of the United States by force of circumstances have become global in character.''[15] Upon his return to the United States, Ambassador Jessup, on April 13, addressed the nation over ABC. Again he cited the requirements for a larger policy to stem the tide of aggression in Asia. There was no need, he began, to explain Asia's importance to the United States. "I think most Americans realize that Asia is important," he added, ". . . because Soviet communism is clearly out to capture and colonize the continent.''[16]

From this conceptualization of Communist aggression in Asia, the Truman administration moved logically into its standard rationale for the Korean War. The North Korean invasion was simply another demonstration of Soviet imperialism in Asia. "The attack upon the Republic of Korea," said the president on July 19, "makes it plain beyond all doubt that the international Communist movement is prepared to use armed invasion to conquer independent nations. We must, therefore, recognize the possibility that armed aggression may take place in other areas.''[17] Similarly, State Department adviser John Foster Dulles, in a CBS interview, assured the nation that the North Koreans did not attack "purely on their own but as part of the world strategy of international communism.''[18] To meet the challenge, the president ordered troops to Korea and the Seventh Fleet to Formosa; he speeded up military assistance to Indochina and the Philippines. Many Far Eastern experts argued that the Soviet commitment to Korea was limited and that the Korea-type aggression would not occur elsewhere. For Truman, however, it was essential that the United States protect the credibility of Western determination to prevent Communist-led aggression in Asia. As he explained to the allies:

> Firmness now would be the only way to deter new actions in other portions of the world. Not only in Asia but in Europe, the Middle East, and elsewhere the confidence of people in countries adjacent to the Soviet Union would be very adversely affected . . . if we failed to take action to protect a country

established under our auspices and confirmed in its freedom by action of the United Nations.

United States officials, in attributing the Korean War to Soviet imperialism, placed enormous faith in China's decision to abstain. Such abstinence would demonstrate the actuality of Chinese independence. Acheson revealed his confidence in the good judgment and resistance of the Chinese in a CBS telecast of mid-September 1950. For the Chinese to enter the war, he said, would be sheer madness. "And since there is nothing in it for them," he added, "I don't see why they should yield to what is undoubtedly pressure from the Communist movement to get into the Korean row."[19] At Wake Island, in October, General Douglas MacArthur assured the president that China would not enter the Korean War.

Such expressions of hope proved to be a poor prediction of Chinese action, but they explain why the Chinese advance across the Yalu in November 1950 produced a traumatic reaction in Washington. China's intervention seemed to demonstrate, at last, not only Peking's irrationality but also the absolute sway which Moscow had gained over China and China's external policies. "Those who control the Soviet Union and the international Communist movement," Acheson warned the country in a nationwide radio address on November 29, "have made clear their fundamental design." Truman declared the following day: "We hope that the Chinese people will not continue to be forced or deceived into serving the ends of Russian colonial policy in Asia."[20] Chinese behavior seemed to substantiate Stanley K. Hornbeck's observation in October: "The conflict in Korea is not a 'civil conflict.' The conflict between China's Communists and China's Nationalists is not a 'civil conflict.' The attacking forces in both cases bear a made-from-by-and-for Moscow stamp."[21] Even the *New York Times* proclaimed on December 8: "The Chinese Communist dictatorship will eventually go down in history as the men who sold out their country to the foreigners, in this case the Russians, rather than as those who rescued China from foreign 'imperialism.'"

Thus Korea perfected the notion of Chinese subservience

to Moscow. Truman reminded the American people, in his
State of the Union message of January 8, 1951, "Our men
are fighting . . . because they know, as we do, that the agres-
sion in Korea is part of the attempt of the Russian Communist dictatorship to take over the world, step by step."[22] It
was left for Dean Rusk, assistant secretary of state for Far
Eastern affairs, and John Foster Dulles to carry the fears
of Soviet aggression in the Far East to their ultimate conceptualization. Both men, as top spokesmen for the State
Department, accepted without question the existence of a
monolithic Communist enemy, with its center in Moscow.
Their analyses transformed nationalism from a legitimate
quest for self-determination into a fraudulent device for
Soviet expansion.

To achieve its ultimate success the Soviet program of
world conquest required, first, the amalgamation of China's
millions. "To this end," Dulles informed a New York audience in May 1951, "a Chinese Communist party was formed
under the guiding direction of the Russian, Borodin. That
party, Soviet Russia has nurtured until it has matured into
today's regime of Mao Tse-tung, which serves as the instrument of Soviet communism." Certainly, said Dulles, the
Soviet government would not have paid so great a price to
bring the Chinese Communists to power unless it intended to
serve the Russian interest thereby. "By the test of conception, birth, nurture, and obedience," Dulles concluded, "the
Mao Tse-tung regime is a creature of the Moscow Politburo,
and it is in behalf of Moscow, not of China, that it is destroy-
ing the friendship of the Chinese people toward the United
States." Ostensibly the Chinese Communists had whipped up
anti-American sentiment in the interest of national independence. But actually, Dulles informed his listeners, the hysteria was merely the front behind which the Chinese people
were "being betrayed into amalgamation with the mass which
serves Moscow."[23]

But the pattern of Soviet subversion now appeared equally
clear elsewhere in Asia. Disturbances throughout the Pacific
and Asian areas, from the war in Korea to the activities of the
Communist-controlled United States maritime unions, said

Dulles, were "part of a single pattern . . . of violence planned and plotted for 25 years and finally brought to a consummation of fighting and disorder in the whole vast area extending from Korea down through China into Indochina, Malaya, the Philippines, and west into Tibet and the borders of Burma, India, and Pakistan."[24]

This concept of a Kremlin-controlled monolith created the ultimate rationale for rejecting Peking from membership in the United Nations and denying it the recognition of the United States. In a dramatic statement before the China Institute of New York, on May 18, 1951, Rusk announced that this nation would not recognize the Peking regime. His reasoning was clear: The rulers of China were the puppets of Moscow. "We do not recognize the authorities in Peiping for what they pretend to be," he said. "The Peiping regime may be a colonial Russian government—a Slavic Manchukuo on a larger scale. It is not the Government of China. It does not pass the first test. It is not Chinese."[25] Dulles reaffirmed that decision before the same audience: "We should treat the Mao Tse-tung regime for what it is—a puppet regime."

To President Dwight D. Eisenhower and Secretary of State Dulles, the world they inherited was scarcely reassuring. Early in 1953 the new president declared that the nation stood in greater peril than at any time in its history. On February 9, six days after he assumed his new office, Dulles asked the American people to awaken to the dangers before them. "Already our proclaimed enemies," he told a national radio and television audience, "control one-third of all the people of the world." The Soviet strategy, he continued, "has been to pick up one country after another by getting control of its government, by political warfare and indirect aggression. And they have been making very great progress. At the end of the Second World War, only a little over 7 years ago, they only controlled about 200 million people. Today, they control 800 million people and they're hard at work to get control of other parts of the world."[26]

What gave this perception of massive danger its only

sustaining rationale was the concept of the international Communist monolith. Ambassador Rankin in Taipei saw this clearly when he wrote to Ambassador George V. Allen in New Delhi during July 1953. He reminded Allen that the United States could maintain its anti-Peking posture only as long as it denied that Mao enjoyed any independence from Moscow. Whether or not this was true, wrote Rankin, the Chinese Nationalists on Formosa feared that the United States might accept Peking's independence as true and there-after follow the course of Britain and India in recognizing the mainland regime. "Only so long as they are persuaded that Americans continue to regard Mao simply as a Soviet tool," ran Rankin's final warning, "will they feel reasonably assured as to our China policy."[27] Moscow's powerful influence had transformed China from a revolutionary into an expansionist state; no less than the perpetuation of that assumption would sustain China's role as an aggressor.

Dulles's Washington never denied the close relationship be-tween Peking and Moscow, although with time it dropped the earlier concept of total Chinese subservience for that of a Sino-Soviet partnership. The secretary expressed his view of that relationship in an interview in July 1957: "As far as we can judge, the nations which are within the Sino-Soviet bloc are all dominated by what can fairly be called international communism, a single group which provides a guiding force." The State Department sustained that judgment in its August 1958 memorandum to all United States missions abroad. Attacking the notion that the recognition of Peking might weaken that regime's ties with Moscow, the memorandum declared: "The alliance between Moscow and Peiping is one of long standing; it traces its origin to the very founding of the Chinese Communist Party in 1921, in which representa-tives of the Comintern played an important role. It is based on a common ideology and on mutually held objectives with respect to the non-Communist world."[28] Even as the Eisen-hower administration entered its final months, Under Secre-tary of State Robert Murphy assured a New York audience: "Some day this might become a most uneasy partnership. However, this day seems far in the future, and in the present in which we must operate there is little doubt but that both Moscow and Peiping regard the continuation of their close alliance as being of overriding importance."[29] This new perception of the Sino-Soviet amalgam elevated China to the status of an aggressor in its own right.

Indeed, during the late 1950s, as Nikita Khrushchev managed to establish more reassuring relationships with the United States, China emerged as the dominant threat to Asian stability—the major partner in the Asian Communist monolith. In his noted San Francisco address of June 1957, Dulles reminded his audience that China "fought the United Nations in Korea; it supported the Communist war in Indochina; it took Tibet by force. It fomented the Communist Huk rebellion in the Philippines and the Communists' insurrection in Malaya." Peking did not disguise its expansionist ambitions. It was, said Dulles, bitterly hateful of the United States, which it considered the principal obstacle in its path of conquest.[30] Later that year William J. Sebald, ambassador to Australia, condemned China in what had become standard phraseology. The core of the problem in the Pacific, he said, "is the deadly hostility of the Chinese Communist regime with its unwavering espousal of the principles of Marxism-Leninism. These principles, as we know, envisage the conquest of the non-Communist world and the destruction of free institutions."[31] The subservient China of midcentury, with its aggressiveness dictated by Moscow, had now replaced Russia as the primary source of Asia's turmoil.

Still China, in American eyes, had not achieved full independence from the Kremlin, for the acknowledgment of Chinese independence would have destroyed the major rationale for nonrecognition. However grave the Chinese threat to Asia, nonrecognition carried the chief burden for both the containment and the eventual liberation of the mainland. Even as the perception of China's Asian role changed during the 1950s, nonrecognition required perennial denial that the Peking regime represented the Chinese people. Since a traditional, non-Communist government in Peking would pose no danger to Asia, official American rhetoric continued to accuse the mainland leadership of imposing an alien minority rule on an intimidated Chinese populace. As late as March 1959, Walter S. Robertson, assistant secretary of state for Far Eastern affairs, reminded a Canadian audience: "Let no one say that representation is being denied to 600 million mainland Chinese. The fanatical Marxists of Peiping come no closer to representing the will and aspirations of the Chinese people than the puppet regime of Budapest comes to representing the will and aspirations of the Hungarian people or William Z. Foster comes to representing the will and aspirations of the American people."[32]

Long before 1960 the evidence pouring out of Moscow and Peking dramatized the growing tensions between the two countries over a wide range of historic and ideological issues. Even in the early fifties Sino-Soviet relations did not fit Washington's official description, for throughout the twentieth century Russia and China had sustained a high level of animosity in their exchanges. Still, those disagreements which did exist after 1950 did not break into open controversy; as late as the mid-fifties Peking continued to cultivate cordial relations with the USSR. Perhaps the years from 1953 to 1958 comprised the golden age in Sino-Soviet diplomacy, although before that period ended the cordiality had begun to wear thin. Symbolically, the break came in 1956 with Khrushchev's condemnation of Stalinist policies and his plea for a more realistic and less ideological—an economic rather than a military—competition between the Soviets and the non-Soviet world. China's denunciation of Soviet ideological moderation embraced claims to ideological purity, but it revealed as well vast differences in timing and character between the Russian and Chinese revolutions and the resulting divergence in national purposes.

At the policy level, the Quemoy crisis of August 1958 clarified the growing conflict in Sino-Soviet perceptions of the Asian danger and the chasm dividing Russian from Chinese interests. Peking coordinated its attack on the offshore islands with an effort to invoke its treaty arrangments with the USSR. With the launching of the first Soviet sputnik in the immediate background, the Peking government pressed the Kremlin to support its objectives in the Formosa Strait with some form of nuclear diplomacy. This pressure carried with it an essential test of the character and value of the Sino-Soviet alliance. Soviet abstinence, accompanied by clear warnings that Peking's troubles with the Republic of China were and would remain China's own, demonstrated the limited efficacy of any Chinese reliance on Soviet military power. Thereafter, Chinese leaders condemned the Soviet emphasis on "peaceful coexistence" and demanded cooperative policies of opposition to the United States, especially in the Far East. Early in 1960 Peking warned Moscow that the socialist camp could be built only "on a basis of brotherly alliance of equality, mutual respect, mutual assistance, and the common goal of socialism and communism." To China's spokesmen, the Russians had abandoned a socialist ally to improve their relations with the imperialists. The impact of this split on the Communist parties of Asia was profound. Its impact on United States perceptions of danger to Asia was scarcely apparent at all.

Despite the universal evidence of the Sino-Soviet rift which broke into the open after 1960, the new administration of John F. Kennedy accepted the assumptions and postures inherited from the Eisenhower years with little attempt at reexamination. To Democratic Washington, the Moscow-Peking axis remained united on essentials and therefore dangerous. Secretary of State Dean Rusk denied in July 1961 that the prospects of a Sino-Soviet break could serve as the basis of sound policy. "I think," he declared, "there is solid evidence of some tensions between Moscow and Peiping, but I would use a little caution in trying to estimate the width of such gap as might be developing between them. . . . [H]ere are two great systems of power which are united in general in certain doctrinal framework and which together have certain common interests vis-à-vis the rest of the world."[33] Whatever differences separated Peking from Moscow, the disagreements, ran Washington's official view, were over means, not ends. As one administration spokesman remarked in February 1963, "A dispute over how to bury the West is no

grounds for Western rejoicing." Shortly thereafter, Rusk
warned the country in a NBC interview to be "careful about
taking premature comfort from arguments within the Communist world as to how best to bury us."[34] Averell Harriman
that year likewise limited the Sino-Soviet quarrel to methods,
not objectives. "Both Moscow and Peiping," he said, "are
determined that communism shall sweep the world, but there
is a deep difference between them concerning the methods to
be employed."[35]

Beginning with the late Eisenhower years, China emerged
as an ever-increasing threat to the small countries of Asia.
The Kennedy administration carried that assumption into the
sixties. Assistant Secretary Roger W. Hilsman defined the
Democratic administration's standard view of China in an
address of June 1963: "In Asia the greatest danger to independent nations comes from Communist China, with its 700
million people forced into the service of an aggressive Communist Party. . . . Communist China lies in direct contact
with, or very close to, a whole series of free nations. . . . All
these free nations must deal with the facts of Communist
China and its ambitions."[36] Kennedy applied these assumptions of Chinese expansionism to the problem of Vietnam.
He not only claimed validity for the domino theory but logically attributed the danger of falling dominoes to China.
"China is so large, looms so high just beyond the frontiers,"
he warned, "that if South Vietnam went, it would not only
give them an improved geographic position for a guerrilla as-
sault on Malaya, but would also give them the impression
that the wave of the future in Southeast Asia was China and
the Communists. So I believe it [the domino theory]."[37]
Indeed, as Hilsman made clear, the American struggle in
Vietnam remained essentially an effort to contain the power
and influence of mainland China.[38]

United States opposition to recognition of the Peking regime, as well as the corresponding commitment to Taiwan,
remained firm. During their first months in office, Kennedy
and Rusk reiterated this country's continued support for
the Republic of China. But the Kennedy administration—as
did the Lyndon B. Johnson administration which followed—

based its rationale for nonrecognition less on China's subservience to Moscow than on Chinese aggressiveness and misbehavior. No longer did nonrecognition carry the promise of containment in Asia. The Kennedy and Johnson administrations acknowledged both the strength and the permanence of the mainland government, albeit with a perennial tone of regret.

Adlai Stevenson, in his argument before the United Nations in December 1961, established the Kennedy rationale for prolonging the fight against recognition. No country, he said, could be more aware of the existence of the Peking regime than the United States. But to bow to the demands of that government to expel and replace the Republic of China in the United Nations "would be ignoring the warlike character and aggressive behavior of the rulers who dominate 600 million people and who talk of the inevitability of war as an article of faith and refuse to renounce the use of force."[39] It would be wrong, he said, to give "implicit blessing to an aggressive and bloody war against those Chinese who are still free in Taiwan." All nations, added Stevenson, were aware of the high standards of conduct and contributions of the Republic of China to the principles and success of the U.N. "The notion of expelling the Republic of China," declared Stevenson, "is thus absurd and unthinkable."[40] In his widely heralded address before the Commonwealth Club of California in December 1963, Hilsman repeated the standard formula for nonrecognition and the search for stability in Asia. China remained a danger to its neighbors. Peking and Moscow shared the goal of communizing the world. A robust Taiwan served as an alternative model for Chinese development. The hope for a peaceful Orient lay, then, in the prospects for change in the Chinese Communist hierarchy.[41]

Against the background of the growing American involvement in Vietnam, the Johnson administration became even more determined in its opposition to mainland China. In November 1965, Arthur Goldberg again carried the official American position before the U.N. He denounced Peking for laying down its own conditions for membership. "The oldest of Peiping's conditions," he reminded the General

Assembly, "is the expulsion of the Republic of China. How can this Assembly even consider meeting that condition?" But what mattered even more was China's aggressiveness and its continued defiance of the principles of the United Nations Charter. "The admission of Peiping," warned Goldberg, "would bring into our midst a force determined to destroy the orderly and progressive world which the United Nations has been helping to build over the past 20 years."[42] Recognition would only encourage Peking on its path of violence by rewarding it for its international misbehavior and confirming its belief in the righteousness of its ideology, an ideology which "commends rather than condemns settlement of issues by armed force."

What confirmed Washington's perception of a dangerous and aggressive China was Marshal Lin Piao's doctrinal article which appeared in the Peking press on September 3, 1965. This manifesto by the Chinese defense minister proclaimed a worldwide people's war against the West and thereby reaffirmed Peking's commitment to global revolution. For Lin the countryside—the underdeveloped regions of Asia, Africa, and Latin America—would provide the revolutionary bases from which the revolutionaries would go forward to final victory over the cities—the industrialized regions of North America and Western Europe. This revolution, admitted Lin, would be long and costly, but it would triumph. For as he explained,

> however highly developed modern weapons and technical equipment may be, and however complicated the methods of modern warfare, in the final analysis the outcome of a war will be decided by the sustained fighting of the ground forces, by the fighting at close quarters on battlefields, by the political consciousness of the men, by their courage and spirit of sacrifice. The spiritual atom bomb that the revolutionary people possess is a far more powerful and useful weapon than the physical atom bomb.[43]

United States officials and their supporters in the press

acknowledged Lin's statement with profound seriousness. Here was the ultimate reason for a policy of universal opposition to the Peking regime, for Lin had announced to the world, in concrete terms, both the ends and the means of Chinese expansion. True, the doctrine called for revolution by the natives of each country—thus it was largely a "do-it-yourself" program. "But," warned Rusk in April 1966, "Peking is prepared to train and indoctrinate the leaders of these revolutions and to support them with funds, arms, and propaganda, as well as politically. It is even prepared to manufacture these revolutionary movements out of whole cloth." The mainland regime, said Rusk, had encouraged and assisted the aggressions in Vietnam and Laos; it had supported the national liberation forces in Thailand. Malaysia reportedly was next on the list. But the aggressions had gone far beyond Asia; they had penetrated Africa and Latin America as well.[44] Peking's new challenge, warned the secretary, would lead to catastrophe if not met by a timely response.

China's foreign policy reached its highest stage of militancy and revolutionary zeal amid the Chinese Cultural Revolution of the mid-sixties. So belligerent became the "Red Guard" diplomacy that it alienated Asian, African, and Western nations alike through its systematic insults and clumsy efforts at subversion. Peking recalled much of its diplomatic corps for reindoctrination in the goals of the Cultural Revolution. Throughout Asia, Chinese nationals rioted against foreign governments. Within China itself, Chinese revolutionaries seized embassies and attacked foreign emissaries. During August 1967, they sacked the British embassy and conducted mass demonstrations outside the Soviet embassy. Peking seemed determined to earn the enmity and distrust of the entire world. By 1968 formal Chinese relations with other countries were virtually nonexistent. Chinese prestige and trade had fallen to an all-time low. Such behavior did not enhance the American image of China. Rusk observed in November 1967, that

within the next decade or two, there will be a billion Chinese on the Mainland, armed with nuclear

weapons, with no certainty about what their attitude toward the rest of Asia will be. . . . The militancy of China has isolated China within the Communist World. . . . Now, we believe that the free
nations of Asia must brace themselves, get themselves set with secure, progressive, stable institutions of their own.[45]

Clearly Chinese belligerency had gone too far. By 1968
observers within the United States anticipated a change in
China's outlook which could result in better United States–
Chinese relations. "The Cultural Revolution and all its implications," observed the Congressional Quarterly Service,
"could well influence the course of Sino-American relations
for the last third of the 20th Century. For out of China's
political crisis could emerge the great disaster the world has
been able to avoid since 1945. Or there could arise a new
leadership, more attuned to the tenor of world events."[46]

One administration later, the perception of an aggressive
China, meriting every American effort to isolate it diplomati-
cally, politically, and economically, had vanished amid a
revolution in Washington's official outlook—a revolution
planned and executed by President Richard M. Nixon. Behind the accumulation of more moderate judgments of China
and its foreign policies was the widespread realization that
official American reactions to China after midcentury had
little relationship to reality. Still, if the normalization of
United States–Chinese relationships demanded new attitudes
and perceptions in Washington, it required as well conditions
elsewhere which would encourage China to identify its deep-
est interests with that normalization. No American initiatives
toward China would have succeeded without the knowledge
that they would be received with some graciousness. Even
then, those Far Eastern scholars who argued for the recognition of the Peking regime before the Senate Foreign Relations Committee during March 1966 agreed that American
initiatives would benefit the United States only by casting

the blame for China's isolation on Peking and not on Washington. What lay behind the ping-pong diplomacy of the early seventies was Peking's admission that past antagonisms would prevent any beneficial response to the new, more promising international environment. Among those factors which encouraged the new Chinese pragmatism were the pervading nature of the Sino-Soviet rift, which official American rhetoric had persistently denied; the reemergence of Japan; the Nixon Doctrine; and the expectation of peace in Vietnam.

Nixon's new approach to China, which commenced as early as 1969, culminated in his trip to Peking in February 1972 and in the establishment of a permanent United States "liaison office" in Peking during 1973. This changing relationship reflected the president's conviction that peace in Asia required both the recognition of China as a major power and some positive Chinese contribution to the stability and progress of Asia. By acknowledging the legitimacy of the Chinese government—which four previous administrations had refused to do—Nixon expected Peking to admit the legitimacy of the existing diplomatic order and the limits of proper political conduct. The new American approach to China assumed a general equilibrium in Far Eastern affairs and a fundamental desire in Peking to accept the conditions then prevailing in Asia.

Late in 1971 the Peking government replaced the Republic of China in the United Nations without producing distress among the American people or bringing disaster to either the U.N. or the free nations of Asia. Whatever the purpose or the necessity of the earlier tensions between the United States and China, those antagonisms never disintegrated into open conflict. Yet the perennial posture of nonrecognition and the language which underwrote it were not without their costs. For, as Walter Lippmann observed, they made China the enemy and propelled the country into a wide variety of treaties and guarantees around the eastern fringes of the Pacific with consequences that could require a generation to correct.

That the president's new diplomacy enjoyed the almost universal approval of the American people was not strange.

For many, the older attitudes and intentions toward mainland China, defended with such flamboyant phraseology,
never made much sense. Indeed, that rhetoric belonged
largely to a minority which had a direct political and emotional stake in this country's special attachment to the Republic of China. Long before the seventies, the charges of
Chinese aggression had ceased to carry much conviction. Public attitudes had moved ahead of official policy. As Walter
Lippmann observed in October 1971: "The old anti-Communist crusading in which you had to outlaw and blackball anything Chinese had been dead for some time."[47] Similarly,
William Pfaff, writing in the *New Yorker* of June 3, 1972,
believed that Nixon's China initiative, while apparently dar-
ing enough, merely capitalized on a suppressed popular im-
pulse for change. "It reversed," wrote Pfaff, "an American
China policy that under a succession of previous Administrations had delivered blows, bluster, and grand denunciations in
the name of democracy and liberty. That way of conducting
ourselves before the world . . . had become so corrupt in
recent years, so sterile and thick with hypocrisy, that the
country was ready for some Metternichian realism."[48]

Clearly the Asia of the seventies scarcely resembled the
former vision of a continent engulfed by a dangerous and
revolutionary bipolar conflict. The developments of the early
seventies suggested that the lines of major tension in Asia
were receding before a realignment of world power. Washington's initiatives toward Moscow and Peking in 1972 encouraged Japan to establish closer relationships with both China
and Russia. Japan's influence in Asia expanded with that
country's trade and investment around the continent's eastern and southern rim. For hard economic reasons, the powerful bonds between the United States and Japan showed signs
of strain. China and the USSR were in direct confrontation
everywhere across Asia. As early as 1969 Moscow offered
defense pacts to the countries of Southeast Asia against an
allegedly aggressive China. Peking retaliated in 1972 by inviting the United States to maintain its bases in Southeast Asia
as a guarantee against Soviet encroachment.

Much of the president's new pentagonal world embraced

Asia, where four powers competed in a fluid relationship. Nothing dramatized more clearly the revolution in the American perception of Asia and the world than the president's assumption of a new balance of power. "We must remember," he declared in January 1972, "the only time in the history of the world that we have had any extended period of peace is when there has been a balance of power. . . . I think it will be a safer world and a better world if we have a strong, healthy United States, Europe, Soviet Union, China, Japan— each balancing the other."[49]

Thereafter, the new American outlook toward Asia set the stage for a limited, ordered relationship with China. What continued to mar that relationship, however, was the issue of Taiwan. The Chinese seemed determined to avoid full diplomatic links until the United States terminated its special arrangements with the Nationalists and recognized Peking's sovereignty over all China, including Taiwan. The United States agreed not to challenge the thesis, shared by all Chinese, that there was "but one China and that Taiwan is a part of China." But Kissinger, in repeated trips to Peking, could discover no formula that would bridge the opposing views regarding the disposition of the island. What eliminated much of the earlier cordiality, secondly, was the continuing American pursuit of detente with the USSR, for the Chinese viewed the Soviet Union as a special danger to Asia. Faced with the absence of any agreement on these two major issues, President Gerald Ford knew that his trip to Peking in late November 1975 could be no more than ceremonial. Indeed, the divergence of opinion on detente was sufficient to rule out any joint communique to end the summit. Still the Chinese-American relationship remained generally satisfactory, for the two nations shared a wide spectrum of purposes which again denied the validity of the earlier notion of a binding Moscow-Peking-Hanoi axis. For what concerned Peking above all was the need to limit the ambitions of both Moscow and Hanoi in Asia.

4

AMERICAN RELATIONS WITH THE
REPUBLIC OF CHINA

Douglas H. Mendel, Jr.

Professor of Political Science,
University of Wisconsin, Milwaukee

Ever since July 15, 1975, when the news broke of Richard Nixon's plan to accept the invitation of Peking to visit the People's Republic of China (PRC), the Republic of China (ROC) on Taiwan has wondered about its ties with the United States. Would the U.S. maintain the 1954 security treaty? Would it switch its embassy from Taipei to Peking, as many other nations did following the admission of the PRC into the United Nations in late 1971? The Nixon visit to the PRC opened a Pandora's box of problems for the ROC, most of which it has valiantly solved by substituting unofficial for official relations, maintaining a foreign trade almost equal to its gross national product, and increasing the contrasts between itself and the PRC in terms of social, economic, and political freedoms and an open society. But its relations with the United States remain cloudy. Taipei, notably Foreign Minister Shen Chang-huan, protested both President Gerald Ford's flight to Peking in early December 1975 and Ford's reliance on Henry Kissinger's advice regarding the "Japan formula" for normalizing relations between the U.S. and the PRC by moving the American embassy from Taipei to Peking but retaining nominally unofficial liaison offices in Taiwan, while the ROC also opened nominally unofficial liaison offices in the United States.[1] This had been Japan's method of transferring political recognition from Taipei to Peking while retaining full economic and cultural links with Taiwan, as only 8 percent of the Japanese public, in a mid-1974 national poll, wanted the Communists to take over Taiwan.[2]

But when Dr. Kissinger mentioned during the December 1975 Peking visit that the U.S. planned to adopt the "Japan formula," which was acceptable to Peking, and President Ford announced a new Pacific Doctrine including "normalization of relations with the People's Republic of China," Taipei worried that it might suffer the great strategic loss of the United States' security commitment to Taiwan. Other governments with no such security link could substitute unofficial trade, travel, air, and other agreements through unofficial liaison offices. But the security commitment, which differs from trade or cultural links in that it depends upon official recognition, was a cause of concern to the ROC; specifically, it feared that the U.S. might switch its embassy from Taipei to Peking, as Senator Henry Jackson had urged after his 1974 visit to mainland China.[3]

This chapter is designed to show how fickle the United States has been toward the ROC during the decades since the start of the second Sino-Japanese war of 1937, and how determined a majority of American citizens are to defend the ROC (as evidenced in recent Gallup polls and by the majority petition of the House of Representatives requesting President Ford not to compromise U.S. relations with Taipei during his Peking visit).

It may be advisable to trace briefly the record of U.S.-ROC relations during two periods: 1937–49, before the victory of the Chinese Communists, and 1949–71, before the Nixon shocks that transformed him from the ROC's best-liked American to its most-disliked American. Those periods, especially the latter, reveal the limited nature of U.S. support for the ROC and the gap between rhetoric and policy. We should also caution the reader at the outset that there are severe differences of opinion within Washington and Taipei (as well as in Peking) on how far to trust the American government's commitments to the ROC. After analyzing the 1937–49 and 1949–71 record, we can better predict the future based on the changes in American relations with both Taipei and Peking since the 1971 Nixon trip announcement.

U.S.–ROC Relations before the Communist Takeover

Those old enough to recall the decade of the 1930s easily remember the widespread American sympathy for the Nationalist Chinese government in the face of Japanese military aggression—in Manchuria in 1931, later in North China, and finally in 1937 throughout the mainland. Most Japanese naval officers and diplomats with China experience opposed the Japanese aggression, and even Hitler sent a warning to Tokyo that its military adventures in the mainland would only help the Communists. Mao himself predicted that Japan would defeat the Nationalists, that the United States would subsequently defeat Japan, and that the Communists could then take over. Just as the French kept the Vietnamese divided, the British and Japanese kept the Chinese divided to benefit their imperialistic designs. But most Americans of the 1930s were isolationists, opposed even to aiding the British and French after Hitler invaded Poland. The United States has always been Europe-oriented, and before Pearl Harbor the Soviet Union gave more military aid to the ROC than did the United States. Moreover, Washington did not place an embargo on trade with Japan until Japan moved into Vietnam as a southern route to China. Some might say that Vietnam was the trigger of the Pacific war, since the United States had not taken such drastic steps against Japanese moves on the mainland.

Nor did Washington during the Pacific war plan any invasion of the mainland. It preferred to use air and sea power to defeat the Japanese by island-hopping in the Pacific and blockading the Japanese islands. Research after the war proved that the two atomic bombs were not needed and that Tokyo would have surrendered by late 1945 without the atomic bombs, the Soviet Union's entry into the war, or the planned invasion of southern Japan. Washington decided not to invade Taiwan because Okinawa was a smaller island, easier to capture and use as a base to invade southern Japan, although American bombers did attack targets in Taiwan.

The United States agreed at the 1943 Cairo conference to return all lands taken by Japan from China, such as Taiwan and the Pescadores, but in the secret Yalta Conference of 1945 Washington agreed to turn over to the Soviet Union not only islands taken by Japan but some islands never before claimed by the Soviet Union. It also agreed to give the Soviet Union the former czarist rights in Manchuria as an induce-ment to enter the war against Japan. That concession angered both the Chinese Nationalists and their Communist oppo-nents, as neither really liked the Russians. Moscow had im-prisoned Chiang Ching-kuo when his father, Chiang Kai-shek, expelled all Russians in 1927, and Stalin had never liked the Maoist faction of the Chinese Communist party, although he did turn over much of the captured Japanese arms in Man-churia when the Soviet Union took over that part of China and helped the Communists (not Nationalists) enter it.

American policy in World War II was aimed mainly at the defeat of Germany and Japan, not at preventing or solving any postwar problems caused by the power vacuums left by the defeated Axis powers. Few Americans knew the history of Russian expansionism in the Far East or even the history of Asian nations, and it is true to say that the United States was probably the least imperialistic power in China before 1945. The U.S. opposed the carving-up of China even after the British gave up their Open Door policy, and Wilson was very opposed to Japanese incursions into the ex-German concession and sphere of interest in China after 1917. The American role was mainly economic and missionary, not official, despite the presence of a Yangtse River patrol and naval units stationed in Shanghai. Japan was a better trading partner than China before as well as after World War II, and many American families who had lived in both China and Japan preferred life in the latter (before the antiforeignism of the 1930s). Thus, we can see that the United States did its best to keep the Nationalist Chinese government in the war by sending aid across Burma and having a military mission in the wartime capital of Chungking, but Washington also had a liaison mission of diplomats and military officers in the Chinese Communist capital of Yenan (the "Dixie mission"). The whole story of the American relations with the Chinese Nationalists and Communists has been told elsewhere.[4]

The Truman plan to send General Marshall to mediate the Chinese civil war was hopeless from the outset. Both Chinese factions had expected to fight each other again after Japan's defeat. Anyone who worked with either the Chinese Nationalists or Communists knew they had fought bitterly from 1927 to 1936 and never really cooperated much in their common struggle against Japanese invaders, because the Communists knew the Nationalists would be blamed for failure to halt the invasion while the Communists could reap all the benefits of Nationalist weaknesses. The Japanese invasion pushed the Nationalist government from the populous coastal areas into the western hills, and the return of the Nationalists to the cities meant hopeless struggle against the inflation which was the major cause of Nationalist collapse. Many Nationalist leaders, after the move to Taiwan in 1949, admitted their weaknesses in the mainland—economic, social, and military.

Nationalist misrule in Taiwan was reported by American and other diplomats in Taipei, and when the Nationalist regime fled the mainland in 1949, the Soviet embassy followed the Nationalist government from Nanking to Canton while the U.S. embassy remained in Nanking, a rather serious slight to the ROC and another evidence of the fickle nature of American policy. In 1949, the Department of State drafted a White Paper on China which blamed the Nationalists for all their problems, whereas in reality these problems had been mostly caused by the Japanese invasion and were due only secondarily to Nationalist weaknesses, the Communists' deception of the public, and the latter's exploitation of Nationalist mistakes. Only minor roles were played by the Soviet Union and the United States. Both superpowers were far more interested in Western Europe during 1947–49; and the cold war started in Europe. The Soviet Union had also been more afraid of Hitler than of Japan in the 1930s, and had made concessions to the Japanese in Manchuria and China in order to devote its full attention to Europe.

Some Washington officials wanted to recognize the Chinese Communist regime after it was established in Peking on October 1, 1949. President Truman and his secretary of state, Dean Acheson, more or less washed their hands of the China problem and wanted to "let the dust settle." They worried mainly about Soviet threats in Europe and the Middle East.

After the outbreak of the Korean War in June 1950, the whole American containment policy was extended to the Far East, with more aid to the French in Vietnam. Occupation orders were given to the Japanese government to begin rearmament, previously forbidden by every known means, and President Truman ordered the Seventh Fleet to patrol the Taiwan Straits to prevent either the Communists or the Nationalists from resuming their civil war. Actually, Allen Whiting and others claimed that the only Communist preparations to attack Taiwan were made in the spring of 1950, but an epidemic swept the coast and aborted that effort. In one sense, therefore, the Korean War, which was Stalin's effort to probe U.S. commitments to South Korea at a time when all evidence pointed to a lack of unilateral commitment and the success of the European containment policy, helped to defend the ROC in its island bastion of Taiwan.

The Truman administration also resumed economic and small-scale military defensive aid to the Republic of China in 1950–51, and the Asian containment program was set for the next two decades. However, Washington did not accept any Nationalist troops to fight on the United Nations side of the Korean conflict, partly because it feared Peking reactions; nor did Washington or Saigon ask for any Nationalist troops to fight in Vietnam during the 1965–72 period of heavy American involvement there. But one must recall that General Douglas MacArthur had also assured President Truman that the Chinese Communists could not intervene in Korea, only to be proven wrong later the same year when hordes of Chinese Communist volunteers pushed the U.S.-U.N. forces back below the 38th parallel. When given a chance, of course, large numbers of North Korean and Chinese Communist prisoners of war opted to stay away from their Communist homelands. Thousands went to Taiwan, and their decision is commemorated in the annual Freedom Day celebrations in Taipei.[5]

American foreign policy was still mainly Europe-oriented even after the start of the Korean defense action in June 1950. When Korea spurred NATO allies to ask for a NATO joint military command under an American general, Washington not only complied by sending General Dwight D. Eisenhower to command the joint force, but also began sending $15 billion in arms to the NATO partners and pressured them to admit Greece, Turkey, and West Germany to the alliance. Aid to the ROC remained small until the 1953 Korean truce, and gradually increased thereafter as the ROC improved its domestic and foreign image.

Relations in the 1949–71 Years: Alliance and Aid

The greatest success of the Republic of China since its removal to Taiwan in 1949 has been economic and social progress, stemming mainly from the work ethic of Chinese people everywhere but aided by the encouragement of free enterprise given by the American AID advisors and the $1.6 billion in economic assistance (mostly grants) that ended in 1965. The best study of U.S. aid to Taiwan was by Neil H. Jacoby, *U.S. Aid to Taiwan: A Study of Foreign Aid Self-Help and Development* (New York, 1966), based on Jacoby's official report for the American government done at the termination of the grant-aid program. Much of the other $2.5 billion in military aid from the United States was also of indirect benefit to the economy in that it provided jobs, infrastructure, and a greater sense of security.

One indication of the success of the economic programs was the rise in per-capita income from $100 in 1952 to $700 in 1975—about four or five times higher than income in mainland China, where the Communist system discourages farmer and worker productivity by forcing long hours of work at low wages (average of $30 per month). There has always been a gap between lower agricultural income and higher urban income, but Taipei started programs to balance the two in the 1970s. Part of the U.S. economic aid went into the very effective Joint Commission on Rural Reconstruction (JCRR), whose tasks included the laudable land reform of 1952–57 and diversification of commercial crops to expand the export markets for agriculture (usually to Japan, but later to the United States and Europe), plus mechanization of small-scale farming. In 1961–62 water buffalo were a common sight, but by 1974–75 they almost disappeared. Naturally, inflation, especially in the early 1970s, reduced the rise of real income, but wages rose a great deal and will continue to increase.

The U.S. economic aid program, as Jacoby notes in his book, did not attempt to promote political democracy or use economic aid as a lever to secure political changes, but it did encourage private enterprise which tended to strengthen the hold of the native Taiwanese businessmen over the economy. For example, the few big landlords received shares in government businesses turned over to private hands in the early 1950s, and it later became all too true that the private wealth in Taiwan was in native Taiwanese hands. The Republic of China retained official control of a few key industries such as wine, tobacco, salt, and sugar, but those had traditionally been government monopolies in all Asian lands. Land reform, which was extended to urban land owned by rural landlords in the early 1960s, gave the farmers a stake in society by building up the agricultural cooperative societies, which grew into semipolitical organs later as many rural children migrated to the cities. The official American policy in all allied countries was to avoid interference in their internal politics even to promote democracy; nevertheless, by supporting private enterprise in Taiwan, AID and other American agencies did strengthen the hands of the native businessmen.

Some of the American economic aid went into social overhead, such as improvement of rail equipment, the purchase of railcars from Japan (since Japan had built most of the original railways in Taiwan), harbor expansion—especially in Kaohsiung, where the annual percentage of shipping and freight (total island cargo tonnage was 30 million in 1973) topped those of the other ports—and highway development. The AID also encouraged birth control, in the face of serious opposition in national Taipei circles from conservatives who thought that more children would better enable the ROC to keep up the military strength necessary to challenge the much more populous Communist mainland. (Estimated 1976 mainland population was 800 million, compared to 16.2 million in Taiwan.) But the provincial Taiwan government was more receptive to the birth-control program, and the intra-uterine loop became very popular among native wives. Net population growth was slowed from about 3.5 percent in the early 1950s to 2 percent in the early 1970s, and urbanization will slow it further.

That industrialization had been the major effort of the 1960s was very evident to anyone who visited Taiwan in 1974 after an absence of a decade. Industrial production quadrupled from 1966 to 1973, while electric machinery and appliance production rose 1,900 percent during that period. Exports by 1975 were about $6 billion, compared with $120 million in 1952 and $1.5 billion in 1970. Total foreign trade was close to $12.5 billion in 1975 and is likely to expand as the world recession abates. Any nation that has a foreign-trade total close to its GNP runs the danger of subjecting itself to the perils of recessions in other countries, and the Republic of China is planning to reduce the export share of its economy in the next decade. Another AID effort was to raise living standards so that the people would have more of a stake in a non-Communist future and so that enough people would realize more than $1,000 in annual income to permit a greater shift of taxation toward direct levies such as the income tax. In 1973, direct taxes accounted for 27 percent of the total tax revenues, while indirect taxes (on imports, sales, and related items) provided 73 percent. The government is planning a further reduction of indirect taxes, which tend to fall on the poorer segment of the population. Incomes in 1975 were taxed at rates running from 15 percent to 60 percent, another reform urged by many AID advisors.[6]

Military aid constituted a large portion of the American program for the Republic of China, but has been less open to

public scrutiny. The best available source of information is
*Hearings before the Subcommittee on United States Security
Agreements and Commitments Abroad of the Senate Committee on Foreign Relations*, published in 1971 in two vol-
umes. The hearings on Republic of China military relations
(vol. 1, pp. 918–1146) include much relevant data but omit
classified information. Many witnesses confirmed that there
were often points of friction between the ROC military and
the U.S. military advisors, especially in regard to the ROC's
asking for more than the U.S. could give. American policy
had been limited to supplying defensive arms and protective
agreements against a Communist attack, and did not extend
to assisting the Nationalists in recovering the mainland. This
defensive posture was implied in the exchange of notes between Secretary Dulles and Nationalist Foreign Minister
George Yeh on December 10, 1954, requiring joint agreement for any "use of force from either of [the areas under
the mutual defense treaty . . . except for] action of an emer-
gency character which is clearly an exercise of inherent right
of self-defense."[7] As a matter of fact, Washington persuaded
the ROC to withdraw from the small Tachen island group
before the 1954 security treaty, and provided defensive
weapons such as Sidewinder missiles for Nationalist planes
during the Quemoy crisis of 1958. President John F. Kennedy told his U.N. ambassador, Adlai Stevenson, when the
ROC threatened to use its Security Council veto to bar admission of Outer Mongolia: "You have the hardest thing in
the world to sell—the idea that Taiwan represents China. . . .
We'll have to get people to make it clear to Chiang Kai-shek
that he can't expect to make a domestic political issue out
of our strategy in the U.N."[8]

In 1962, when there were rumors inside Taiwan that the
ROC planned to attack the mainland due to the latter's weaknesses after the failure of the Great Leap, President Kennedy
told his ambassador in Warsaw, who conducted ambassadorial
talks with his Chinese Communist counterpart there, to "tell
Peking that the United States would not support any such
undertaking by the Chinese Nationalists, but on the other
hand would defend Taiwan if Peking mistakenly resorted to

force." The signal went through and the crisis was abated. "This may well have been the most valuable single consequence of the ambassadorial talks," wrote Kenneth Young, an expert on U.S.–PRC relations.[9]

Escalation of American military use of Taiwan during the Vietnam War, especially during 1966–72, was a prime motive for the Symington subcommittee hearings cited above, which delved into the possible transfer of B-52 bombers from Okinawa (after reversion in 1972) to Taiwan. By 1975, the forces had been reduced from a Vietnam high of 9,000 to about 2,000, and Premier Chiang Ching-kuo said that total withdrawal would not damage ROC security so long as the security treaty remained in effect. "We do not need American troops to fight for us. We will need only material and spiritual support from the United States—we have adequate manpower to defend ourselves without asking for help from troops from other countries," Chiang said.[10] He also denied any intention of acquiring nuclear weapons directly or through use of radioactive waste from the several nuclear power plants scheduled for Taiwan in the next decade.

Finally, we should take note of the political relations of the U.S. with the Republic of China during the 1960s, up to the announcement of the Nixon plan to visit Peking. First, the U.S. had never deported any Taiwanese independence activists back to Taiwan, as the Sato cabinet in Japan did on two occasions, and some members of Congress spoke favorably of the independence movement. Congress passed annual resolutions throughout the 1960s opposing any change in the U.N. representation of China, and a majority of congressmen still opposed abandonment of the ROC in 1976. But when A. T. Steele, former Asian area correspondent, spent a year studying American public views of China policy for the Council on Foreign Relations, he discovered that 28 percent did not know that the Communists controlled the mainland, while only 60 percent of those who did know about the PRC knew there was another Chinese government on Taiwan.[11]

The TIM, or Taiwan Independence Movement, was described and analyzed in this writer's book *The Politics of Formosan Nationalism* (Berkeley and Los Angeles, 1970).[12]

Fewer than 10 percent of the Taiwanese in Japan and the United States participated in the independence movement actively, although many others sympathized with it; and the movement was as fractured into different factions as are most other emigré political movements. Even though few Americans knew of Taiwan in 1970, they would have been turned off by an attempted political assassination of Chiang Ching-kuo—who was characterized by the State Department in 1975 as a man who could bring more Taiwanese into the government and continue to meet native demands, as he had done so well since 1972. After the spate of political assassinations in the United States which took the lives of the two Kennedy brothers, Dr. Martin Luther King, Jr., and Malcolm X, the American public wanted no more of terrorist activities. However, Washington did allow any of the 10,000 or more Taiwanese who had come to this country for graduate education to engage in demonstrations at the U.N., near the ROC embassy in Washington, or elsewhere.

Throughout the Vietnam War, Washington viewed Peking as a menace. After American opinion turned against the war, however, Nixon knew it would have to be ended, and he made that promise in his successful attempt to win the 1968 presidential election. He also promised to end the U.S. hard line on Peking, and began to refer to that government by its official name, the People's Republic of China. By 1971 he had relaxed the U.S. trade embargo, and American visitors to Hong Kong were allowed to bring back some mainland products. Peking made the first overtures to Washington knowing that it would have to deal with Nixon, since the leftists and radicals had no power in Washington. The Kunming Papers, a document from the Kunming party, published an explanation of the Nixon trip in 1973 in order to counter complaints by Chinese Communists who opposed inviting a man with such a hard-line anti-Communist record. That document explained that Nixon was a "transitional man" who could open the doors to Chinese propaganda in the United States, counter the Soviet military challenge that had been Peking's main concern since 1968, weaken U.S.-Japan ties by appearing to rush into China ahead of Tokyo, and otherwise weaken U.S. alliances in Asia, especially the U.S. tie to the ROC.[13]

After the Nixon trip, following the secret Kissinger flight from Pakistan to Peking, Taipei cooled toward Nixon as Peking waxed enthusiastic over its ability to use him for its own purposes. When the U.N. General Assembly refused to accept a two-China arrangement in the fall of 1971, the Nationalists walked out, and the General Assembly overwhelmingly voted to give the PRC the Chinese seat. By 1974 the ROC had managed to substitute unofficial relations for its lost diplomatic ties.

How have U.S.-Taiwan relations changed since the Nixon visit to Peking in February 1972? Now that we have surveyed the past record to that critical date, it is time to focus on the developments since 1972 and the most likely future of U.S.-ROC relations.

Fluid Policy since 1972 and Future Prospects

The Nixon visit to mainland China in February 1972 produced a Shanghai Communique, in which the United States specifically did not challenge the position taken by "all Chinese on either side of the Taiwan Strait" that "there is but one China and that Taiwan is part of China." The communique further stated that the United States would withdraw its military forces from Taiwan as tensions relaxed in the region, and also reaffirmed its interest in achieving "a peaceful settlement of the Taiwan question by the Chinese themselves." The latter statement, which implied negotiation between the two Chinese governments, raised much turmoil in Taipei because the latter had no intention of negotiating with the Communist regime, although it had proposed a 70-percent political and 30-percent military formula for "recovering" the mainland. (Peking had a similar doctrine, less clearly articulated.) To encourage the two regimes to unite, in Taipei's view, was tantamount to encouraging the 16 million people on Taiwan to succumb to the totalitarian rule of the mainland, where the freedoms recently expanded under the Chiang Ching-kuo administration would soon disappear. The communique seemed reminiscent of the 1947 Marshall mission to China, when that general wanted the two sides to combine—something neither of them intended to do.

In late 1975, when President Ford stopped in Honolulu to speak at the East-West Center of the University of Hawaii, he said, "I visited China to build on the dialogue started nearly four years ago. . . . There were, as expected, differences of perspective . . . but we did find common ground. . . . I re-affirmed the determination of the United States to complete the normalization of relations with the People's Republic of China on the basis of the Shanghai Communique . . . our rela-tionship is becoming a permanent feature of the international landscape. It benefits not only our two peoples but all the peoples of the region and the entire world."[14] This enuncia-tion of a Pacific Doctrine was as vague as President Nixon's Guam Doctrine of 1969, which implied a lower U.S. military profile in Asia—while the Asian states were expected to de-fend themselves and their friends.

What happened to U.S. relations with the ROC between the February 1972 Shanghai Communique and the December 1975 Ford-Kissinger promise to complete the normalization of relations with the PRC? The lack of a specific timetable for the latter implied that Washington did not plan to close its Taipai embassy quickly or cancel its security commitment to defend Taiwan, but in true Kissinger style it implied a switch of diplomatic ties in the near future from the ROC to the PRC.

After his 1972 trip to mainland China, President Nixon affirmed that he would not abandon old friends and allies—a statement repeated by President Ford in the traumatic days of early 1975 when all of Indochina fell to Communist con-trol. But the United States never had a direct treaty commit-ment to the Indochinese governments, as it has had with the Republics of Korea and China. Washington has been explicit in repeating its commitment to Seoul—a commitment openly supported by the Miki cabinet of Tokyo—but more muted in its support for the Republic of China. The Nixon visit to mainland China was preceded and followed by the relaxation of passport restrictions on travel to China, the removal of the ban on noncommercial imports, the granting of permission for subsidiaries of U.S. firms to trade with China in non-strategic goods and for the PRC to ship cargoes in American vessels between non-Chinese ports, and the establishment of a more open policy regarding imports from the mainland to the U.S.[15] Yet, in the four years since that time, American trade with Taiwan has risen far more than trade with the mainland and averages three times the value of the latter. (The 1974 figures were $3.5 billion and $1 billion, respectively, with an even greater gap in 1975, when Peking bought less grain.)

American trade with the mainland in 1974 was $819 million in exports ($665 million in agricultural products) and $115 million in imports. In 1975, U.S. grain exports to China dropped sharply as a result of better Chinese harvests, and two-way trade between the U.S. and the PRC amounted to less than $500 million. Japan remains Peking's biggest trading partner, as it was for years before the 1972 diplomatic normalization.

Let us look first at economic relations. American businessmen tend to agree with the conclusion of Ray Cline, former chief of the State Department Bureau of Intelligence and Research, that the ROC is one of the most stable polities in the world. American trade with Taiwan in 1974 was over $3.5 billion, with $600 million more imports than exports—up from $2.5 billion in 1973 and $1.8 billion in 1972.[16] The worldwide recession, which has tended to encourage protectionism in all countries, slowed the rate of trade increase in 1975; but the rate improved again in 1976, when first-quarter two-way trade reached the record value of $1 billion. An article in the December 15, 1975, issue of *Business Week* described the "remarkable allure of Taiwan for U.S. business."[17] The total foreign investment in Taiwan is about $1.3 billion—less than the $1.6 billion in recent foreign exchange reserves. One-third of the foreign investment comes from the United States, 17 percent from Japan, and 28 percent from overseas Chinese (who are very welcome in the ROC). The rate of domestic savings in Taiwan is 29 percent of the gross domestic product, a figure that can be attributed to the thrifty habits of Asians and to the fact that two-year tax-free savings accounts in banks yield over 12 percent annually. In one recent year, National Distillers decided to invest $10 million in a polyethylene plant, Amoco Chemicals $75 million in the polyester fiber industry, and Union Carbide $100 million in a petrochemical project financed by five American and Canadian banks. "The major concern of U.S. investors in Taiwan would be political," said the chairman of National Distillers' local subsidiary, "but we are not worried to the point that we are fearful about our investment."

Why are they not worried? First, they doubt that Peking would risk antagonizing the United States, on whom it relies as a counterbalance to the Soviet Union, by attacking Taiwan militarily or in other ways. Second, they doubt that either Taipei or Peking has the military capability to invade the other. Third, they think that "the mainland Chinese will not disturb [Taiwan's] business relationship because, like Hong Kong, it provides an open door to the Western world" and that a thriving Taiwan would be an asset to China in any eventual settlement of the sovereignty issue. Surely Peking knows how high the Taiwan living standards are when 86 percent of Taipei households have television sets, 69 percent refrigerators, 35 percent washing machines, and 23 percent telephones, while there are more private cars in Taipei than on the entire mainland.

Fox Butterfield, who formerly had been very critical of the Nationalist regime, revisited Taipei in 1975 and reported that "Taiwan at present appears to enjoy greater political stability than any other country in Asia . . . and is likely to grow stronger economically and politically."[18] Many other American and other foreign visitors to Taiwan would agree. Former Secretary of the Treasury David Kennedy said, during his March 1975 Taipei visit, that the U.S. would never restrict foreign investment in the ROC by U.S. companies, and that detente between Washington and Peking would not affect American business interests in Taiwan. Former U.S. Ambassador Everett Drumwright returned to Taipei in September 1975 and claimed that Taipei's "real" relations with other countries were stronger than they had been seventeen years before, when he had arrived as ambassador, and he urged all Americans to see the conditions in Taiwan for themselves.

The United States has become the biggest buyer of Taiwan exports, including textiles, television sets and other appliances, and canned foods. Japan is the biggest supplier, but Taipei has tried to reduce its perennial trade deficit with Japan by encouraging her to buy more goods and by switching to Europe and the United States as sources of items traditionally imported from Japan. Yet the Republic of China has never wished to harm its economy by decreasing trade for political reasons, and one of its strongest economic assets is the series of ten capital-investment projects planned for the coming decade. These projects include port expansion, rail improvement, a superhighway from north to south, an integrated steel mill, a petrochemical complex in the southern port city of Kaohsiung, and several nuclear plants to reduce dependence on Arab oil (although Taipei has excellent relations with Saudi Arabia). The U.S. Export-Import Bank agreed in 1974 to loan $924 million for those ten projects at an annual interest rate of 8 percent. Japanese also top the Taiwan tourist list, sending about 500,000 tourists annually compared to about 140,000 Americans in 1973 and somewhat more in 1974. (The recent recession, during which U.S. unemployment rates were higher than those of either Japan or Taiwan, caused a decrease in overseas travel by Americans. Airlines also offer lower transatlantic plane fares, which commonly include special excursion rates not available on Pacific flights, and so encourage Americans to travel to Europe where there are likely to feel more at home culturally.) The costs of tourist life are usually less in Taiwan than in Japan or even Hong Kong.

We have discussed the military relationship between Washington and Taipei and the differences within each nation's military circle. Now we should discuss the actual military relations after 1972, when President Nixon promised to scale down the American presence in Taiwan. Troop levels fell from about 9,000 in 1972 to under 2,000 in 1976. (The U.S. Air Force maintains some support units, the Army a communications outfit, and the Navy a small unit.) Jet fighters were removed in 1975, against the wishes of many American generals; Premier Chiang insisted, however, that his 500,000-man force, in combination with 2.2 million reservists and a pledge of strategic defense by Washington, obviated the need for American troops. In 1972, Washington sold Taipei seventeen warships (fifteen destroyers and two submarines), and Taipei purchased additional vessels. Grant military aid stopped and was replaced by long-term credit sales, including $150 to $200 million in credits for the building of F-5 fighters to counter the MIG fighters in the Communist mainland. Military aid in terms of credit sales in fiscal 1973 was $102 million; this figure was reduced in 1974 to $92 million and to $3.5 million in 1975. Taipei also benefited from claiming and repairing used American weapons from the Vietnam War, keeping some and selling others.

Peking objects to any American military aid to the Nationalists, and would prefer to have a U.S. embassy in its own territory in order to further isolate the ROC government. While Peking favors the American security treaty with Japan, opposes North Korean force against the ROK, and even claims that it approves the stationing of American forces in the Philippines and Thailand if those governments wish them, it considers Taiwan an internal problem because it is Chinese territory. If Taipei were subsequently to make overtures to the Soviet Union, perhaps inviting a Soviet freighter to stop occasionally in a Taiwan port for rest and recreation, Peking might think twice about urging an American military withdrawal. While no Taipei government would be likely to ally itself with the Soviet Union—considered an enemy by all Chinese—the government has printed items from the Soviet press and allowed some Soviet correspondents to visit.

The Taipei government has confidence in its U.S. military commitment, despite the views held by some of its legislators that the security treaty is a less vital factor than ROC forces or the Soviet threat to Peking.[19] Ambassador Leonard Unger, whose appointment to Taipei aroused PRC anger because of his stature, often reiterated the strong American ties to the ROC, but occasionally referred to the mainland by its official title—which is never done in Taiwan. Vice-Admiral

Edwin Snyder, the top American commander in Taiwan as head of the U.S.–Taiwan Defense Command, insisted that Congressional repeal of the 1955 Taiwan resolution had not affected the 1954 security treaty, and he pledged to work to maintain the security link despite Washington's efforts to normalize relations with the PRC.[20] But American military officers do not determine foreign policy. Most of the American military officers in East Asia would prefer that the U.S. keep its treaty with the ROC, which has always been a defensive one and is not involved in the Nationalist goal to retake the mainland. Peking has refused to renounce the use of force against Taiwan, just as the Taipei government has refused to renounce force in its policy, but in practice (which is always more important than a nation's rhetoric) there have been no military efforts by either side against the other beyond the occasional shelling duels at Quemoy.

Senator Hiram Fong, the only Chinese-American in the U.S. Senate, urged Washington to give more advanced weaponry to Taipei in a late-1974 talk. Fong praised the regime as giving the people of Taiwan a life of dignity, free enterprise, and democracy, saying that, "along that line, the government and the people of the Republic of China have made great progress . . . compared with the mainland people, who are under completely different political, economic, and social systems."[21] As previously noted, the sales credits for the F-5 fighters, now in production, were part of the post-Nixon-era pledge to Taiwan defense. It may be true, as American and Chinese Nationalist experts agree, that the PRC has neither the capacity nor the will to attack Taiwan, and that the Nationalists know they must rely on an uprising on the mainland to trigger any move of their own to return. Younger mainlanders in Taiwan, those brought over at a young age or born on the island, tend to discount the mainland recovery goal.

Finally, political relations between the United States and the Republic of China remain very complex. As part of its worldwide program to substitute unofficial for official relations and to meet the Communist Chinese cultural offensive within the United States, Taipei opened four new U.S.

consulates, making a total of fourteen by mid-1974.[22] The ROC also has expanded the number of information officers at the major consulates, realizing that the Nixon visit to the mainland in 1973 made it popular for even conservative Americans to be pro-Peking. One retired foreign-service officer with experience in Hong Kong said in early 1974, "Who cares about a little island like Taiwan when we have doors to China open?" Dr. Henry Kissinger told a Washington audience of groups promoting trade and exchanges with the People's Republic in June 1974 that the United States "has and will continue to have an interest in a strong People's Republic of China. . . . No policy has had greater bipartisan support than normalization of relations with that country."[23]

Yet there is a great deal of disagreement in Congress and within the State Department and Pentagon on such a shift in American China policy. House Speaker Carl Albert, for example, told a Hong Kong press conference, after he and John Rhodes, House minority leader, had visited mainland China, "There certainly cannot be any diplomatic relations between the United States and Communist China under the present circumstances."[24] Rhodes was aware of this writer's Japan survey results of 1974, showing that only 8 percent of the Japanese favored a Communist future for Taiwan, and he and Albert agreed on the need to maintain relations with Taipei.

Senator Jacob Javits, no friend of either the Soviet Union or the PRC, returned from Peking in mid-1975 and said, "Our diplomatic relations [with Peking] have gone about as far as they can now," although he predicted that the mainland would stress economic development which could expand trade with the United States.[25] Javits also said that Peking understood that the U.S. would not relinquish its security commitment to the Nationalist government, but that he was nevertheless surprised by the late-1975 Kissinger-Ford comments in Peking, promising to adopt the Japan model.

Many other congressmen and senators who have visited the mainland continue to oppose establishing diplomatic relations with Peking at the expense of Taiwan, and twenty-nine of them signed a petition to President Ford agreeing with the majority in the House of Representatives which was opposed to switching diplomatic relations from Taipei to Peking.[26] These legislators included not only such conservatives as Barry Goldwater, John Tower, and Strom Thurmond, but also such liberals as Mark Hatfield, Edward Brooke, and Howard Baker. Senators Jackson and Fulbright have called for the switch in diplomatic relations—thinking, perhaps, along the Kissinger line, that, because Moscow is worse and more dangerous than Peking, it would be good for the United States to get closer to the PRC in order to worry the Soviet Union. Henry Jackson's explicit suggestion to move the U.S. embassy to Peking and the liaison office to Taipei was made in 1974 after his visit to Peking: "We should try to reverse the location of our embassy and the liaison office—there are many areas in which American relations parallel those of the Chinese."[27] Senators Mike Mansfield and J. William Fulbright agreed with Jackson, but such anti-Soviet senators have little reason to praise Peking or dump the ROC, other than the political reason that impelled Richard Nixon to visit Peking: They know that the American public is more anti-Moscow than anti-Peking.

After the collapse of Indochina under communism, and even before that event, the general American public was opposed to establishing diplomatic relations with mainland China at the expense of Taiwan. A Gallup poll in August 1974 showed that a majority was opposed to switching embassies and to cancelling the American defense commitment to the Republic of China.[28] When approximately 1,600 Americans were polled on their views about many foreign nations, about half of them underestimated both the economic and political stability of Taiwan and Taiwan's affection for the United States, since very few had ever been to Taiwan or read much about it. However, 72 percent opposed Peking's conditions for diplomatic relations (such as breaking ties with Taipei), against only 11 percent in favor of them; about 50 percent favored American efforts to improve relations with Peking. On the security treaty with Taiwan, 48 percent favored honoring it while 35 percent were opposed. Younger people were more likely to be opposed, as would probably also be true in Japan and other countries.

A similar Gallup poll conducted in October 1975 showed that 58 percent thought that the collapse of Indochina had led other Asian nations to doubt U.S. treaty credibility, but that 70 percent favored continuing formal diplomatic relations with the Republic of China.[29] In overall attitudes, 53 percent had favorable views of the ROC, compared to only 27 percent who were favorably disposed toward mainland China. Those results may explain why 61 percent favored normalizing relations with Peking, against 23 percent opposed. When asked if Washington should cut its diplomatic ties with the ROC to open them with the mainland, however, 70 percent said "No" while 14 percent said "Yes." Such results, one would think, should have deterred Kissinger and Ford from saying in Peking during their December 1975 visit that the United States would adopt the Japan model. In regard to the ROC treaty commitment, the 1975 Gallup sample was divided 47 percent "pro" and 31 percent "con"; the sample's views of the political and economic stability of Taiwan were more favorable than in 1974, as were estimates of ROC friendship for the United States (53 percent positive and 31 percent negative). As a place to visit, Taiwan drew a 35 percent positive to 57 percent negative vote, showing how few Americans have visited the Far East or know the truth about the beauty, economy, safety, and hospitality of Taiwan.

What arguments can be used by those favoring and by those opposing a switch in diplomatic relations from Taipei to Peking? On the "pro" side, many who hate the Soviet Union think that China is a better country, with more hardworking people, and that it is deserving of full diplomatic recognition as the most populous nation in the world. "Oil for the lamps of China," "800 million customers," and similar sentiments echo the pro-Chinese sentiments of the 1930s, and many American youth who have visited the mainland were brainwashed into believing that it really is a people's democracy. Peking was more open to critical visitors in 1972 and 1973, but then discovered that such Americans as Robert Scalapino, Alfred Jenkins (who formerly served at the U.S. liaison office in Peking), and others reported very unfavorably, as did Michael Lindsay, the British sinologist, and his wife. Jenkins said he was not allowed to speak freely with the common people of China, as he was in pre-Communist times or as anyone is free to do inside Taiwan. Another argument stressed by the China experts who visited the mainland in 1972–73 was that Peking was only using the United States as a counterweight to the Soviet Union, in conformance with the traditional Chinese strategy of being friendly to distant powers but hostile to neighboring ones. For these and other reasons, such as domestic turmoil, Peking became much more selective of the Americans it admitted in 1974 and 1975. For example, it refused to admit Professor Allen Whiting for ten months' study, although Whiting had often predicted a merger of Taiwan into the mainland regime; Taipei, on the other hand, allowed him to study for a year there. Members of the U.S.–China People's Friendship Association, which some believe is subsidized partially or indirectly by Peking, organized group trips to the mainland for which each participant had to pay $60 per day—more than double what they would pay in Taiwan or other parts of Asia.[30]

Another reason for supporting full diplomatic ties with Peking could be the desire to neutralize Peking support for liberation movements in Asia. That was a motive of the Thai, Philippine, and Malaysian governments in extending full recognition in 1975, but they could not rely on such Peking links to defuse internal rebellions. Each government would have to solve its own internal problems, since every government in Southeast Asia except Singapore discriminates against resident Chinese and other minorities. What a Communist regime says is not always what it does, and because each Communist government operates on a state-to-state basis as well as a party-to-party basis and a people-to-people basis, it can use a triple strategy. Few Americans are familiar with the nature of the Chinese Communist system and the need for every non-Communist Asian government to unify its people, raise living standards, eliminate corruption, and do the other things Premier Chiang Ching-kuo has done in Taiwan. Proponents of Peking recognition might also cite better trade opportunities, cultural exchanges, and other

nonpolitical advantages, but they should look at the Japanese
example to see that mere diplomatic relations do not necessarily lead to other benefits. Nor does any other nation have
the kind of security commitment to the Republic of China
which the U.S. has as a result of its 1954 treaty. Other mo-
tives might include the world rush to Peking after the Nixon
visit, the U.N. seating, the personal interest Dr. Kissinger and
others have shown in mainland China (but not in Taiwan),
and a variety of more detailed reasons that pro-Peking people
might mention.

On the other side, President Ford himself told a press conference in May 1975 that it was his aim to "tie more closely
together South Korea and the U.S., to reaffirm our commitments to Taiwan, to work more closely with Indonesia, with
the Philippines and with other Pacific nations."[31] Officials
claimed that the president's words had been carefully thought
out in advance, but probably not by Secretary of State
Kissinger. Defense Secretary James Schlesinger, who subsequently left the Ford administration in late 1975, also said
at a May 1975 press conference, "We have treaty obligations
with Taiwan, and as long as those treaties continue to guide
this country and be the law of the land, Formosa will be
protected." President Ford also told the American Society
of Newspaper Editors convention in April 1975 that the U.S.
was concerned about the security and stability of the Republic of China, and that his administration considered "relationship and cooperation with the Republic of China a matter of
very, very great importance to us."

It is difficult for any person acquainted with international
law and the history of mutual-security treaties to contemplate
having a security treaty with a nation that is not diplomati-
cally recognized. That is the biggest argument against switching diplomatic missions from Taipei to Peking, even if one
thinks that significant benefits would be realized from the
move. It is this writer's contention that Peking's only real motive is to deter a Soviet attack by drawing the U.S. closer to
it, and that there is little reason to expect Peking to change its
policies of economic self-reliance and diversification of trade—
getting the best products where it can buy them cheaply.

Peking did promise Australian Labor party leader Gough Whitlam that it would buy more Australian wheat if he became premier and switched diplomatic relations. After he did so, Whitlam's popularity plummeted during the following two years, and he was removed from office in late 1975.

The former U.S. ambassador to Taipei, Walter McConaughy, told a New York audience in late 1975, "The U.S. policy of friendship and close cooperation with the Republic of China . . . is a national consensus, on which a majority of the American people and their representatives in both houses of Congress seem agreed without regard to party affiliation."[32] At the same meeting, professors Richard Walker and Paul K. T. Sih, as well as Anthony Kubek, Michael Lindsay, and former congressman Walter Judd, defended a status quo in U.S.-China policy.

It is true that a majority of the House of Representatives and about one-third of the U.S. Senate urged President Ford not to alter American ties to the Republic of China. However, American foreign policy since 1969 has been largely in the hands of Dr. Henry Kissinger, who once angered NATO allies by commenting that he often could get along better with adversary nations (presumably the Soviet Union and China) than with some allies.

In an article printed in the *Mainichi Daily News* (Tokyo) in July 1975, "The Ally We Have to Trust," a Chinese reporter in Taipei admitted that "for the more emotional young nationalists, the standard line nowadays is 'The United States is unreliable; we have to depend on ourselves' . . . an attitude that began in 1971 and gathered momentum with the collapse of Cambodia and South Vietnam. . . . After the U.S. failure in Indochina [said Premier Chiang], there are even hopes that the 'appeasement trend' in America will be dampened. . . . Chiang Ching-kuo said that 'Even though we emphasize self-reliance and the concept that only those who help themselves can be helped by others, we do not exclude the opportunity of group security and defense cooperation with allies.' For the cool-headed officials, at least, the United States is still the most important ally that Taiwan has, and an ally Taiwan has to trust."[33]

Dr. Frederick Chien, former director of the Taipei Government Information Office and since early 1975 vice-minister of foreign affairs, told a Taipei seminar that "normalization of relations between the United States and the Chinese Communists is strewn with obstacles and cannot be achieved quickly. . . . American policy is still concerned mainly with the Russians, so Maoist detente plays only second fiddle. . . . We do face difficulties on the diplomatic front, but the government is sticking to its principles and developing other kinds of relations to smash the Chinese Communist plot to isolate the Republic of China."[34]

On the subject of an eventual peaceful merger of Taiwan into the mainland, through some kind of deal in which the Nationalists would retain nominal control of the island but recognize Peking's sovereignty, Taipei denies all such rumors, and claims it would never make such a deal. Many American diplomats agree, as did William Overholt of the Hudson Institute in an article, "Would Chiang Find Mao an Unacceptably Strange Bedfellow?," in *Asian Survey*.[35] Overholt qualified his prediction—as anyone must, in such a case—citing the uncertainties of the nature of the Communist government after Mao's death and of the subsequent succession struggle (since struggle has always been a theme of the Peking government). But, what with the periodic turmoil on the mainland, the critical reports from sinologists who visit the mainland and then praise the conditions in Taiwan, and the majority sentiment in Congress and in U.S. citizens against cutting ties with the ROC in order to formalize relations with the PRC, it is difficult to foresee a major change in American policy in the near future. As an Arizona travel association leader urged in Taiwan in late 1975, the ROC should make itself better known in the United States and that, rather than tolerate the propaganda that everyone is happy under Communist rule on the mainland, it should send more exhibits and troupes, welcome more U.S. visitors, and publicize the wide contrasts between life in Taiwan and that on the mainland.[36] The success of this strategy, of course, would depend on the temper of the U.S. public, the attitude of the news media, and the types of reform promoted in the ROC to win foreign applause.

The future is hard to predict, and the history of U.S.-ROC relations contains many examples of policy mistakes and misperceptions. Yet there is a strong bond of common interest linking the Chinese in Taiwan to the United States in terms of lifestyle, culture, respect for freedom, and agreement about the strategic importance of Taiwan to the defense of Japan and other allies in Asia. Those who favor continued warm bonds between the ROC and the United States should emphasize those common interests and expose the selfish motivation of the Chinese Communists in their drive for normalization with Washington.

Part 2
American-Japanese Relations

5

Good Intentions and Political Tension in Japanese-American Relations

James W. White

*Associate Professor of Political Science,
University of North Carolina at Chapel Hill*

The political relationship between the United States and Japan, though calm today, was characterized during the last five years by a greater degree of friction than has existed at any time since the end of World War II. Both partners are voluble in their protestations of goodwill, and efforts to reach amicable settlement of the few outstanding problems are incessant.[1] Nevertheless, both military and economic issues have divided us and will do so again; such issues are inevitable and increasingly politicized, and neither past performance nor future prospect gives reason for any great optimism about the smooth resolution of such problems.

During the late 1950s and early 1960s the United States could afford to look upon Japan with indulgence. Japanese trade practices were questionable and Japan's apparent free ride under the American nuclear umbrella may have seemed unprincipled to some; but Japan was still a minor force economically, and Asia did not appear to be an area of immediate threat to global peace. America could easily tolerate the efforts of those hard-working little Orientals to better themselves. For their part, the Japanese were primarily

concentrating on economic betterment and were quite happy
to let political and military issues lie dormant.

Of late, conditions have changed. An economy that is now
third in the world has an impact which cannot be overlooked,
especially when it is currently running at a sizable trade surplus vis-à-vis the United States. Although Japan's practices
could be tolerated before, now they appear critical to certain
sectors of our economy; in this country, the natural reaction
in such cases is political protest. And with U.S. forces largely
out of Southeast Asia, the adamant refusal by Japan to participate in the full defense of its own territory—much less in
any sort of regional security arrangement which would
lighten the American military load—rings increasingly hollow
to American ears. The Japanese, on the other hand, feel that
they are being penalized for their economic success and that
they are being pressured to involve themselves militarily at
precisely a time when the United States claims that international tension is declining. Furthermore, this involvement
will be quite expensive, may well entangle them in conflicts
not of their making, and will be almost certainly unconstitu-
tional.

Most of the potential political problems between the
United States and Japan today are derived from two broad
issue areas: economics and security. Since both are treated
elsewhere in this volume, I will deal with them only briefly;
I will, rather, stress the politicization and political consequences of actions in these spheres, mention a few characteristics of both Japanese political behavior and Japanese-
American interaction which have an impact upon the political substance of the relationship between us, and suggest
some future possibilities regarding that relationship.

The Economic Relationship

Politically, three aspects of Japanese-American economic ties
are important: the crucial role of foreign trade in Japanese
economic survival; the objective impact of Japanese foreign
trade; and the peculiarly Japanese way of trading, which
seems specifically designed to create political friction.

In terms of its proportion of total gross national product,

foreign trade appears of minor importance to Japan—roughly 10 percent of its GNP—more than is the case for the United States, but less than most of the countries of Europe. Japan's prosperity has been generated by internal demand, not by a flood of exports. However, foreign trade occupies a position which gives it an importance wholly disproportionate to its absolute size. Two examples suffice: Japan imports over 95 percent of her petroleum and iron ore; stoppage of these alone would cripple Japan, energywise, and paralyze such industries as petrochemicals, automobiles, steel, and machinery.[2] Trade failures would be economically fatal; the Japanese are acutely aware of and sometimes a bit paranoid about this condition. Needless to say, economic threats are political threats as well.

Such sensitivity can lead to political friction in another way. Foreigners have tended to emphasize Japanese GNP figures and picture a solid economic giant; the Japanese are more aware of their own vulnerability and therefore decry foreign assertions that Japan is now in the economic big leagues and no longer deserves special treatment. Japanese self-description as a "poor country" can easily sound hypocritical, if indeed it is heard at all above the usually humming economy.

For the last two decades the Japanese, while working to achieve prosperity and to overcome, insofar as possible, their vulnerability, have attempted to isolate economics from politics. Economic affairs could be quantified and calculated, and mutual economic benefit, it was hoped, would be apparent to any rational trade partner. Politics, on the other hand, was an area of friction, conflict, and ambiguity which could affect economic relations adversely and was, moreover, an area in which the insular Japanese were not at their most adept. While their economy was too small to constitute a threat to any of the great powers they were allowed to avoid political complications; that stage has now passed.

Impact

During the 1960s total world trade grew at the rate of approximately 9 percent per year; during the same period

Japanese imports grew at about 15 percent per year and exports at about 17 percent. From 1966 to 1970 the latter rate increased to roughly 20 percent per year.[3] That another country's share of world trade decreased does not necessarily mean that the absolute value of its trade diminished, but in many cases it may be assumed that foreign traders have been squeezed out of markets by the Japanese. The natural reaction by such traders is to seek alternative markets or other forms of economic relief; with the Japanese seemingly in all markets and with economic competition unsuccessful, the American reaction has often been to seek political relief, especially in light of Japanese trade practices. A further political implication is that the ever-growing web of Japanese trade not only keeps the country prosperous but also enmeshes Japan increasingly in the affairs of her trade partners.[4] Although Japan's stake in the political stability of her partners will hopefully never approach that of the United States in Latin America in its consequences, the historical example is suggestive.

Practices

Another aspect of the impact of Japanese trade—and also one aspect of Japanese trading practices—is its concentration in certain sectors of the economies of her trading partners. Rather than spreading her exports across all sectors, the Japanese seek out areas in which high potential demand can be inferred, or in which domestic supply is for some reason insufficient, or in which Japan's relative advantage is great. Then, after extensive market research and product testing, Japanese exporters hit the target country with what seems like a blitz designed to wipe out one segment of domestic industry.[5] The speed and magnitude of the initiative (despite its limitation to a small economic area) give the impression of a trade offensive; belligerent responses should thus be no surprise.

Other Japanese trade practices are no less rational, from a coldly economic point of view. To a country that lives or dies with its foreign trade, market and resource security is more important than profits; as a result, Japanese traders are sometimes willing to take a beating in profits to maintain their share of a given market or to get a foothold in a new one. Equally rational is the widespread collusion between government and business in Japan which has given rise to the epithet, "Japan, Inc." The epithet is without foundation, but Japanese practices do include many actions which are contrary to American notions and laws concerning business behavior and government intervention in business.

Export cartels expressly designed to set prices of Japanese exports and to prevent "excessive competition," subsidies to exporters, and export tax incentives have, in the past, given foreigners the impression that they cannot compete effectively without governmental help of their own. Additional friction has arisen from Japanese foreign-aid programs, which, being tied to purchase of Japanese products and utilization of Japanese expertise, have been decried as being, not aid at all, but rather trade promotion.

All these activities, as mentioned, have proven quite rational from the point of view of a nation to which economic growth has been almost the benchmark of success since defeat in the war. The Japanese have certainly proven their ability to achieve their economic goals. In fact, they have, insofar as possible, limited their international behavior to the economic sphere, honing a set of skills which are essentially entrepreneurial and hardly, if at all, diplomatic. Unfortunately, these same skills, exercised without regard to political considerations, have brought on political problems.[6]

To be sure, not all the friction is due to Japanese economism. A variety of Japanese industries have been realistic enough to curb voluntarily their exports to Western Europe and the U.S. The United States has fought hard (largely, perhaps, in response to the pleas of lobbyists and of industrialists calling in their political IOUs) to maintain, in the case of the textile industry, a sector in which a nation as advanced as the United States has no economically rational reason in being involved.[7] The Japanese apparently recognize this fact; Japanese textile companies are diversifying rapidly, and the time is not far off when textiles will offer no comparative advantage to Japan either. Thus the United States appears to be willing to jeopardize its ties with a major trading partner for the sake of an industry which is destined to decline. Obviously, in this case some tradeoff of domestic and international interests entails great domestic political conflict, but to preserve domestic peace in this area may entail great international costs too.[8]

In addition, American practices have on occasion been, to say the least, heavy-handed. The "Nixon shocks" of 1971 and the soybean embargo of 1973 came as unwarranted surprises to an ostensibly trusted ally, and subsequent American economic measures seem to have been aimed directly at Japan—a fact which strikes the normally sensitive Japanese as at best discriminatory and at worst as a racist attempt to prevent her from attaining great-power status. The dispatching of John Connally as economic emissary to Japan was like dispatching a bull to a china shop, given the Japanese preference for allusion, nuance, and conference over frankness and confrontation.

Unfortunately, this preference has on occasion led directly to confrontation. Rather than make a domestically unpalatable decision to limit exports of, e.g., steel and textiles, the Japanese procrastinated in the face of American requests until the United States felt that the only way to reach a resolution of the problem was to deliver an ultimatum. Presented with the prospect of protectionist American legislation, the Japanese capitulated and established "voluntary" export quotas. The result satisfied no one. The Japanese felt coerced economically and politically, and, since Japanese exporters diverted their energies immediately to types of steel and textiles not covered by the agreements, American competitors felt as if they had gained little protection. Moreover, increasing political hostility between the Japanese government and its industries will make any further quotas increasingly difficult to realize and will make future confrontation with America more likely.

Since the early 1970s, numerous measures have been taken to minimize economic conflict and to enable amicable settlement of issues before they become conflictual. Ongoing, standing negotiating bodies, both public and private, are numerous; high-level contacts between the governments (not the least of which is Secretary of State Henry Kissinger's recently increased solicitude for Japanese feelings) have been almost unceasing during the last two years, and such public relations–oriented bodies as the recently created Japan Foundation promise to play a large role in promoting cultural exchange and international understanding.

On the other hand, the form of resolution of most recent economic disagreements offers limited hope of positive contribution to political relationships from that direction. The "voluntary" steel and textile quotas have been mentioned; the American import surtax and revaluation of 1971 were equally distasteful to the Japanese; and interactions in general have exhibited a basic discrepancy in political style which has made preemptive settlement of incipient problems very difficult.[9]

Military Dimensions

The major sources of political friction stemming from military relations between Japan and the United States are the Mutual Security Treaty between these two nations (and its accompanying arrangements) and the current pullback of United States military forces from East Asia.[10] As in the case of economic ties, friction in this instance has arisen both from the relationship between the United States and Japan and, as a result of changes in the international relationship, from Japanese domestic politics.

The Japan–United States security setup basically provides the United States with bases on Japanese territory, in exchange for which the United States extends its nuclear deterrent to protect Japan against attack. The treaty has provided Japan with high security at a very low cost; until recently the United States has not begrudged her this arrangement. Of late, however, with Japan's increasing affluence, it has become apparent to the United States that Japan could well afford to shoulder more of her own defense burden. Moreover, with the United States out of Indochina, many

Americans have suggested that Japan should take a larger role in regional as well as national defense, not only out of self-interest but also to redress a situation which looks more and more to the United States like Japanese freeloading.

That this situation has produced political friction between the United States and Japan is due both to objective structural features of the two countries and to their perceptions of each other. First, the dispatching of troops overseas is contrary to Japanese interpretations of their constitution; numerous comments by American political figures suggest either that the latter are unaware of these legal restraints or that for some reason they are interested in putting pressure on Japan to change or circumvent its laws or that they are trying to score domestic political points by arousing anti-Japanese sentiment.[11]

Second, as a development stemming initially from Japan's immediate postwar military impotence and lack of political autonomy but later from her desire to trade freely with all nations, regardless of their political systems, Japan has endeavored to make her defense policies as unprovocative as possible toward all, and especially toward her Soviet and Chinese neighbors.[12] Thus, clear inconsistency between Japan's objective military needs and her military posture is possible, dictated by economic strategy; to outsiders, especially those looking on from a purely military perspective, such inconsistency can appear either as naiveté or as a politically intentional effort to continue the free ride enjoyed so far at American expense.

Third, Japan's postwar defense policies have been directed as much inward as outward.[13] Fears of general strikes (note, again, the political relevance of economic phenomena) and internal subversion, as well as of popular nonsupport of the regime in time of crisis, have prompted the Japanese government to create a military establishment far better equipped to deal with internal uprising than with external invasion. In fact, the most recent Japanese defense contingency plan sketched two alternative forms of military crisis: conventional invasion by the USSR and internal subversion instigated by China. The extreme concern over a small handful of radicals seems unrealistic in light of the general state of social stability; one can easily see how this preoccupation could create friction with an ally whose fears are international and nuclear. However, this is the way the Japanese see their defense needs, and failure to appreciate their peculiar fears can lead only to misunderstanding and mutual recrimination.

In addition, a number of Japanese perceptions of the world in general and national defense in particular either conflict with American interests or are overlooked by the U.S., leading either to tension which could be approached through bilateral discussion or, worse, to unnecessary political friction between well-meaning allies.

First, the Japanese see the Mutual Security Treaty as a basically fair exchange, in light of international conditions. They see little or no threat to themselves from abroad; in such a situation the United States umbrella doesn't look as valuable to them as it seems to an American that it should. Given this condition, the grant of much-needed land and the allowance for the stationing of foreign troops seem to them to be considerable sacrifices. In fact, many Japanese think that they are getting less out of the treaty than is the United States. Numerous opinion polls indicate that the Japanese tend to see the bases less as evidence of an American commitment to defend Japan than as targets or magnets which will draw Japan into any war involving the United States. In the aftermath of America's precipitate withdrawal from Indochina, reduced faith in the firmness of U.S. commitments is understandable. They also see the bases as being more a part of America's self-interested defense of its far-flung military commitments than as an element in Japan's defense, and doubts regarding America's real willingness to come to Japan's defense in a crisis are widespread. Finally, while Americans see the treaty as unequal in terms of the relative military commitments of the two signatories, the Japanese see it as unequal in the sense that the United States is clearly the dominant partner and Japan the protegé.[14]

The interaction of these structural and perceptual features of United States–Japanese military relations has produced extensive political conflict in Japan, with a consequent hesitance on the part of the Japanese government to take any bold steps in the area even if smooth political relations with the United States demand them. A very vociferous sector of articulate Japanese opinion and politics is adamantly opposed to any sort of military growth, qualitative change in weaponry, overseas military commitment, and/or the entire Mutual Security Treaty arrangement itself. Any movement in any of these areas is sure to stir up loud opposition in parliament and probably demonstrations in the streets as well. None of this is sufficient to shake a government or defeat legislation, but, if opposition becomes enmeshed with such domestic political factors as are discussed below, it can at least delay the already overloaded and hurried legislative agenda and at most create complete paralysis in government.

Part of this opposition is ideological; some stems from experiences in World War II; some purportedly stems from the pacifist elements in postwar education; and some no doubt results from the widespread opinion that no country in the world constitutes a military threat to Japan. I suspect that the final factor is crucial: the Japanese are acutely nation-conscious, and if a clear and immediate military or economic threat were to appear—one which was unquestionably real and verifiable by anyone—then I suspect that much antiwar and antimilitary feeling would evaporate overnight, even along the leftist sectors of the political spectrum.[15] But for the present there is no such compelling force, and pacifist moods govern the political opposition and much of the public mind. Consequently, the United States can be certain that any move to pressure Japan to increase her armaments disproportionately to the growth of the economy as a whole, or to embark on costly military ventures of any kind, will encounter either reluctance or outright opposition from a Japanese government at all times sensitive to its own weaknesses in the face of external, and even intragovernmental, opposition. Recent American suggestions that Japan augment her antisubmarine and antiaircraft defenses and logistical capabilities reflect sensitivity on this point, but any American insistence on positive military moves is an open invitation to political friction, regardless of the degree to which the

United States sees its policy as being in the best interests of the Japanese.[16]

The Domestic Ingredients of International Friction

Elements of domestic Japanese politics are important to any understanding of the tension in present-day Japanese-American relations in two areas: first, Japanese decision-making style in general and the foreign-policy process in particular; second, the international behavior of the Japanese per se.

Decision and Leadership

Contemporary Japanese foreign-policy decision making can be summed up with two words: consensus and coalition. The traditional cultural norm of consensual rather than majoritarian decision making remains strong in all sectors of Japanese society; and the government, not surprisingly, feels considerable pressure to arrive at decisions ostensibly reflecting the unified will of not only the entire ruling party but of the nation as a whole. Partial, sectarian viewpoints (even if those of a majority) have never enjoyed the legitimacy of unanimous ones, and any government desiring popular support for its foreign policy would have to go to great lengths to incorporate both allies and opposition into the final compromise.

Unfortunately, political realities in postwar Japan have made the attainment of a consensus sufficiently strong to support bold initiatives in the foreign-policy field almost impossible. Thus, old patterns of policy persist even though new realities make changes advantageous to both Japan and her partners; and her inability to adapt to changes in internal and international conditions may well seem, to anyone not well aware of Japanese domestic politics, either clumsy or simply duplicitous.

First, the ruling Liberal Democratic party is in fact not a solid political party at all but a coalition of factions, cooperation between the heads of which is essential to the achievement of intraparty and intragovernmental consensus. Differences of opinion and the dictates of factional infighting, which is designed to bring to the head of each faction the party presidency and to his followers the spoils of victory, combine to fragment the party leadership and make consensus almost impossible except on routine, low-risk, noncontroversial policies.[17] Since party leaders must marshal majority support within the party for any proposed policy, bold leadership in any area is impossible because it invites opposition; since consensus must be achieved and maintained continuously, decision making becomes very slow, especially on divisive questions. On especially sticky issues decision is simply postponed in hope that either eventually a consensus can be engineered or that the problem will solve itself or go away in time. This type of procrastination has been of singular importance in recent Japanese–United States wrangles over Japanese exports of textiles and steel, in which the Japanese gave the impression that they were simply stalling for time in the face of America's just requests, which with time and impatience became demands.

The overall effect of this combination of fragmentation and consensualism has been a Japanese foreign policy which is shortsighted (because short-term policies are more probably capable of realization and because long-term proposals stir up more opposition than do incremental, ad hoc ones), tentative, inconsistent, and rather inept. The situation is compounded because in foreign policy, more than in other fields, national interests are manifestly at stake, making some sort of national consensus desirable. On several occasions the LDP has interpreted election results as mandates for its foreign policies; the low salience of foreign policy in popular eyes and the prevalent fashion in which foreign policy works against the LDP to the extent that it is, and among those to whom it is, a lively issue area, make such interpretations transparent. Even were this not so, the political opposition is continuously engaged in demonstrating that it and all those it claims to represent are adamantly opposed to almost anything the LDP may attempt in foreign policy.

As mentioned, the parliamentary opposition, even with its extraparliamentary allies, is not strong enough to block concerted LDP efforts to pass any policy. On occasion, however, divisive issues are utilized by factional leaders in the LDP in its intraparty power struggles, and concerted party action becomes impossible. In the best of times the parliamentary agenda is overcrowded. The many days of delay caused by intraparliamentary opposition and obstruction over a particular foreign-policy bill can be so costly in terms of other important legislation not dealt with that even minority opposition can be an effective deterrent to LDP initiative. In either case the result is the same: the continuation of old policies (however obsolete and however galling to Japan's partners) because any new one will arouse some opposition.

For these reasons, and for the economic reasons already mentioned, Japan has for many years actually tried to avoid having any political foreign policy at all. As Japan has become increasingly entangled in the internal affairs of her trade partners and as her successful export policies have created political problems in other countries, other nations are less and less willing to tolerate the dilatory, apparently evasive, ad hoc political responses of the Japanese government.[18] However, as long as the present political structure and long-established cultural norms contribute to a condition of fragmented consensualism, Japan's partners cannot realistically look forward to anything in the way of bold, positive leadership and prompt, imaginative solutions to outstanding problems.

Unfortunately, Japan's partners sometimes let impatience and the influence of lobbyists replace realism, and domestic Japanese political trends will in all probability make realistic perception more essential than ever. Specifically, the waning power of the Liberal Democratic party and the increasing ability of the opposition to delay the parliamentary process— both of which one may expect to continue—could well produce a decision-making situation even more time consuming and tentative than the present one. This immobilist portent is eminently debatable, but is nevertheless worthy of attention by American leaders, economic and political.[19]

The aforementioned difficulties are compounded by two more indigenous factors. First is the peculiar place that foreign trade occupies in the Japanese political consciousness. Traditional cultural factors make an adequate response to

foreign economic demands difficult; the foreseeable foreign
reaction is stiffness, harsher terms, and perhaps a tinge of real
animosity. But such a reaction, in the life-or-death area of
foreign trade, can be expected to arouse in the Japanese both
fear and belligerent defensiveness, which can add to the normally cumbersome decisional process an element of hostility
and wounded innocence in which rationality easily might go
out the window.[20] In the event of a major foreign-trade crisis,
such a process may easily escalate.

A second factor is the relevance, already noted, of tradition in Japanese politics. The importance of tradition in Japanese politics has been often overestimated; however, to the
extent that it is still a significant factor it constitutes an area
of potential trouble in the event of any major political or
economic crisis.[21] A single example suffices here—that of the
decisional process sketched above. The time-consuming process of consensus building is a luxury the Japanese can afford
in times of rapid economic growth and minimal external tension, as are factional backbiting and irresponsible leadership
(the concomitants of unanimous decisions reached without
vote). In that they give everyone a feeling of participation in
decisions, offer minorities influence out of all proportion to
their strength, and provide the Japanese with a strong norma-
tive continuity during a time of rapid change, such decisional
norms can in fact be beneficial for Japanese society. But this
is a hothouse beneficence; in a time of crisis the same norms
under pressure may cause complete political paralysis, and
the pervasiveness of these norms throughout society could
turn a sectoral—e.g., economic—crisis into a systemic one,
turning economic immobilism into political immobilism, with
implications for other areas of policy which would involve
the nation as a whole in a breakdown in political effectiveness and performance.

The International Arena

Traditional norms are equally noteworthy in their influence
upon the behavior of the Japanese in their interactions with
foreigners. The most important indigenous factors in this regard are nationalism, hierarchicalism, and insularity; with the

possible exception of the last, all of these factors are presently becoming stronger in their role in Japanese international behavior.

The Japanese have for centuries had at least some sort of national identity; this has become, in the last century, a sharp sense of national and racial consciousness—sometimes manifested as pride, sometimes as shame, sometimes as orthodox or even extreme political nationalism. Coupled with a traditionally hierarchical social and political outlook, this sense leads to an intense preoccupation with Japan's international status. After the defeats and disillusionments of World War II, Japanese national pride was slow in reviving, and the international position to which Japan could realistically and rightfully aspire was unclear. Now, however, economic growth has created a Japan which is overwhelmingly dominant in East Asia and a power to reckon with all over the world. Clearly, now, Japan seems to the Japanese entitled to a major seat among the powers, at least as the apex of any Asian hierarchy with, as a start, a permanent seat in the United Nations Security Council.

The relevance of this growing nationalism for Japanese-American relations is triple. First, the acuteness of the hierarchical outlook makes the Japanese very sensitive to real or implied threats to Japan's assumption of her proper station in the world. Coupled with the racial factor of Japaneseness, this state creates the heightened possibility for the perception of racial slights; the recurrent rumor that Japan's political leadership suspects anti-Japanese sentiment in Washington is simply one manifestation of this condition, a plausible reaction of the Japanese to foreign criticism. Second, hierarchicalism linked to economic growth impels the Japanese outward into ever-proliferating relationships with other nations as the Japanese expand their economic net and try to translate their affluence in some fashion (as yet unspecified and probably unknown to them) into an international status which proves satisfactory. However, the proliferation of external relationships by a nation so markedly deficient in foreign-policy expertise and effectiveness simply increases the possibility and likelihood of friction.

Third, in special reference to the United States, with increasing Japanese growth and pride comes increasing dissatisfaction with what the Japanese see as their inferior position vis-à-vis the United States. Militarily, Japan has clearly long been an American client; for nationalistic Japanese it does not require militarist ideas to feel dissatisfaction with this relationship. Economically, too, the Japanese feel subordinate. To Americans the significant fact is that Japan is running a substantial trade advantage with the United States; to the Japanese the salient fact is that United States–Japan trade is far more important to them than to us in terms of economic survival, and that in terms of interdependence Japan is still at our economic mercy.[22]

Finally, Japan is perhaps the most insular—in all senses of the word—of the world's major nations, on both the mass and elite levels. In much of Southeast Asia the "Ugly Japanese" who arrive on Japan Air Lines, stay in Japanese hotels, eat in Japanese restaurants, play golf only with each other, go to Japanese bars, and sightsee in closed groups, have replaced the Americans as symbols of international gaucherie. The inability of Americans to understand the political idiosyncrasies of the Japanese is more than matched by the ability of the Japanese to study deeply and travel widely and still return home with little understanding of the nations they have seen. Language problems are certainly one cause, but there is also a national egocentrism and a sense of apartness which make Japanese empathy with foreigners extremely difficult regardless of their good intentions.

Moreover, insularity is tied to the sense of vulnerability in natural resources and to racial consciousness, both of which heighten Japanese sensitivity to foreign behavior. The resultant attitude is not that of a chip on the shoulder but rather one of apprehensive goodwill, well meaning but slightly defensive. And thus the circle is closed: Some indigenous elements impel the Japanese outward into ever-increasing participation in the international arena; while other, related factors make a smooth performance in that arena difficult indeed.

Prospect, Precedent, Plea

Despite the present calm, the prospect in Japanese–United States relations in the future is for recurrent, and possibly increasing, political friction, resulting both from objective structural aspects of the relationship and from mutual misunderstanding and misperceptions—despite the good intentions of both sides—in a context marked by three trends.

First, the Japanese economy will continue to grow, though at a reduced rate, as will Japanese export efforts (at a possibly increased rate, given domestic recession). The underdeveloped state of social overhead facilities—sanitation, utilities, public housing, etc.—is receiving increased attention in Japan, as is the rapidly deteriorating environment; both will make larger demands on available resources in the future, but the basic commitment to stable economic growth will remain.[23] Consequently, the defensiveness of Japan's trading partners will also remain, and the possibilities of protectionism will remain high unless the Japanese continue the sharp self-restriction of certain of their exports. Some efforts are being made in this area, but European and American fears seem to be growing faster.

Moreover, the structure of the Japanese economy is changing in such a way as to compete more directly with that of the United States, and the present absence of conflictual trade issues should not obscure this fact. Increasing concentration on sophisticated electronics, machine industries, chemicals, and other technology- and knowledge-intensive industries will create a challenge, not in essentially outdated fields such as textiles, but in areas where American supremacy has as yet gone unchallenged.[24] The basic Japanese-American interdependence will continue, but in tandem with a divergence of interests in many instances; thus, economic rationalism will still dictate cooperation and amity, while narrower points of view will emphasize differences in priorities and interests and perhaps advocate the assertion of national rather than bilateral goals. Given the potential for decisional problems and mutual misperceptions, the possibilities

for political mischief and economic irrationality in the un-
trammeled pursuit of narrow unilateral interests are great.

Directional changes in the Japanese economy will enhance
the chances of political friction with the United States in
one further way, unless Americans acquire more empathy
with Japanese efforts to improve the general quality of life
and prevent irretrievable destruction of their environment.
Japanese initiatives in these two areas will surely be taken,
and they will be expensive. As a result, the Japanese will
be more and more loath to adopt any foreign policy which
promises to be costly.[25] Vague American suggestions concerning Japan's regional security responsibilities imply considerable outlays, the limits of which can perhaps be imagined from the money expended by the United States in Indochina. Needless to say, in the absence of some acute external
threat the Japanese—alleged revivals of militarism notwithstanding—are hardly likely to be enthusiastic about any such
arrangement. Fortunately, there are signs that the United
States is beginning to understand this attitude.[26]

The second trend is the increasing Japanese participation
in the international community, combined with the continuing inability of the Japanese to act decisively and positively in
this community (with the exception of such innocuous steps
as the Osaka Exposition and the Olympics). Japanese foreign
policy will become more autonomous, in the sense that Japanese goals and priorities will play a larger role in determining
international behavior; at the same time, this behavior will
continue to be largely reactive, coming as the result of external stimuli rather than internally generated motivation.[27]
And, with particular relevance to the United States, this more
autonomous Japan will probably never again feel the past
sense of trust in the credibility of America. Two "Nixon
shocks" and the crude coercion of the textile "agreement"—
all of which underscored Japanese weakness in the face of
American resolve and undercut the credibility of the Japanese government in the eyes of the people—have probably
damaged the United States–Japanese relationship irretriev-
ably, as has the rather rude American abandonment of her
putative allies in Indochina.

This change is not necessarily for the worse. Some such change is needed if the Japanese are to become truly independent in their international behavior, and it is probably unhealthy for such a power as Japan to be anyone's client. Nevertheless, a new coolness and critical faculty presage a more conflictual relationship in the future.

The third trend is Japan's continuing search for some satisfying position in the international system.[28] What rank Japan should occupy, how her international role is defined—politically, culturally, economically, or militarily—and how she should try to realize it are all unanswered questions at present. But define it she will, and Japanese pride and hierarchicalism dictate that she will devote great energy to reaching her chosen spot and will look with great apprehension upon any measure taken by any nation which seems designed—purposely or not—to frustrate her accession to her proper station.

All of these trends portend a rockier American-Japanese road over the long run—or perhaps one should say, rather, a less artificially euphoric relationship, since some tension is unavoidable between powerful nations in close interaction in a context of great cultural disparity. Multiple efforts are being made to minimize conflict: Henry Kissinger deals with the Japanese much more frequently than before; ongoing negotiating bodies abound; the Japanese are making definite efforts to reduce protectionism and limit exports; the yen and the dollar have been extensively revalued; and the recently established Japan Foundation promises to launch a far-ranging program of cultural exchange which, while it cannot guarantee that Americans and Japanese will like each other, certainly holds some hope in the area of mutual understanding.

On the other hand, none of the measures taken to date promises to eliminate significant sources of conflict. Revaluation was a half-step at best and a misstep at worst: While revaluation increases the cost of Japanese exports, it simultaneously lowers the cost of the imports from which the export goods are made; in addition, the incredibly complex Japanese system of wholesaling and distribution has a way of absorbing

lower import prices to such a degree that Japanese consumers
enjoy little benefit from the lower import price of goods. Of
greater importance, however, is the frequent failure of either
Japanese or Americans to exercise much foresight in their
relations. Both sides have in the past been willing to let pressure build up on an issue until a graceful solution is impossible, political elements have intruded, and the eventual resolution is at least moderately coercive to some of the parties
(leaving them angry) and never completely satisfying to the
others. Business interests in particular have been largely unable to solve their problems within the economic sphere; one
side calls upon its government for help and so, in response,
does the other, politicizing and publicizing the issue and leaving the residue of ill will on both sides.

Nevertheless, the most probable course in the near future
is one of continued close Japanese–United States cooperation
and interdependence in military, economic, and political
fields, while the Japanese try as much as possible to equalize
the degree of dependence on each side of the relationship by
spreading their commitments, maintaining amicable ties with
both Russia and China, and finding alternative markets and
sources of raw materials outside the United States. Still, a
number of alternate arrangements of varying probability can
be imagined. An ideological breakdown would align the
United States and Japan and bar any strong ties between
either of these states and either China or Russia. If, on the
other hand, the economic complementarity which comes
with the parallel stage of development exercises greater influence, then the USSR could conceivably become a third partner in a Japanese-American-Soviet economic (and perhaps
security) triangle. If the classic tenet of international politics—your neighbor is your enemy, your neighbor's neighbor
is your friend—holds, a Soviet-Japanese detente could be
matched with a close Sino-American relationship. The latter
was obviously feared by the Japanese after Nixon's announcement of his visit to Peking; the fear has no doubt re-
ceded now that Japan has established diplomatic ties with the
People's Republic, while the United States still wrestles with
the problem of Taiwan. The Soviet Union, on the contrary,

would love to have some counterweight to China, but overtures to Japan have been vacillant to date.

If, as some suggest, race is more important than ideology or GNP, then a Sino-Japanese bloc pitted against the Soviets and Americans is possible in East Asia. Many Japanese seem to feel that they, as Asians, can interact more smoothly with Chinese than with Americans. In the light of previous Japanese experiences in Asia, I find this proposition highly unlikely. This leaves one last alternative arrangement, which is extremely unlikely also, but for which there is historical precedent: the confrontation of Japan against all other nations.

This last situation flies in the face of economic rationality and political advisability, but it is precisely what happened in the 1930s. The Japanese, having learned imperialism from the West, saw themselves encircled by discriminatory, racist nations bent on frustrating Japan's attempts to reach her proper station, forbidding her to practice that which they had themselves practiced in their own imperialist epochs, and threatening to destroy her economically if she resisted. The intentions of the actors at that time were not all good: There were out-and-out expansionists, war lovers, and cynical would-be imperialists in Japan; and racists and established, jealous old imperialist powers abroad. The significant point is that Japan, perceiving hostile encirclement and operating from perceptions of resource vulnerability and national superiority, departed from active, reasoned attempts to avoid conflict and let events snowball until national interests did in fact demand military initiatives.

These last characteristics remain today. A wave of international protectionism, intentionally directed (at least in part) against Japan, would arouse desperate feelings. The proliferation of Japanese economic ties with foreign countries, especially in the politically unstable area of Southeast Asia, gives Japan a stake in the political fortunes of these states;[29] the multiplication of such situations increases the possibility that a legitimate threat to the objective national interest will appear. And, as suggested above, the national conscious reaction to such a threat might well be the wholesale conversion of the Japanese people from their purported pacifism and the overnight cure of their "nuclear allergy."

In such a situation, moreover, the decisional handicaps and racist tendencies of the Japanese themselves would come to the fore; no amount of face-to-face negotiation and effort at mutual understanding could be surely expected to overcome the deep-seated fears and wounded pride of the Japanese in such an instance.

Obviously, today is far distant from the 1930s in many respects, and today's United States–Japanese friction is no way comparable to that of those years.[30] Nevertheless, national and geopolitical characteristics persist, and so does the potential for conflict; and our attention must be turned to this potential if events are not to be allowed to drift. Thus a plea for attention, a plea to American leaders, is in order. In general, despite its present even keel, our relationship with the Japanese will require unending negotiation, clarification, and searching for solutions. Understanding, self-restraint, and foresight are absolutely essential, as will be some degree of indulgence. This last derives, not from any paternalistic need for the United States to shepherd its protegé into the international arena, but, rather, from the reality of Japanese inexperience in this area and the reality of Japanese apprehensions and sensitivities. It may be at times in our long-term self-interest to accept the Japanese double standard which permits them to be protectionist while demanding free trading opportunities in other countries, however galling such acceptance may be in the short run. The exigencies of domestic American politics cannot be ignored by any practical politician, but the advisability of extending the life of essentially obsolete American industries such as textiles must be closely examined from an international political perspective as well. The reason such indulgence and sensitivity are necessary is because, above all single-industry considerations, it is in the overriding interest of the United States to have a prosperous, politically stable Japan. Japan is *the* economic power of East Asia, and if there is to be any political stability in that area, it will be possible only if Japan is stable.[31] And, given the political cruciality of economics in Japan, forceful measures designed to get Japan to do our bidding—however justified from the point of view of equitable trade practices—could, if not executed with consummate tact, bring on political hostility and economic desperation, the latter of which would lead inevitably to political desperation as well. And, as mentioned above, Japan is poorly equipped to deal with such situations. It is thus in our interest to help the Japanese in all possible ways to avoid crises, even if this requires some self-abnegation. Friction must be expected and accepted; good intentions, skillfully implemented, will, one can hope, enable us to avoid its aggravation.

6

TRADE RELATIONS BETWEEN THE UNITED STATES AND JAPAN: THE PAST AND THE FUTURE

Kazuo Sato

*Professor of Economics,
State University of New York at Buffalo*

Problems of yesteryear are easily forgotten. Trade problems between the United States and Japan are no exception. Early in this decade, the United States suffered from a serious disequilibrium in its balance of payments. Since the American deficits were the largest with Japan, Japan was considered the major culprit in this American problem of the day. A political confrontation ensued; emotions rose on both sides of the Pacific. Many trade talks were held between the two governments in an attempt to rectify the imbalance, but they turned out to be futile. More than piecemeal measures had to be taken. Currency realignments since December 1971 and the subsequent floating of exchange rates were such measures. In the meantime, new problems arose in quick succession. Violent rises in primary prices in world trade through 1973 and into 1974, the oil crisis in the 1973–74 winter, the world inflation, and then the world recession in 1974 and 1975 became immediate and pressing issues. These events led to a dissolution of the bilateral disequilibrium in U.S.-Japan trade from 1973 to 1975.

This may seem to indicate that an equilibrium has been reestablished in trade between the two nations. However,

129

there is no such thing as a permanent equilibrium in international trade. Indeed, by its own nature, international trade is a reflection of disequilibria among nations. Countries trade with one another because they differ. Economic development alters their economies and, by the same token, their need to trade. Trade problems that arose between the United States and Japan through the three decades since the end of World War II are manifestations of such changes. They include requests for "voluntary" restrictions on Japan's exports of textiles and steel products, recurrent charges of Japanese dumping in the U.S. markets, protective tariffs and nontariff barriers to trade in both countries, impediments to free flows of capital, and the American embargo on soybeans in the summer of 1973. There are logical reasons for these problems; they emanate from long-term changes in the two countries' economic positions. Since changes continue to take place, the current state of peace may well be transitory. Unless basic factors change, one may have to expect another flare of excitement sooner or later.

Preventive medicine is not yet in practice in this field; a cure is applied only after the patient shows acute symptoms of illness. U.S.-Japan trade relations in the early 1970s are a case in point. Events since 1971 helped to reshape U.S.-Japan relations in general, but one must be prepared to do better in the next round.

Through the postwar years, Japan had been regarded as a protegé and a faithful ally by the United States. However, in the short span of thirty years, Japan has grown into an economic superpower that can compete with the United States on equal footing and will possibly exceed it in per-capita GNP sometime in the not-too-distant future. A sudden change in the American perception of Japan—to that of a formidable rival—aggravated the matter considerably in the early seventies. It was a time when their economic and other relations should have been reviewed and realigned by the two nations.

In this paper, I shall review economic changes that led to the climax in 1971–72 before a truce was reached, probe their causes, and offer a conjecture on the future course of trade relations between the United States and Japan. While there are many interrelated aspects in trade relations, I confine my discussion mostly to commodity trade.

The United States and Japan as Trade Partners: A Long-Term Review

As is well known, Japan maintained a national policy of isolation from the rest of the world for three centuries during the Tokugawa regime. The only link of trade with the Western world was with Holland. In 1853, Commodore M. C. Perry came to Japan with the American squadron of four "black ships" to negotiate opening Japanese ports for foreign trade. On March 31, 1854, Japan's first treaty of friendship and commerce was signed with the United States. In spite of many vicissitudes over the 120 years since then, Japan–U.S. trade continued to grow in importance. Long-term changes in this trade reflect changes in the relative positions of the two economies. In order to understand where U.S.–Japan trade stands in the 1970s, we may begin by getting a historical perspective.

Table 1 shows quinquennial averages of the shares of both the United States and Japan in each other's exports and imports over the past hundred years.[1] Looking at the figures from the Japanese side, we note that the U.S. has been important to Japan as an export market from the very beginning; 20 to 40 percent of Japan's exports initially went to the United States. Though there were some fluctuations, the U.S. share was 30 to 40 percent till the 1920s. That proportion declined precipitously in the 1930s as a consequence of the Great Depression and the subsequent militarization of Japan. Japan's trade returned to normalcy in the early 1950s, after it recovered from the devastations of World War II. During the next two decades, the U.S. share continued to rise steadily until, by the latter half of the sixties, it exceeded 30 percent. The United States has been the most important single market to Japanese exporters. The only other market comparable in importance is Southeast Asia as a whole. However, the latter's importance as Japan's customer has been steadily waning, its share in Japan's exports having fallen from 36 percent in 1955 to 22 percent in 1974.

Table 1. Relative Positions of the U.S. and Japan
          as Trade Partners

Period	Japan's trade			U.S.'s trade		
	U.S.'s share in			Japan's share in		
	Japan's exports	Japan's imports	U.S. J. U.S. J.	U.S.'s exports	U.S.'s imports	J. U.S. J. U.S.
	(1)	(2)	(3)	(4)	(5)	(6)
1873-75	32.7	4.8	.214	.2	1.3	.180
1876-80	29.9	7.3	.288	.3	2.5	.164
1881-85	39.3	9.1	.199	.3	2.0	.197
1886-90	39.2	8.9	.229	.5	2.7	.225
1891-95	38.3	8.5	.202	.5	2.9	.177
1896-00	29.2	15.1	.744	1.4	3.7	.644
1901-05	29.9	17.2	.697	1.9	4.3	.657
1906-10	30.5	15.3	.515	1.9	4.9	.512
1911-15	31.0	17.7	.591	2.1	5.3	.524
1916-20	31.1	34.4	1.032	3.7	8.9	.790
1921-25	42.2	29.2	.842	5.5	9.8	..722
1926-30	40.6	29.2	.781	5.1	9.4	.649
1931-35	27.0	32.4	1.329	8.4	8.7	1.145
1936-40	18.3	33.8	1.839	7.5	6.6	1.450
1951-55	18.1	34.0	2.763	4.3	2.6	2.343
1956-60	24.9	34.3	1.606	6.0	5.7	1.457
1961-65	27.6	31.5	1.288	7.8	9.0	1.154
1966-70	30.5	27.8	.908	8.9	12.7	.777
1971-72	31.1	25.1	.662	9.6	16.2	.550
1973-74	24.3	22.3	.986	11.3	13.1	.863

Sources:
  (1) to (3): Bank of Japan, Hundred-Year Statistics of the Japanese Economy
             (1966); Bank of Japan, Economic Statistics Annual, 1971; Economic
             Planning Agency, Japanese Economic Indicators, August 1975.

  (4) to (6): Department of Commerce, Historical Statistics of the United
             States (1971); Department of Commerce, 1971 Business Statistics;
             Department of Commerce, Survey of Current Business, September
             1975.

In contrast, the United States was not important to Japan
as a supplier of goods at the beginning. Only after the Sino-
Japanese war (1894-95) did the U.S. share of Japan's imports
exceed 15 percent. That share exceeded 30 percent during
the trade disruption caused by World War I, and hovered at
around 30 percent from that time until the end of the thir-
ties. It is interesting to note that the United States' role as a
supplier expanded in the 1930s, unlike Japan's exports to the
U.S. The ratio remained at 1:3 in the 1950s but declined considerably during the next dozen years.

    From an American perspective, Japan has been a marginal
buyer and seller because of the great economic disparity between the two countries at the outset. Not until the 1920s

did Japan begin absorbing more than 5 percent of the U.S. world exports, and only in the 1960s did Japan's purchases approach the 10 percent level. In the first half of the 1970s, Japan's share finally broke the 10 percent barrier. While, on the other hand, U.S. imports from Japan were somewhat more important, not until the late 1960s did Japan's share exceed 10 percent. That share registered a very rapid increase in the decade following 1961, however. Indeed, the increase during this period was such that out of each additional dollar in U.S. imports, 25 cents came from Japan. This drastic change in the trade structure was the factor that made Americans cry havoc.

In terms of the bilateral balance of trade, export surpluses were maintained by Japan over the United States until the 1920s; import surpluses followed in the 1930s, continuing into the postwar years until the early sixties. Japan again started to have export surpluses with the U.S. after the mid-sixties. What had been alarming to both countries was that the trade gap had continued to expand. This was the most pressing issue in U.S.–Japan trade relations during the early 1970s.

Why did this radical change take place in U.S.–Japan trade? Because basic economic changes had been occurring in each of the countries, slowly but steadily, since the end of World War II. Two countries trade with each other because they are different in one way or another. Trade patterns change when the two countries change their basic characteristics.

In concluding this brief review, we may comment on changes in the commodity composition of trade. Japan initially exported primary commodities—in particular, raw silk and tea. That country followed the typical pattern of a nation on the path of industrialization in that it emphasized import substitution and export promotion of industrial goods. Exports of manufactured goods (the bulk of which initially consisted of fabricated raw materials, including raw silk) exceeded 75 percent of total exports at the turn of the century; the proportion rose to more than 90 percent in the postwar decades. Japan's exports to the United States followed the same pattern of change. By the same token, Japan's imports shifted from industrial products to industrial raw materials. Japan's typical trade pattern—that of importing raw materials and exporting fabricated products—was firmly set by the 1920s and was intensified during the postwar decades. Bilateral trade between the United States and Japan changed in the same way, and is very much different from the trade pattern usually observed among industrial countries, which trade industrial goods among themselves. This is a primary cause of the disequilibrium in U.S.-Japan trade.

Changes in U.S.-Japan Trade since the 1950s

Macroeconomic Balances

In the preceding section, we presented a bird's-eye view of U.S.-Japan trade over the past century. We now focus our attention on changes that have taken place during the past two decades. Immediately after the end of World War II, Japan's domestic production suffered a precipitous fall—partly because of the destruction of productive facilities during the war, but mainly because of the nearly complete stoppage of imports of raw materials. By 1951, imports had risen to some 10 percent of Japan's GNP, the normal level in subsequent years. The prewar peak levels of production and consumption had been regained by 1954.

With this background in mind, we examine total trade figures of the United States and Japan since 1951 in Tables 2 to 4. Whichever table we look at, we notice that the export surplus of the U.S. continued to decrease in percentage terms. The trade balance between the two favored Japan for the first time in 1965, and that imbalance reached a gigantic proportion in 1971 and 1972. It is asserted that no other two countries have maintained such a huge imbalance in bilateral trade.

This imbalance was primarily due to the very rapid expansion of Japan's exports to the United States. While Japan increased its exports to the U.S. by 50 percent from 1970 to 1972, exports from the U.S. to Japan showed an absolute decline from 1970 to 1971 and registered only a 7 percent

Table 2. Japan's Position in Trade of the U.S.

Year	Trade of the U.S. (Mn.$)		(2) (1) (3)	% of resp. total (U.S.)	
	Exports to Japan (1)	Imports from Japan (2)		Exports to Japan (4)	Imports from Japan (5)
1951	601.4	204.9	.341	4.0	1.9
1952	632.7	229.3	.362	4.2	2.1
1953	686.4	261.5	.381	4.4	2.4
1954	692.7	279.0	.403	4.6	2.7
1955	682.5	431.9	.633	4.4	3.8
1956	997.8	557.9	.559	5.2	4.4
1957	1319.3	600.5	.455	6.3	4.6
1958	986.9	666.5	.675	5.5	5.1
1959	1079.5	1028.7	.953	6.2	6.8
1960	1447.2	1148.8	.794	7.0	7.6
1961	1837.3	1054.8	.574	8.7	7.2
1962	1573.8	1358.0	.863	7.3	8.3
1963	1843.6	1497.8	.812	7.9	8.7
1964	2009.3	1768.1	.880	7.6	9.5
1965	2080.1	2413.8	1.160	7.6	11.3
1966	2363.5	2962.8	1.254	7.8	11.6
1967	2695.0	2998.7	1.113	8.5	11.2
1968	2954.3	4054.4	1.372	8.5	12.2
1969	3489.7	4888.2	1.401	9.2	13.6
1970	4652.0	5875.3	1.263	10.8	14.7
1971	4054.8	7258.8	1.790	9.2	15.9
1972	4940.5	9094.7	1.841	9.9	16.4
1973	8313.1	9676.2	1.164	11.7	13.9
1974	10678.6	12337.6	1.155	10.8	12.3

Source: Department of Commerce (U.S.), *1971 Business Statistics* (1971); *Survey of Current Business*, September 1975.

increase from 1970 to 1972. This lopsided development in 1970–72 was, however, nothing like a sudden change; it was a culmination of a long-term shift gradually taking place during the two decades under review. While Japan's share in the total exports of the U.S. steadily rose from 4 percent in 1951 until it came to a standstill at 10 percent in 1969–72, Japan's share in total U.S. imports started from a mere 2 percent in 1951, rose rapidly to a plateau of 11 percent in 1965–67, and again showed a rise to 16 percent in 1972 (see Table 2). Japan's relative position registered a sharp reversal during the next two years, however, when U.S. exports to Japan expanded while U.S. imports from Japan significantly declined as a proportion of total trade. Hence, the imbalance between exports and imports has been substantially reduced.

Table 3. The U.S.'s Position in Trade of Japan

Year	Trade of Japan (Mn. $)		(1)/(2)	% of resp. total (Japan)	
	Exports to U.S.	Imports from U.S.		Exports to U.S.	Imports from U.S.
	(1)	(2)	(3)	(4)	(5)
1951	185	695	.266	13.6	33.9
1952	234	768	.305	18.4	37.9
1953	234	760	.308	18.3	31.5
1954	283	849	.333	17.3	35.4
1955	456	774	.589	22.7	31.3
1956	550	1067	.516	22.0	33.0
1957	604	1623	.372	21.1	37.9
1958	690	1056	.654	24.0	34.8
1959	1047	1116	.938	30.3	31.0
1960	1102	1554	.709	27.2	34.6
1961	1067	2096	.509	25.2	36.1
1962	1400	1809	.774	28.5	32.1
1963	1507	2077	.725	27.6	30.8
1964	1842	2336	.788	27.6	29.4
1965	2479	2366	1.048	29.3	29.0
1966	2969	2658	1.117	30.4	27.9
1967	3012	3212	.938	28.8	27.6
1968	4086	3527	1.158	31.5	27.9
1969	4958	4090	1.212	31.0	27.2
1970	5940	5560	1.068	30.8	29.5
1971	7495	4978	1.506	31.2	25.3
1972	8848	5852	1.512	30.9	24.9
1973	9449	9270	1.019	25.6	24.2
1974	12799	12682	1.009	23.0	20.4

Source: Bank of Japan, Economic Statistics Annual, 1971 (March 1972);
         Economic Planning Agency, Japanese Economic Indicators
         (August 1975).

As Table 3 shows, the United States bought less than 20 percent of Japan's total exports in the early fifties, subsequently increased its share to 30 percent, and remained at that level during 1965–72. The proportion then significantly declined and was slightly below 20 percent in 1975. On the other hand, the U.S. continued to supply more than 30 percent of Japan's imports, but the ratio fell below 30 percent in 1964 and has continued on a downward slide since then, now hovering at slightly above 20 percent.

U.S.-Japan trade is actually a mirror image of each country's position in world trade. Table 4 presents each country's trade with the world since 1961. The United States maintained export surpluses until 1970. These surpluses, sustained

Table 4. Trade Balance of the U.S. and Japan (Mn. $)

(A) United States

Year	Exports to world	Imports from world	X-M	of which Japan
1961	20999	14714	6285	783
1962	21700	16380	5320	216
1963	23347	17138	6209	346
1964	26508	18684	7824	241
1965	27478	21366	6112	-334
1966	30320	25542	4778	-599
1967	31526	26812	4714	-304
1968	34636	33226	1410	-1100
1969	38006	36043	1963	-1399
1970	43224	39952	3272	-1223
1971	44130	45563	-1433	-3204
1972	49768	55555	-5787	-4154
1973	71339	69476	1863	-1363
1974	98507	100251	-1744	-1659

(B) Japan

Year	Exports to world	Imports from world	X-M	of which U.S.
1961	4236	5810	-1574	-1029
1962	4916	5637	-721	-409
1963	5452	6736	-1284	-570
1964	6673	7938	-1265	-494
1965	8452	8169	283	113
1966	9776	9523	253	311
1967	10442	11663	-1221	-200
1968	12972	12987	-15	559
1969	15990	15024	966	868
1970	19318	18881	437	380
1971	24019	19712	4307	2517
1972	28591	23471	5120	2996
1973	36930	38314	-1384	179
1974	55536	62110	-6574	117

Sources: (A) Department of Commerce (U.S.), 1971 Business Statistics; Survey of Current Business.

(B) Bank of Japan, Economic Statistics Annual, 1971; Economic Planning Agency, Japanese Economic Indicators.

throughout the postwar decades, helped the U.S. to finance its foreign aid and overseas investment. But we notice their shrinkage over time. Nonetheless, it was only in the beginning two years of the 1970s that import surpluses actually emerged. Export surpluses had come to an end much earlier, in 1964; since then, the trade gap between the two countries has kept on widening. What is clear is that basic factors responsible for disequilibrium in overall U.S. trade with the world had also been working, in a more pronounced way, upon U.S. trade with Japan. One consequence of this was that in 1972 Japan accounted for nearly 75 percent of the deficit in the U.S. trade balance. Not surprisingly, many Americans believed at that time that Japan was primarily responsible for their country's trade deficit. But it is important to look at the U.S. deficit with Japan in the overall framework of U.S. trade with the world. In 1973 the U.S. balance of trade was in the black, but it was again in the red in 1974, primarily with Japan.

Japan exhibited changes completely different from those that occurred in the United States, in that the former country has maintained import surpluses in commodity trade since the end of World War II. These surpluses were offset by income from nontrade services through the 1950s. Up to 1965, Japan's rapid economic growth was periodically punctured by disequilibria in the balance of trade. The sequence of events was thus: rapid growth — temporary cutdown in growth — export surplus — rapid growth. This typical growth cycle, usually of three or four years' duration, was in effect until 1965 and reappeared in 1970. Japan came to sustain chronic export surpluses (except in 1967), which were amassed in Japan's foreign reserves. The Japanese government found itself at a loss about what to do with its huge liquid assets, and its inability aggravated the international monetary crisis. The oil crisis of 1973 and the inflation of primary prices in the international markets led to a tremendous inflation in Japan from late 1973 to mid-1974. Mismanaged monetary policy, as a result of the excess liquidity, worsened the situation. Thus, Japan's imports expanded more than exports, exceeding 15 percent of the country's GNP. Trade deficits developed in 1973 and 1974, almost wiping out the trade surpluses of 1971 and 1972. The changes in Japan's balance of trade with the world were exactly reflected in its bilateral balance with the United States.

Commodity Composition

Japan's trade pattern has been to import raw materials and export finished goods; 70 percent of Japan's imports have consisted of food, crude materials, and fuels. This ratio tended to decline somewhat in the sixties, but the decline was mostly accounted for by an increase in imports of processed materials. Apart from these, imported manufactured goods are mainly producer goods. Very little consumer goods have been imported into Japan. In contrast, more than 90 percent of Japan's exports are manufactured goods. The steady shift from light manufactures, such as textiles, to heavy manufactures, such as automobiles and steel products, reflects changes in the industrial structure of Japan.

This trade pattern has been accurately reflected in U.S.-Japan trade (see Table 5). Japan imports relatively more manufactured goods from the United States than from the rest of the world. Among primary commodities, Japan imports a great deal of cereals and oil seeds from the U.S. For a number of commodities, the U.S. share in Japan's imports is very high; in 1971, it was 91 percent for soybeans, 70 percent for iron and steel scraps, 56 percent for softwood logs, 54 percent for corn, 52 percent for wheat, and 24 percent for raw cotton. Among manufactured goods, machinery is the most important category. As for exports from Japan, automobiles have become increasingly important in recent years. Among light manufactures, consumer electronic products, china, dinnerware, and other sundry goods have been important.

While Japan's trade with the United States is not basically different from its trade with the world in terms of commodity composition, U.S. trade with Japan differs significantly from U.S. trade with the rest of the world. Primary commodities occupy a substantial position in the U.S. world imports, though their proportion of the total declined from more than

Table 5. Commodity Composition of Trade: U.S. and Japan

1965

SITC[a]	United States				Japan			
	Imports from world	Imports from Japan	Exports to world	Exports to Japan	Imports from world	Imports from U.S.	Exports to world	Exports to U.S.
0+1 Food, beverages & tobacco	18.6	3.9	16.6	24.6	19.3	24.6	4.1	3.9
cereals	.1		9.0	18.4	9.8	18.4		
2+4 Crude materials	15.0	2.4	12.2	32.4	36.5	32.4	3.0	2.4
26 textile fibres	2.2	...	2.3	6.3	11.3	6.3	...	...
28 ores and scraps	4.5	...	1.6	6.5	9.4	6.5	...	...
3 Fuels	10.1	.1	3.5	6.8	19.0	6.8	.4	.1
5~8 Manufactured goods	55.6	92.8	63.8	34.7	24.6	34.7	92.0	92.8
5 Chemical products	3.3	1.8	8.8	7.2	5.2	7.2	6.5	1.8
7 Machinery & transport equip.	15.7	22.9	36.9	20.0	9.6	20.0	31.2	22.9
road passenger vehicles and parts	4.6	5.8	1.5	.4	.4	.4	3.6	5.8
6+8 Other manufactured goods	36.6	68.1	18.1	7.5	9.8	7.5	54.3	68.1
65 textile yarns & fabrics	3.9	9.2	1.9	.2	.6	.2	13.5	9.2
67 iron & steel	6.2	20.3	2.3	.2	1.5	.2	15.3	20.3
68 nonferrous metals	6.3	1.9	2.0	7.5	3.7	7.5	1.5	1.9
other metal products	1.6	4.6	2.1	.4	.2	.4	3.0	4.6
0~9 total	100.0	100.0	100.0	100.0	100.0	100.0	100.0	100.0

<u>1970</u>

SITC		United States				Japan			
		Imports from world	Imports from Japan	Exports to world	Exports to Japan	Imports from world	Imports from U.S.	Exports to world	Exports to U.S.
0+1	Food, beverages & tobacco	14.7	2.4	11.9	15.8	14.1	15.8	3.4	2.4
	cereals	.1	...	5.6	11.3	5.5	11.3	...	...
2+4	Crude materials	8.6	.6	12.0	29.1	33.0	29.1	1.8	.6
22	oil seeds	.2	...	3.0	6.8	3.1	6.8	...	...
26	textile fibres	.6	.2	1.3	2.0	5.5	2.0	1.0	.2
27	crude fertilizers	.7	...	.8	.9	1.2	.9	...	...
28	ores & scraps	2.8	...	2.2	7.9	12.9	7.9	...	...
4	oils and fats	.3	...	1.2	.8	.4	.8	...	...
3	Fuels	8.3	.0	3.7	11.3	20.1	11.3	.2	.0
5~8	Manufactured goods	67.4	95.7	69.0	42.3	31.7	42.3	93.7	95.7
5	Chemical products	3.2	2.7	9.0	6.9	5.1	6.9	6.4	2.7
7	Machinery & transport equip.	29.7	40.2	42.0	24.9	12.0	24.9	40.5	40.2
	passenger road vehicles and parts	10.3	13.1	2.0	.4	.3	.4	7.0	13.1
6+8	Other manufactured goods	34.5	52.8	18.0	10.5	14.6	10.5	46.8	52.8
65	textile yarns & fabrics	3.1	5.1	1.4	.4	1.3	.4	9.0	5.1
67	iron & steel	5.4	15.1	3.0	.5	1.5	.5	14.7	15.1
68	nonferrous metals	4.3	1.2	2.1	1.9	5.3	1.9	1.1	1.2
	other metals products	1.8	4.2	1.8	.4	.3	.4	3.1	4.2
84	clothing	3.2	4.6	.5	.07	.8	.07	2.4	4.6
0~9	total	100.0	100.0	100.0	100.0	100.0	100.0	100.0	100.0

1973

		United States				Japan			
		Imports from[b]		Exports to		Imports from[b]		Exports to	
SITC		World	Japan	World	Japan	World	U.S.	World	U.S.
0+1	Food, beverage & tobacco	13.1	2.7	18.4	23.5	16.1	16.4	2.3	2.8
	cereals	.1	...	11.6	16.1	4.5	9.7	...	...
2+4	Crude materials	7.7	.5	12.9	31.1	29.4	28.4	1.9	.6
22	oil seeds	.1	...	4.2	8.9	3.1	7.8	...	...
26	textile fibres	.4	.2	1.9	2.5	6.7	2.6	1.2	.2
27	crude fertilizers	.5	...	.6	.6	1.0	1.0	...	...
28	ores and scraps	2.0	...	1.5	4.5	9.2	3.0	...	...
4	oils and fats	.3	...	1.0	.9	.3	.7	.2	...
3	Fuels	9.9	.1	2.4	6.1	23.6	8.9	.2	1.9
5~8	Manufactured goods	68.5	95.5	63.7	38.3	29.6	45.1	94.5	95.1
5	Chemical products	3.4	2.7	8.2	7.7	4.6	.6	5.8	2.5
7	Machinery & transport equipment	32.6	49.9	39.7	18.2	10.6	25.4	49.3	53.1
	passenger road vehicles & parts	11.8	21.0	2.6	.7	.4	.5	10.3	20.9
6+8	Other manufactured goods	32.4	42.8	15.8	12.3	14.4	13.4	39.4	39.5
65	textile yarns & fabrics	3.1	3.6	1.7	1.5	1.7	1.1	6.6	2.8
67	iron & steel	5.4	11.6	1.9	.2	.5	.2	14.4	10.2
68	nonferrous metals	3.6	.9	1.5	2.4	3.8	1.9	.8	.8
	other metal products	1.7	4.3	1.6	.5	.3	.4	2.8	4.8
84	clothing	3.3	3.1	.4	.2	1.0	.1	1.0	2.5
0~9	Total	100.0	100.0	100.0	100.0	100.0	100.0	100.0	100.0

a Standard International Trade Classification.   b 1972.

Source: United Nations, Monthly Bulletin of Statistics, May 1968, April 1972, July 1972, September 1974, April 1975, July 1975; UNCTAD, Handbook of International Trade and Development Statistics, 1972.

40 percent in 1965 to a little above 30 percent in 1970 and 1973. However, American imports from Japan were concentrated in manufactures, and Japan's exports to the U.S. consequently have increased significantly since the mid-sixties. In 1971, Japan's share in U.S. imports was 82 percent for motorcycles, 81 percent for phonographs and tape recorders, 78 percent for television sets, 66 percent for radio receivers, 61 percent for pianos, and 40 percent for steel.

Exports from the U.S. to the world are one-third primary and two-thirds manufactured goods; however, when it comes to trade with Japan, the proportions are reversed. In other words, the United States is primarily important to Japan as a supplier of crude materials and food. In particular, Japan is an important customer for U.S. cereals, oil seeds, scraps, lumber, coal, and petroleum products. By the same token, Japan has not been a good customer for American manufacturers.

Next, we examine the importance of each country as a supplier of goods to the other in terms of major commodity groups (see Table 6). Japan's share in U.S. imports is much higher when the comparison is limited to manufactures. We may note that while Japan's share in textiles declined, its steel share made a dramatic increase. It is also worthwhile to note that although Japan's share in total U.S. imports has registered a substantial increase since 1965, the comparable figure for manufactures has shown only a modest increase. In other words, one of the causes for disequilibrium in U.S.-Japan trade is located here.

As for imports into Japan, the United States has been an important supplier of crude materials. About two-thirds of Japan's imports of cereals, oil seeds, and ores and scraps come from the U.S. However, a more interesting point is that the U.S. accounts for 40 to 50 percent of Japan's imports of manufactures. (The ratio fell to 30 percent in 1973.) This proportion is particularly high in machinery and metal products. In other words, while Japan does not import much in the way of manufactured goods, what little it does import comes mainly from the United States.

Table 6. Trade Shares by Major Commodity Group, Japan and the U.S. (%)

SITC		Japan — World / U.S.					U.S. — World / Japan				
		1955	1960	1965	1970	1973	1955	1960	1965	1970	1973
0+1	Food, beverages & tobacco	1.5	2.3	2.5	2.5	3.1	30.4	21.6	38.6	34.1	34.6
	cereals	...	...	...	...	...			56.7	61.9	70.6
2+4	Crude materials	2.0	1.4	1.9	1.1	1.1	26.2	35.5	26.8	26.7	25.5
22	oil seeds									67.0	65.8
26	textile fibres				5.6	9.6			16.9	10.8	10.0
27	crude fertilizers									23.3	15.5
28	ores & scraps								21.1	18.7	12.1
4	oils and fats									49.1	48.4
3	Fuels	-	.3	.1	.1	.2	25.9	24.5	10.8	17.0	6.2
5~8	Manufactured goods	8.4	14.7	20.1	21.9	20.3	47.2	48.9	42.7	40.6	29.9
5	Chemical products	2.1	3.8	6.8	12.9	10.6	41.0	54.2	42.3	41.0	38.9
7	Machinery & transport equipment	3.7	9.6	17.5	20.9	23.2	63.6	58.8	62.9	63.2	54.2
	road passenger vehicles & parts			14.9	19.7	27.1			38.4	42.6	41.4
6+8	Other manufactured goods	9.7	17.7	22.4	22.7	18.2	31.6	32.6	23.1	21.9	16.5
65	textile yarns & fabrics	8.1	16.5	28.0	25.6	17.4	77.8		11.6	10.0	10.6
67	iron & steel	1.1	1.3	39.2	43.1	32.7	10.0	28.6	3.8	10.4	7.3
68	nonferrous metals			3.6	4.4	3.2		32.4	10.8	10.9	13.7
	other metal products			34.3	37.0	38.2			58.8	43.5	32.2
84	clothing				21.8	11.1				2.5	2.3
0~9	total	4.0	7.5	12.0	15.4	13.7	31.3	37.1	30.3	30.4	23.7

Source: See Table 5.

Table 7. Exports and Production of Manufactured Goods by Major Industrial Countries[a]

Year	Value of Exports (bn. $)					Volume Index of Exports			Unit Value Index of Exports			Manufacturing Production Index		
	total	U.S.	(%)	Japan	(%)	total	U.S.	Japan	total	U.S.	Japan	total	U.S.	Japan
1951	29.30	8.75	(29.9)	1.19	(4.1)	48	71	17	94	84	125	57	66	20
1952	30.24	9.66	(31.9)	1.07	(3.5)	48	78	18	96	85	123	59	69	21
1953	31.55	11.08	(35.1)	1.05	(3.3)	51	90	19	93	85	115	63	74	26
1954	32.51	10.10	(31.1)	1.39	(4.3)	55	82	26	91	84	111	63	69	29
1955	35.62	10.00	(28.1)	1.75	(4.9)	59	80	34	92	86	105	70	78	31
1956	40.68	11.88	(29.2)	2.18	(5.4)	66	91	41	96	90	108	73	81	39
1957	44.71	12.85	(28.7)	2.54	(5.7)	70	93	46	98	95	112	75	81	46
1958	43.88	11.72	(26.7)	2.52	(5.7)	69	84	48	97	96	107	72	75	45
1959	47.02	11.31	(24.1)	3.04	(6.5)	75	79	58	96	99	107	80	85	55
1960	54.02	13.00	(24.1)	3.62	(6.7)	84	90	67	98	100	109	86	87	69
1961	56.54	12.87	(22.8)	3.76	(6.7)	87	88	73	99	101	105	89	88	83
1962	60.34	13.88	(23.0)	4.39	(7.3)	93	95	87	99	100	102	95	95	90
1963	65.21	14.47	(22.2)	4.95	(7.6)	100	100	100	100	100	100	100	100	100
1964	74.34	16.64	(22.4)	6.07	(8.2)	113	114	124	101	101	99	108	107	116
1965	83.27	17.26	(20.7)	7.83	(9.4)	124	114	161	103	104	98	116	118	121
1966	93.12	19.12	(20.5)	9.05	(9.7)	135	123	188	106	107	97	125	130	137
1967	99.75	20.77	(20.8)	9.76	(9.8)	143	130	196	107	110	101	128	132	164
1968	114.81	23.65	(20.6)	12.19	(10.6)	165	145	243	107	113	101	138	139	189
1969	134.59	26.78	(19.9)	14.97	(11.1)	187	158	286	110	118	106	149	146	220
1970	155.00	29.37	(18.9)	18.12	(11.7)	203	164	327	117	124	112	151	139	251
1971	177.69	30.45	(17.4)	22.63	(12.7)	222	166	394	123	127	116	154	139	257
1972	210.11	33.77	(16.1)	27.09	(12.9)	242	181	421	133	129	130	163	150	276
1973	278.55	44.73	(16.1)	34.89	(12.5)	270	221	446	158	140	158	180	165	326
1974	372.88	63.53	(16.1)	52.44	(14.1)	298	258	522	192	170	203	181	164	311

a Belgium-Luxembourg, Canada, France, Italy, Japan, Netherlands, Sweden, Switzerland, United Kingdom, United States, and West Germany.

Source: United Nations, Monthly Bulletin of Statistics; The Growth of World Industry.

Changes in International Competitiveness up to 1971

We have pointed out that recent changes in the U.S.–Japan bilateral trade balance must be examined in the framework of each country's trade with the world, even though they are also subject to various factors specific to each country. The reason for the turnabout in the two countries' respective balance-of-trade positions in the latter half of the 1960s must be found in persistent differentials in economic growth and in the productivity changes of each country vis-à-vis other industrial nations. We shall consider this point with respect to manufactured goods.

Table 7 shows the relative positions of the United States and Japan among eleven major industrial countries whose exports of manufactures account for 85 percent of all manufactured exports of developed market economies.[2] The U.S. share declined from 35 percent in 1953 to 17.4 percent in 1971 and stabilized at 16.1 percent in 1972–74. Both the United States and the United Kingdom lost their leading positions in the world trade of manufactures. It is obvious that this slippage is a long-term phenomenon. In contrast, Japan has increased its share steadily over the past two decades. From 1960 to 1974, Japan's share more than doubled, going from 6.7 percent to 14.1 percent.

These changes must be attributed to differences in the international competitiveness of these countries in relation to other countries. International competitiveness is hard to quantify. Though prices are a basic factor, they are not necessarily the dominant one; nonprice competition may weigh more than price competition in certain instances. In any case, U.S. export prices registered an above-average increase, while Japan's export prices showed a decline in the 1950s and remained stable for most of the 1960s. With the fixed exchange rates, the dollar tended to be overvalued and the yen undervalued. The persistently widening differentials in currency values no doubt contributed toward shifting world demand away from American products to Japanese goods.

More important than this, however, are real factors concerning development of supply potentials and introduction of new commodities. Countries trade with each other because each of them produces different or differentiated commodities. In the case of manufactured goods, a country can maintain its leading position as a seller in the international market only by continually introducing new commodities. That such product innovations were particularly notable in the 1950s and the 1960s explains, at least partially, why international trade in industrial products expanded faster than domestic production during those two decades. The United States had long held the leading position as the most industrially advanced economy in the world. Over the last two decades, however, its position has gradually eroded, and latecomers—particularly West Germany and Japan—have caught up. Among the indicators of innovative activities are differentials in the growth rate of industrial production. Rapid industrial expansion is accompanied by creation of new industries and adoption of new products. While the United States lagged very much behind the world average in industrial growth, Japan kept its phenomenal growth about 10 percent per annum through the 1950s and the 1960s. Along with growth, productivity improved tremendously.[3] Japan has developed a great deal of process and product innovations, thanks to technology imports from the United States.

One can note in this connection Japan's industrial policy of "export or perish." The omnipotent Ministry of International Trade and Industry resorted to administrative guidance in giving priority in allocation of investment funds, export subsidies, preferential tax treatment, accelerated depreciation, and other promotional measures to certain key industries, such as automobiles and steel, which the government wanted to develop rapidly. This was in sharp contrast to the situation in the United States, where it is usually the declining industries that lobby most aggressively for government assistance in the form of tariffs, import quotas, and other protective measures. Examples of the latter are the textile and steel industries, which are protected by "voluntary" quotas on exports from Japan and elsewhere.

Domestic industries were long protected in Japan by such devices as tariffs, quotas, cumbersome import licensing of foreign concerns, and restrictions on foreign investment. Such practices were frequently the target of criticism by foreigners, particularly Americans. But most of these devices have been eliminated. The average tariff rate in Japan is similar to rates in the U.S. and Western Europe, and the number of items on the quota list has been drastically reduced during the last few years (except for some agricultural products and electronic computers). Complete liberalization of capital imports was initiated in 1973.

Another feature of Japanese trade is the key role of trading companies. A large proportion of Japan's exports and imports is handled by a few giant trading companies that maintain branch offices all over the world. They serve as sales agents for many small firms that depend very much on exports; otherwise, these firms would not have access to foreign markets. Rapid growth of Japan's exports owes a great deal to the trading companies' intensive sales efforts, e.g., in the United States and Southeast Asia, both of whose total imports did not expand rapidly. The United States has no industry of a comparable character. If we look for a parallel, we might think of multinational corporations that operate on the worldwide scale. But they are quite different in their economic effect on home countries.

So far, we have considered competitiveness in the international market. The same considerations apply to the domestic U.S. market. The latter was invaded by foreign goods toward the end of the 1960s because of the overvalued dollar, a result of domestic inflation and stagnant productivity growth. Evidence for this statement can be found by comparing import expansion with labor productivity changes in U.S. manufacturing industries, particularly in such traditional lines of production as textiles and metals.

Developments since 1971

The disequilibrium in bilateral trade between Japan and the United States became a critical political issue at the beginning of the 1970s. We have already emphasized that changes in the relative positions of the two countries were due primarily to basic differences in their overall economic growth rates.

However, an additional factor was provided by cyclical fluctuations in business activity.

After the balance-of-payments ceiling was lifted from economic growth, Japan enjoyed an uninterrupted five-year upswing in economic activity; GNP grew an average of 12 percent per annum from 1965 to 1970. Not until 1971 did this expansion phase come to a temporary halt, when the growth rate dipped to 6 percent. This downswing produced two effects on Japanese trade. As in any downswing, inventory investment was cut down, and therefore imports did not grow (in real terms). The U.S. share in Japan's imports of crude materials declined. On the other hand, producers attempted to sell surpluses of their products abroad. It is not surprising to find that Japan's sales efforts were stepped up particularly in the U.S. market. Thus, the 1971 recession resulted in a tremendous export surplus in Japan.

In the meantime, foreign imports made substantial inroads into the United States market. In 1971, U.S. exports to the world stagnated, and those to Japan declined. For the first time in eighty years, the U.S. had an import surplus. The overvaluation of the dollar became apparent. The de facto devaluation of the dollar was announced on August 15, 1971. Unfortunately, this devaluation did not immediately help improve the U.S. position. While exports increased substantially in 1972, imports increased even more. The import surplus increased. Apparently, the fundamental internal disequilibrium was so large that a small devaluation had no visible effect.

At this time, Japan had recovered from the 1971 recession. Real GNP grew at a rate of 9.2 percent from 1971 to 1972. Along with this growth, imports started to pick up. However, exports grew even more, and Japan continued to amass foreign exchange reserves, thereby exacerbating the disequilibrium in the distribution of international liquidity.[4]

The culmination of these events was the U.S. import surplus of nearly $6 billion in 1972, more than 70 percent of which was accounted for by Japan. In February 1973 the second round of the currency readjustments was undertaken. Although the yen has been revalued by 30 percent since

1971, the Japanese government has been slow in reacting to new international developments that required prompt action during this time.

The period from 1973 to 1975 witnessed radical changes in the international economic climate. First came the doubling and tripling of primary commodity prices in world markets from 1973 to 1974 as a result of unusually strong excess demand for foodstuffs and crude materials. The United States government placed soybeans under a temporary embargo in the summer of 1973 in order to ensure domestic supply, an action that created strong anger in the Japanese public. This development was followed by the oil crisis in the winter of 1973. The shock of the latter reverberated throughout Japan, because Japan was for the first time forced to realize its extreme dependence on raw-materials supplies from abroad. Japan imports 99 percent of the oil it consumes, most of which goes to electric-power generation and industry use. The quadrupled oil prices exacerbated the inordinately high rate of inflation which was already under way because of easy money. The import price index (in yen) rose by 12 percent in 1973 and 78 percent in 1974. The consumer price index rose by 12 perecnt in 1973 and 25 percent in 1974, while the wholesale price index increased by 16 percent in 1973 and 25 percent in 1974. The export price index in yen was raised by 8 percent in 1973 and 38 percent in 1974. The index in dollars rose by 22 percent in 1973 and 28 percent in 1974. Japanese exports decelerated considerably in growth in 1973 and again in 1975 (see Table 7). Changes in the terms of trade were so large that imports increased their share of GNP from 9 percent in 1972 to 15.5 percent in 1974. Exports fell short of imports in 1973 and 1974, almost liquidating the 1971–72 surpluses.

Trade between the United States and Japan underwent a significant turnabout. American exports to Japan increased by more than 60 percent from 1972 to 1973, while Japanese exports to the U.S. registered only a modest expansion. American exports continued to expand at a substantial rate (more than 25 percent) in 1974. These rapid increases, however, were more apparent than real because of the abnormal price rises in foodstuffs and crude materials. Japanese exports increased at a commensurate rate, but Japan's share in total U.S. imports continued to fall from its high of 16.4 percent in 1972 to 12.3 percent in 1974. Correspondingly, the American share in total Japanese exports fell from above 30 percent in 1968–72 to 23 percent in 1974 and to 19 percent in the first half of 1975. In these recent years, the United States has been of reduced importance as a market to Japan; in fact, the volume of Japanese exports to the U.S. was lower in 1973 and 1974 than it was in 1972. In other words, the trade gap between the United States and Japan was closed in 1973 and 1974, and was even reversed in 1975, because of the change in the terms of trade between primary and manufactured goods and the recession in the two countries. I want to emphasize the very temporary nature of the disappearance of the trade gap.

Future of U.S.–Japan Trade

We have exmained in the preceding section how trade relations between the United States and Japan have changed over two-and-a-half decades. The extreme disequilibrium in the bilateral balance of trade in 1971–72 resulted from basic structural imbalance under the fixed-exchange-rate system. No amount of diplomatic haggling could resolve the imbalance, insofar as the negotiating never did touch upon the basic elements. Events since 1973 have solved the problem by brute force; the question that we now have to ask is whether this solution is permanent or temporary. As we have noted, Japan's export surpluses with the United States in 1971 and 1972 were due mainly to its particular trade pattern of importing crude materials and exporting finished goods. Since this characterization of the Japanese economy will not change, there must always be a basic tendency for Japan to run an export surplus against the U.S., even if the floating exchange rates more or less balance Japan's exports and imports in the aggregate, unless the terms of trade remain in favor of primary goods.

U.S.–Japan Trade Balance

To consider what will happen to trade between the United

States and Japan in, say, the next ten years, we must first
have some idea about how the overall trade of the U.S.,
Japan, and the world will expand. From 1955 to 1970, real
exports and imports expanded at 8 percent per annum while
GNP grew at 5 percent. Trade expansion continued into the
first half of the 1970s, in spite of the world inflations of
1973 and 1974 and the world recession of 1974 and 1975.
Both exports and imports increased their shares of GNPs in
advanced countries. An important question is whether foreign trade can keep on growing faster than domestic production. Since export prices normally increase less than GNP
deflators, trade would expand at a somewhat higher rate—
say, by two percentage points—than GNP in constant prices,
if trade is to maintain a constant proportion of GNP in current prices.

It is generally acknowledged that Japan has now entered a
phase of decelerated growth. In contrast to 12 percent per
annum, the rate at which Japan's real GNP grew from 1965
to 1970, the growth rate of its GNP declined to an average
of 5.7 percent per annum between 1970 and 1974. How fast
Japan will be able to grow after the 1974–75 recession is a
big question mark. Real factors working against rapid growth
are labor shortages (now that all mobile farm labor has been
absorbed into the urban labor force), depletion of ready-
made foreign technologies, and growing problems of environmental pollution. The availability of foodstuffs, energy, and
industrial materials is also an important consideration. Despite these antigrowth factors, the Japanese economy may
still be able to grow at a somewhat faster rate than other
developed nations. This means that its imports and exports
will grow at somewhat higher rates than its GNP, in which
case Japanese exports will grow a little faster than world
trade of manufactures. Imagine that Japanese manufactured
exports expand three percentage points faster than the latter:
Japan's market share would then rise to 19 percent in ten
years from its 1974 level of 14.1 percent. How could this
substantial increase be absorbed?

Imports from Japan are near saturation in Southeast Asia,
and any further inroads into this region could be made only

at the expense of creating friction of serious proportions with importing countries. Other less-developed areas are not very promising for potential market expansion because of their slow growth and limited purchasing power, except for a few oil-rich countries. Centrally planned economies, particularly China and the USSR, may provide outlets, as evidenced by their rapid import expansion in 1974 and 1975, but the future course of trade with them depends on uncertain political and economic elements. Western Europe is one area with high income and rapid trade expansion; Japan now has a very low share of that market. But it is probable that Japan would experience the same sort of export surplus with this region as it has with the United States, since Western Europe cannot supply the crude materials that Japan needs. Furthermore, Western European countries, traditionally resentful of Japan's aggressive encroachment, try to maintain discriminatory restrictions against Japanese goods. In any event, Western Europe as a whole accounted for a virtually constant share of Japan's total exports from 1970 to 1974, in spite of Japan's strong efforts to promote exports into that area (see Table 8).

All this means that the United States is still an extremely attractive market for Japan; there will always be a strong temptation for Japanese exporters to oversell in the U.S. market, in view of Japan's well-established sales network there. The substantial reductions in the U.S. share of Japanese exports from 1973 to 1975 were due initially to the revaluation of the yen and to the Japanese inflation, and later to the prolonged recession in the United States. When the American economy recovers, Japan's share in U.S. imports will again rise.

Since Japan has been losing its comparative advantage in selling light manufactured goods to emerging countries, it must specialize in technology-intensive goods. Automobiles have become a major export good of Japan. It is probable that a strong demand for protection of this industry will arise from both American capital and labor.

The bilateral balance problem will be permanently solved if Japan will sufficiently increase its imports from the United

Table 8. Geographic composition of Japan's exports,
          1970 and 1974 in percentages

	1970	1974
Developed areas	54.2	46.5
U.S.	30.8	22.2
Canada	3.0	2.7
Western Europe	15.1	15.6
Oceania and South Africa	5.4	5.9
Developing areas	40.4	45.6
Southeast Asia	25.0	21.6
Middle East	3.2	7.6
Centrally planned economies	5.3	8.0
China	2.8	3.9
Total	100.0	100.0

Source: Ministry of Finance (Japan), Summary Report
         on External Trade

States. The U.S. has been a major supplier of foodstuffs and
crude materials to Japan; how fast those imports will increase
depends on Japanese demand and American supply. Japan's
demand for crude materials will perhaps not rise very fast as
Japan's technology becomes more sophisticated; there has
been a great deal of talk in Japan about deliberately developing industries that require less imported materials.

Food is another problem. The strength of American agriculture has been tested during the last few years, since the
worldwide food shortage has become a real issue. This is one
area in which the U.S. maintains comparative advantage; on
the other hand, agriculture has been declining in Japan.
Younger workers have virtually deserted the farms. Japan is
self-sufficient only in rice, which has been heavily supported
by the government. In all other crops, Japan has increased
its dependence on imports. Overall, Japan supplies only 40
percent of its food consumption from domestic sources. To
take an extreme example, domestic production of soybeans

accounted for 30 percent of domestic consumption in 1960 but only 4 percent in 1970. While it is definitely not in the economic interests of Japan to attempt to reestablish self-sufficiency in food, a national-security point of view may override economic considerations. Japanese agricultural policy, whichever way it may turn, will have a direct bearing on U.S.-Japan trade.

The trade gap can be filled in if the United States increases its exports of industrial goods, particularly consumer goods. Japan has been buying very few consumer goods from abroad. The latter accounted for only 3 percent of Japan's total imports in 1970, in contrast to 25 percent in the U.S. Affluence, however, seems finally to have broken down Japanese consumer resistance to foreign consumer goods, since this ratio has been rising in recent years. How fast this component will expand is, however, still uncertain. One thing that stands in its way is the complex and imperfectly competitive distribution system in Japan. Any expansion of U.S. exports of consumer goods into Japan requires setting up new sales outlets. However—partly because of Japan's peculiar distribution system, which frustrates any newcomers, particularly foreigners, and because exporting is a marginal activity for most U.S. manufacturers—such efforts cannot be said to have been sufficient.

In passing, we may refer to extensive Japanese discussion in recent years about the need for a shift in national priorities from economic growth to domestic welfare, such as the creation of social overhead capital and attempts to combat pollution. Such a shift would reduce Japan's dependence on foreign trade and, therefore, alleviate the balance-of-trade problem. It is doubtful, however, that a country's economic characteristics can be changed overnight.

Last but not least, one must note the growing impact of unstable world prices of primary commodities, such as was the case in 1973 and 1974. As Japan's economic scale expands, its import requirements soar to a gigantic proportion. Japan's imports would probably account for more than 20 percent of world trade in crude materials (17 percent in 1973) and in petroleum (13 percent in 1973), even if conservation measures were successful. When supplies of primary goods are relatively inelastic or tightly controlled by international oligopolies, increases in demand are likely to lead to the bidding up of prices. Such price increases in key primary goods may easily turn the Japanese export surplus into an import surplus very quickly, as a result of increased payments for imports and the deteriorated competitiveness that follows rises in export prices. In this regard, Japan is much more sensitive to external influences than is the United States.

Rivalry in Trade with the Rest of the World

With Japan approaching the United States in economic scale, it is obvious that the two countries will compete more actively for trade with other countries. So far the clash has not been dramatic. For instance, in the industrial imports of Southeast Asia, Japan's share increased from 18 percent in 1955 to 25 percent in 1973, while the U.S. share decreased from 20 percent to 12 percent over the same period. However, if Japan seeks new markets elsewhere than in Southeast Asia and the U.S., one such market might be Latin America, where the United States had shares of 38 percent and 26 percent of the industrial imports in 1969 and 1973, respectively, against Japan's share of 8 percent. (The comparable figures are 6 percent vs. 2 percent in Western Europe and 5 percent vs. 14 percent in Africa.) In addition, there are the less-familiar markets of Eastern Europe and China, where there has already been competition between U.S. and Japanese firms.

One must also note anticipated changes in Japan's export goods from low-technology to high-technology products. Exports of labor-intensive manufactures, such as textiles and consumer electronics products, have been taken over already by such developing economies as Taiwan and Korea. Japan must shift its exports from these to more sophisticated goods, which have long been the domain of U.S. producers. Whether the United States can maintain its strong edge over Japan in these lines will become a critical issue.

Competition is also probable in imports. This will prove particularly significant in petroleum. Japan depends virtually completely on imported oil for its fuel supply; what with its rapid motorization, the income elasticity of demand has been substantially above unity. Japan may account for 20 percent or an even higher proportion of world imports of petroleum within the next ten years. What happens to American demand for foreign oil depends to a large measure on its success in achieving self-sufficiency. The outcome is uncertain, though there have been optimistic projections. But should the United States have to increase its dependence on oil imports, there might follow a serious strain. Concerted, continued efforts, along the lines set up in recent international negotiations among developed economies, are necessary to reconcile these demands.

Overseas Corporations

One of the most significant developments in the past two decades has been the growth of multinational corporations. While these have been mostly American in origin, European and Japanese firms are now starting on their own. The inducement is particularly strong for Japanese firms to go abroad through direct investment overseas, for a number of reasons. Above all, it becomes more and more necessary to secure stable supplies of key raw materials through direct investment, as Japan's import requirements of these materials expand vis-à-vis world supply. Furthermore, Japanese investors can make use of the abundant and cheaper labor in less-developed countries in labor-intensive lines of manufacturing production. Pollution abatement at home has become an important consideration in the decision to establish production facilities abroad. Another advantage is that, by producing abroad, Japanese manufacturers can bypass restrictions placed on foreign trade by host countries. It has been forecast that Japan will rapidly expand its direct investment abroad during the decade to come. It is quite plausible that American and Japanese firms would then find themselves pitted against each other, not only as traders, but also as worldwide producers.

Conclusion

We have surveyed trade relations between the United States

and Japan in the past and conjectured on their prospects in the near future. We have speculated that, despite their temporary disappearance, there will be a persistent tendency for deficits to exist in the U.S. balance of trade with Japan. In 1971 and 1972, the problem was so acute that the stability of the world order was endangered; it was no longer a two-country, bilateral problem. While the abandonment of the fixed-exchange-rate system seems to have resolved the problem, the resolution may be only temporary, a result of the world inflation and the world recession that took place from 1973 to 1975. The problem may merely be dormant; when the world economy regains its normal state, it may come back—though perhaps not in such a critical form, particularly in the light of expected deceleration in Japan's economic growth. But, unless adequate countermeasures are taken, a persistent imbalance in U.S.-Japan trade may easily evoke American sentiments for a return to protectionism or neo-isolationism, a development that would contribute to the deterioration of relations between the United States and Japan—as the 1973 incident involving the American embargo on soybeans amply suggests.

The United States and Japan will remain important trade partners. Harmony and cooperation between the two countries is essential for the prosperity and peace of the free world.

7

THE UNITED STATES AND JAPAN IN GLOBAL OIL POLITICS: A COMPARISON OF THEIR INTERACTIONS WITH PETROLEUM-EXPORTING NATIONS

Tong-Whan Park

*Associate Professor of Political Science,
Northwestern University*

Never in the history of the U.S.–Japan relationship has the need for cooperation been greater. This need arose in large part from the recent waves of oil crises ignited by several political decisions of the petroleum-exporting nations. The crisis of production cutbacks and embargoes as well as the crisis of prices has dealt a severe blow to the consumer nations which have until recently enjoyed a plentiful supply of cheap petroleum. Moreover, the burden of these "oil shocks" and the concomitant adjustments that the consumers must make appear unevenly distributed.

It is a painful fact that the United States and Japan are located at the opposite ends of the scale in international energy shortages. Though its reliance on foreign oil approached 40 percent of its energy needs in 1975, the United States seems able to survive the crises without too much domestic disturbance, largely because of its relatively strong economy and its wealth of natural resources. On the other hand, Japan is hard hit because it imports nearly 90 percent of its energy requirements, with oil accounting for roughly three-quarters of this total. According to one estimate, a 20-percent decrease in

imports of coal, oil, and other energy sources to the United
States would cause only a 2-percent shortfall in energy
supply.[1] Should the same interruption in imports take place
in Japan, however, over 15 percent of total energy supplies
would be affected.

Confronted with this grave crisis, consumer nations have
embarked on myriad crash programs aimed at reducing their
vulnerability to supply interruption and to price manipula-
tion of imported petroleum. These programs include conservation, technological innovation for alternative energy
sources, and international collaboration. The still-young
International Energy Agency may yet prove to be an important vehicle for facilitating research and planning in these areas.
It is precisely the area of international coordination which
contains great potential for both conflict and competition
among petroleum-importing nations. In this regard, consumers tend to view three major issues as most pivotal in
shaping their collective and individual energy policies.

The first such issue is preparation for emergencies. In principle, most consumers recognize the need to establish emer-
gency sharing plans to cope with new embargoes and to create new financial arrangements for the purpose of recycling
petrodollars. As far as the actual implementation of emer-
gency measures is concerned, however, it is an understate-
ment to say that there are differences of opinion. The central
concern of most consumers is whether the United States will
fulfill the promise of sharing its oil in case of another embargo. This concern is particularly pronounced in Japan,
which observed U.S. behavior during the last embargo. Not
only was there no offer from the United States to share supplies with Japan, but rather there was a frantic launching of
policies aimed at American self-sufficiency. The Japanese are
not convinced that they would receive fair treatment from
the United States in the event of another boycott.

The second issue concerns the ways and means to apply
some pressure upon oil prices. If consumers take collective
actions to reduce domestic consumption and to develop alternative energy sources, the producers are likely to feel pressure to lower prices. Two of the potential shortcomings of

this strategy are that the politico-economic cost of maintaining a common frontier is extremely high, and that once the prices roll back to "normalcy," those who will have made heavy capital investment for technological innovation may be severely penalized.

The last and perhaps the most crucial problem is the strategy of holding negotiations with the producing nations. Because of differences of interest among consumers, the proposals to hold conferences between producers and consumers have not materialized until recently. The first such meeting, which was held in Paris in December 1975, resulted in more rhetoric than agreements on action proposals.

Japan and the United States have areas of both converging and diverging interests concerning the issue of cooperation among consumers. In order to strengthen the cooperation and to mitigate potential conflict between them, it is imperative to identify the areas of possible discord, to unfold the origins and consequences of such discord, and then to explore policy alternatives that will jointly maximize the interests of both nations. The research reported in this study is an attempt to analyze Japanese–U.S. relationships in the context of their interactions with the petroleum-exporting nations (PENs). Utilizing events data on petroleum-related interactions (1947–74), major dimensions of conflictual and cooperative behavior of PENs targeted toward Japan and the United States are investigated. Delineated are not only the general patterns of producer-consumer interactions but also the impact upon these patterns of specific events such as the formation of the Organization of the Petroleum-Exporting Countries (OPEC), Arab-Israeli wars, and important domestic political changes. PENs' behavior toward the United States is systematically compared with that toward Japan, while an attempt is made to build linkages between PENs' external behavior and internal development.

Behavior of Petroleum-Exporting Nations toward the United States and Japan

Caught off guard by a series of blows in international energy markets, consumers in general and Western, developed

societies in particular have come to a painful realization as to
how vulnerable they could be. Many expert opinions have appeared concerning the rapidly diminishing "power" of developed countries relative to that of PENs. These explanations
include:

- the increasing capabilities of PENs in diplomatic bargaining as well as administrative and technical activities;
- the increasing dependence of industrialized countries
  upon petroleum as a result of technological advance
  which relies heavily on petroleum;
- the increasing national assertiveness of public opinion in
  PENs due to increased communication and education;
- the increasing cohesiveness among PENs, as reflected in
  resource cartels like OPEC, and the corresponding rise in
  their collective bargaining strength;
- increasing self-consciousness in the Third World and a
  greater awareness of North-South conflict;
- the experience of temporary oil shortages due to the
  closure of the Suez Canal, tanker shortages, inadequate
  refining capacities, and decreasing United States production; and
- the increasing politicization of oil trade resulting from
  regional conflict.

Though they shed light upon PENs' foreign-policy behavior, these observations lack a coherent and overarching framework which would enable us to describe, explain, and predict
the entire spectrum of interactions between PENs on the one
hand and petroleum-importing nations (PINs) and multinational petroleum companies (MPCs) on the other. One such
framework has been developed utilizing resource nationalism
as the central concept. Resource nationalism is defined as the
behavioral assertion of national interests and control in extractive industries. One of the basic premises of our study is
that resource nationalism progresses through a clearly iden-
tifiable set of stages in PENs' external behavior patterns. It
is further assumed that these stages can be delineated by tracing oil issues which arise in the course of PENs' interactions
with PINs and MPCs. Oil issues include any matter, subject,
or point that either (1) is related to the activities of major

actors within the international petroleum industry or (2) involves the use (actual or potential) of the petroleum industry as an instrument of foreign policy. More abstractly, an oil issue is usually associated with problems, conflicts of interest, or any subject of interest that can become a source or goal of political activity in international oil flows.

Oil issues emerge from both external and internal conditions of the petroleum industry. A brief survey of PENs' oil-related interactions suggests a highly dynamic process which undergoes substantial change over time. At the beginning stages of development in the petroleum industry, oil exporters were primarily concerned with attracting capital investment and securing agreements leading to explorations and subsequent exploitation of their natural resources. Oil issues during this "early" period consisted of demands and requests for minor changes in the behavior of MPCs. As the industry becomes more well developed and profitable, attention has shifted from these early issues and now begins to reflect a greater concern over the control which an exporter can exercise over its own resources vis-à-vis the multinationals. Thus, trade, transportation, marketing, and the pricing of petroleum constitute salient "middle" issues to PENs. Only after PENs have acquired considerable economic strength and experience in international petroleum interactions will the utilization of "oil weapons" and nationalization become more feasible, since these "late" issues generally involve extremely high risks. Table 1 presents the breakdown of the issues for each stage of issue development.

Since our primary concern is to unfold the conflictual and cooperative interactions of PENs in the context of resource nationalism and its development over time, we need both longitudinal and cross-sectional data. The ability to utilize events data represents one recent development that will help capture both the long-term and short-term variations in conflict and cooperation. These data can provide a close interface between attention to specific details and an understanding of general characteristics that a situation may share with others. The present study utilizes an events data coding scheme designed to examine the resource nationalism of PENs. The

Table 1. Oil Issue Categorization

Issue 1 (Early Issues):   Concession Area

                                           Concession Period

                                           Nationality of Employees

                                           Exploration and Development

                                           Investment

Issue 2 (Middle Issues):   Trade, Transportation, and Distribution

                                           Oil Prices

                                           Profits of Oil Companies

                                           Governmental Taxes and Royalties

Issue 3 (Late Issues):   Restriction of Oil Flow

                                           Nationalization

scheme seeks to extract information on the various attributes of actions initiated by PENs and directed toward foreign
actors involving oil issues. The two distinguishing features of
this scheme are that it deals only with petroleum-related
events and that it covers specific issues as components of
these events. An oil event is defined to include all discrete
actions related to oil issues undertaken by major actors engaged in import, export, transport, exploration, discovery,
processing, and/or distribution of petroleum (see Appendix
to this chapter for the PEN coding sheet).

In order to investigate PENs' behavior toward the United
States and Japan, events data were collected on a sample of
PENs from 1947 through the first quarter of 1974. The sample consists of five nations: Iran, Saudi Arabia, Kuwait, Algeria, and Libya. Though it is not a truly representative sample
in the statistical sense, it does reflect an attempt to span a
wide range of cleavages existing among PENs, including geographic location, ideological and cultural gaps, and technological and economic development as well as the unique characteristics of the oil industry in each country. Employing the
PEN coding scheme, events were coded from various chro-
nologies which provide short descriptions of the oil-related

165

behavior of these five countries. The *Middle East Journal* was the primary source for data collection, although the *New York Times* (Daily and Index) and the *Keyhan Havaii* (Iran) were also consulted.

For each PEN in our sample, events were aggregated by quarter for specific targets. These quarterly aggregations represent the frequency of actions and issues for each dyad. Of particular interest to us are the oil events that were targeted toward either the United States or Japan, regardless of the initiators of action.[2] Therefore, only those dyads that have either the United States or Japan as the recipient were selected. These events were then aggregated to produce separate quarterly scores for each recipient (the United States or Japan). For example, when the issue of "restriction of oil flow" to the United States was examined, all the events that make reference to this specific issue were summed for each quarter for all dyads which had the United States as a target. In the following sections, these events will be examined.

The United States

The U.S. involvement in Middle East oil dates as far back as the late 1910s. Seriously disturbed by the depletion of domestic oil reserves during World War I, the American government attempted to share in the exploration and exploitation of oil resources in Iraq. After a series of negotiations with Great Britain and France, which had previously agreed to extract Iraqi oil jointly, a combined enterprise involving some American participation emerged in the form of the Iraq Petroleum Company. This was the beginning, however small, of what is now a gigantic American share in Middle East petroleum. An eloquent testimony to the preponderance of American involvement in the international petroleum market is the fact that among the so-called Seven Sisters, five are U.S.-based MPCs. Until recently, these seven "majors" controlled more than 80 percent of all oil production outside North America and the Soviet bloc. They also controlled more than 70 percent of the refining capacity, and either owned or chartered more than half of the world tanker fleet.[3] Largely through these MPCs, the United States has been in constant interaction with Middle Eastern oil exporters. Especially since the end of World War II, American involvement has gone through exponential growth, and the net imports of crude oil by the United States increased from 142,000 barrels per day (bpd) in 1947 to 1 million bpd in 1960 and to over 3 million bpd in 1973. With this evidence of preponderant American involvement in mind, let us now examine the United States involvement in the Middle East in the context of its event/interactions with our sample PENs.

Figure 1.   Oil Events Directed Toward the U.S.

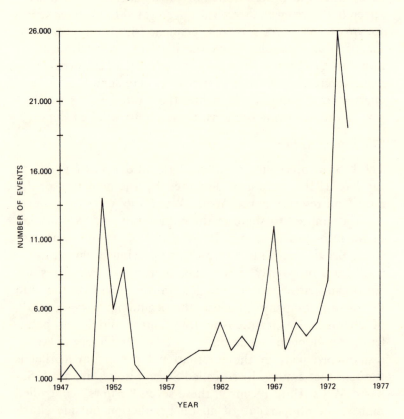

Figure 1 displays the quarterly frequency of oil events which were directed toward the United States during the period from 1947 to 1974. Despite the fact that these frequencies represent the intensity of total interactions between the United States and all five nations in our sample, some salient characteristics of the graph can be gleaned regarding the events of specific PENs as well as those affecting all five sample nations.

The fluctuation in the intensity of the U.S.–targeted interactions was significant during the Iranian oil crisis of 1951–1953, the formation of OPEC in 1960, the Arab-Israeli War of 1967, and the 1974 price rise which followed the October War in the Middle East. United States involvement in the Iranian crisis needs some explanation. Being the oldest oil-producing state in the Middle East, Iran has been a pioneer in obtaining more advantageous agreements from MPCs. Among the five nations under examination, Iran was the first to reverse some of its unequal treaties and agreements with European governments and companies. Influenced by the force of rising nationalism, Iran felt strong enough by 1930 to challenge its primary concessionaire, the Anglo-Iranian Oil Company (AIOC), and its source country, Britain. Although this led to a new agreement in 1933, it did not resolve any of the major issues. World War II forestalled a direct confrontation between Iran and AIOC, but the long-awaited blow came in 1951 when Iran, buoyed by the revolutionary leadership of Mossadegh, nationalized the oil industry and forced the ouster of Britain. During the development of this dispute, the United States also became a target of Iranian hostility because the Eisenhower administration supported Britain's attempt to defeat the policies of Mossadegh. However, the United States had disassociated itself from Britain sufficiently to supplant the British role in Iran through an American-dominated consortium of oil companies which replaced AIOC.

The development of oil issues is presented in Figure 2. Two observations are made from the examination of curves representing Issue Sets 1, 2, and 3. First, there is a recognizable shift in the timing of issue occurrences. It is clear that "earlier" issues tend to precede the "later" ones. This does not preclude overlap among the three issues, however. What is important is that the three issues temporally progress through an ordered phase. Second, the "later" issues seem to contain more frequent interactions than the "earlier" ones. The greater intensity of the "later" issues reflects the fact that they are more fundamental in nature and more difficult to resolve, thus leading to prolonged conflicts and escalations.

Figure 2. Issue Development of U.S.-Directed Interactions

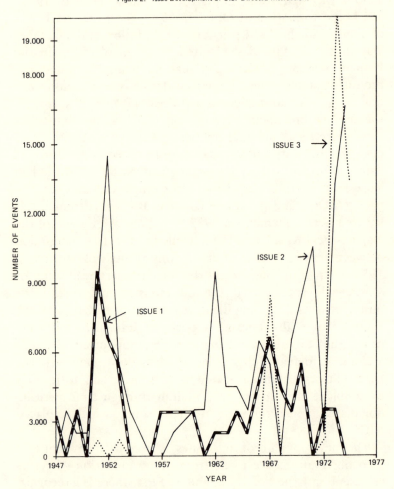

Japan

In contrast to the long history and enormous magnitude of the American share in Middle East oil, Japan has had very little control over the "upstream" activities in the international petroleum industry. It was not until the late 1950s that a Japanese entrepreneur was able to obtain a concession from Saudi Arabia and Kuwait for the rights to explore the neutral zone off Khefji. The Arabian Oil Company was established and subsequently began production in 1961. Since then, it has been supplying one-third of a million barrels of crude per day. Subsequently, another project went into operation in Indonesia yielding close to 7,000 bpd.[4] Perhaps one of the most important additions to Japan's participation in Middle East petroleum is the recent acquisition of British Petroleum's interests in the tiny, oil-rich Abu Dhabi. Continued attempts to increase participation in overseas production notwithstanding, at present about three-quarters of Japan's petroleum supply comes from foreign MPCs, while the remaining quarter is obtained through Japanese channels and sources.

The foreign MPCs operating in Japan control not only the supply of oil but the processing and marketing of it as well. In refining, the formula for Japanese and non-Japanese shares of interest is usually about equal, with each partner getting roughly 50 percent. However, in marketing, a number of MPCs have wholly owned marketing channels. Consider these constraints in light of the fact that Japan has the third-largest refining industry in the world (after the United States and the Soviet bloc), with a capacity of 5.7 million bpd at the end of 1974. The obvious conclusion is that Japan's individual vulnerability to a reduction in supply will remain extremely great for a long time to come.

Figure 3 illustrates the trend of PENs' interactions with Japan. When the quarterly frequency of oil events directed toward Japan is investigated, two points bear discussion. One is the sparse nature of oil interactions. Comparing this graph with total U.S.–directed events (Figure 1), one finds that the level of interaction for Japan has been less than one-quarter of that for the United States. This finding is consistent with the fact that Japan has not cultivated multifaceted arrangements with PENs for sharing in exploration and production. The other point concerns the fluctuations in the intensity of interactions. After the initial concession was made in the late

1950s, peaks occurred during and after the Arab-Israeli wars and the formation of OPEC. The implication of this finding is that the United States and Japan were in the same boat, at least until the first quarter of 1974.

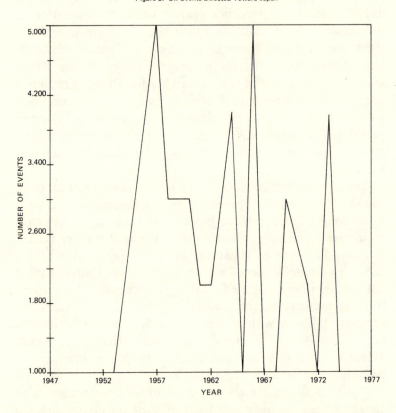

Figure 3. Oil Events Directed Toward Japan

Issue development for the oil events directed at Japan is presented in Figure 4. As in the U.S. case, there is a definite "phasing" in the occurrences of Issues 1, 2, and 3. Most notably, Issue 3 does not appear until the embargo of 1973. Unlike the issues involving the United States, however, there was no step-level increase in the intensity of interaction— implying that the "later" issues were not necessarily more intense than the "earlier" ones. There are two possible explanations for this phenomenon; one is statistical, while the other is substantive. A statistical explanation tells us that there were not enough issues (and consequently events) involving Japan to capture such step-level shifts. The substantive reasoning is based on the hypothesis that nations that have only recently entered the international energy arena (such as Japan) can learn from the experiences of others and thus "speed up" their interactions with PENs. Further research will help to test the validity of this hypothesis.

Figure 4. Issue Development of Japan–Directed Interactions

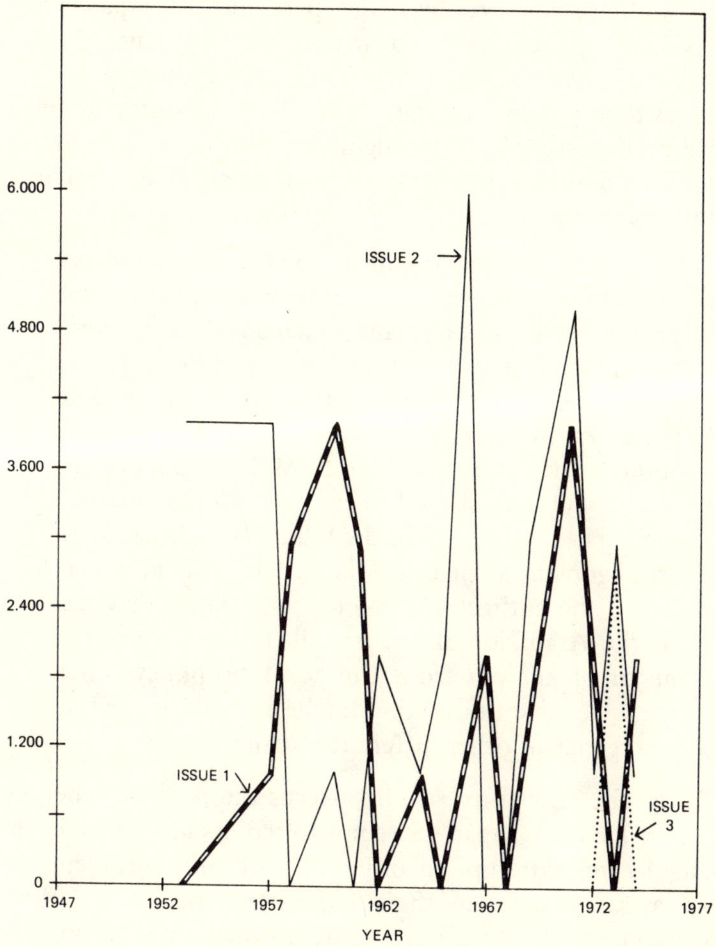

From analyses of PENs' behavior toward the United States
and Japan as well as of the roles of MPCs, one is led to conclude that the triangular relationships among Japan, the
United States, and PENs have not been conducted on co-
equal terms. Specifically, the United States and Middle Eastern exporters were the primary actors, while Japan was on
the receiving end of the outcomes from these U.S.–PENs
interactions. Moreover, the United States has been controlling its relationships with PENs through its vast military and
economic capabilities. The United States was indeed the
dominant force within the triangular structure. Even though
this configuration was in large part due to Japan's own
decision to avoid costly "upstream" involvement, the "oil
shocks" of 1973 signaled a warning to all three parties to
reassess their previous relationships.[5] To Japan this may mean
a radical departure from its alignment with the United States.
Gerard C. Smith, North American chairman of the Trilateral
Commission noted:

> The Arab restraints on oil stunned the Japanese. As
> one official said, his countrymen felt like passen-
> gers on a hijacked airplane. Having no vital interest
> in the Arab-Israeli dispute, they had tried to re-
> main neutral. They felt victimized by Arabs and
> pressured by Americans. They wondered why they
> should suffer because of U.S. Middle East policy.
> Japan will not soon forget the "out-in-the-cold"
> feeling it experienced in the fall of 1973 because of
> its alignment with U.S. Middle East policy, which
> led to the cutback in its oil supply. Japan's switch
> to the Arab side of the Israeli-Arab dispute was a
> major breakaway from United States policy. Like
> the first olive out of the bottle, it could make the
> emergence of other differences easier.[6]

Thus, the crucial question concerns the possible repercussions arising from Japan's attempt to redress imbalance in the
triangular relationship. In order to probe this problem, we
must assess changes in the relative strengths of the three
parties involved. Most important, however, are the rapidly

changing capabilities of petroleum exporters in the Middle East. Once PENs approach a position to receive co-equal behavior from Western, developed societies, the entire structure of global political economy will have to be altered. At present, no other group of countries, including the United States and Japan, has this awesome potential.

Some Dimensions of PENs' Changing Capabilities

The oil embargo and the quadrupling of oil prices following the October War created an image of Arabs financially strangling the PINs and buying up all the treasures of the world. According to the calculations made by the *Economist* of London, at the 1974 rate of capital accumulation due to surplus oil revenues, OPEC could purchase all the companies on the New York Stock Exchange in 9.2 years, all direct U.S. foreign investments in 1.8 years, all Exxon stock in 79 days, and the Rockefeller family wealth in 6 days. In 1976 OPEC received more than $105 billion in oil revenues and had a financial surplus of $40 to $60 billion, depending upon the estimate. Confronted with a massive drain of capital from developed societies, American and Japanese news media were in no position to play down the devastating effects of the oil crises. The result has been an ever-worsening image of PENs as "bad guys," so much so that America came to discuss openly the possible military seizure of Arab oil not so much for the oil itself as for the potential it held for destabilization of the OPEC cartel.[7]

Truly staggering is the magnitude of financial surpluses that will accrue to PENs ($100 to $300 billion by 1980) and the worldwide economic dislocation that it will cause. Especially hard hit are the so-called Fourth World countries, which are nonindustrialized and lack potential energy sources. However, the vision of the global plight engineered by a handful of "inscrutable" Arabs may represent only a part of the whole picture—the part advanced by the consumers of oil. Without going through the entire range of arguments presented by the PENs, several points bear mention:

- It is generally agreed that the price of oil has not kept pace with that of industrial products. In real terms, the price of petroleum was lower in 1973 than in 1959. The prices of major industrial products rose almost 475 percent from 1950 to 1973, while oil prices remained virtually unchanged until 1973.[8]

- The $40 billion surplus of OPEC countries in 1974 constitutes only half of the annual defense budget of the United States and less than half the amount of United States foreign investment.
- Even after OPEC's fourfold price hike, the possible substitutes to Middle East oil, such as North Sea oil, shale oil, and tar sands, are equally, if not more, expensive.
- It is not only the Arab members of OPEC which have been insisting upon high oil prices; in fact, some Arab members have taken initiatives to reduce prices. Many experts have argued that MPCs play a knowing, instrumental role in the implementation of price increases.
- Some experts agree that the U.S. will need at least twenty years before it can become self-sufficient in energy. Japan may never reach this position.

The logical conclusion then is that PENs and PINs will remain interdependent for many decades to come. PINs will need petroleum, while PENs will have to purchase technology for development. If they are to remain interdependent, both sides need a better understanding of the complexities of their respective positions. What is lacking today, in particular, is correct understanding of PENs by PINs. A typical case in point is the now famous prediction made by Western economists that the oil-producing nations would never withhold their petroleum from the international market because "they can't drink it." To bridge this sort of gap in understanding, modest attempts are made in this study to unfold some underlying dimensions in PENs' changing capabilities and to compare them with similar indicators for Japan and the United States.

Like most political entities, PENs have been undergoing dynamic changes in a multitude of socio-politico-economic dimensions. Unlike most polities, however, this change has been occurring at a phenomenally rapid rate. Of particular interest to us are the development of the oil industry in a country and the change experienced in the level of welfare.

The former is directly related to the total capabilities of a PEN, while the latter shows how much of the increased capability is allocated for the well-being of the people. An empirical analysis was undertaken to trace the changes in these two areas, utilizing data compiled by the International Energy Project (IEP) at Northwestern University.[9] From IEP's time-series data on attributes of PENs, we selected ten variables; seven of these measure oil industrialization in a host country, while the remaining three concern the level of wealth. Table 2 lists these variables, the definitions, and their sources. It should be noted that included among the first seven variables were four measures of oil-related exports to Japan and the United States. This conforms with our special interest, which is explored in this chapter, in the role of these two consumers in the PENs' economies. The PENs selected for this analysis were the thirteen OPEC members plus Bahrein. The time span covered a period of fifteen years, from 1960 to 1974. The year 1960 was chosen as the initial point not only because it was the year that marked the formation of OPEC, but also because it represents a past distant enough to put our over-time study into proper perspective and yet close enough to make the analysis relevant for future predictions.

Since our interest was in delineating patterns of development across nations over time, we performed a factor analysis with the data matrix which contained the variables in its columns and the combination of time and nation in its rows. Simply put, think of this arrangement as a super matrix which has fifteen yearly "slices" strung together one behind the other. Each yearly slice contained ten variables in columns and fourteen PENs in rows. This super matrix was factor-analyzed using a principal component solution with orthogonal rotation.[10] The resulting pattern (factor) loading matrix provides the clustering of variables in terms of their similarity in variation over time and nations. Moreover, a pattern (factor) score matrix generates scores for each nation for each year on these patterns.

In contrast to the common usage of factor analysis as a data-reduction technique, we are concerned with the two specific dimensions upon which to trace PENs' development.

Table 2. Variables, Codes, Definitions, and Sources

1. Total oil revenues (REVTOT$). The total amount of revenues accruing to a PEN from its oil industry. Unit = U.S. dollars. Includes royalties, taxes, profits from sale, etc. Source: Petroleum Press Service; Congressional Quarterly.

2. Oil production (PRODCTBL). The amount of crude oil produced. Unit = barrels. World Energy Supply (UN); Petroleum Economist.

3. Oil export in dollars (XPORT$). The total value of crude oil export measured in U.S. dollars. Source: Yearbook of International Trade Statistics (UN); Petroleum Economist.

4. Oil flow to U.S.A. (OILUSABL). The total amount of crude oil transported to the U.S. Unit = barrels. Source: Reports of the Committee of Science and Technology, U.S. House of Representatives; World Energy Supply; International Petroleum Encyclopedia; Petroleum Economist.

5. Oil flow to Japan (OILJAPBL). The total amount of crude oil transported to Japan. See Variable 4 for sources.

6. Export to U.S.A. (XPRTUSA$). The total value of export of goods (including oil and non-oil products) to U.S.A. Unit = U.S. dollars. Source: Direction of International Trade Statistics (UN).

7. Export to Japan (XPRTJAP$). The total value of export of goods to Japan. See Variable 6 for sources.

8. Physicians per capita (PHYSICAP). Physicians refer to registered medical practioners. Source: World Health Statistics Annual (WHO).

9. GNP per capita(GNPCAP). Gross National Product refers to the total value of goods and services produced in a country in a year's time. Unit = U.S. dollars. Source: National Account Statistics (UN); UN Statistical Yearbook.

10. School enrollment ratio (SER). The number of students enrolled in primary and secondary schools as a proportion of total population. Source: UNESCO Statistical Yearbook.

This puts us in a rather unique position of (1) exploring the independence of the two hypothesized dimensions (oil industrialization and welfare), should they emerge, as well as (2) constructing scales for these dimensions. In order to investigate the first point, the varimax orthogonal rotation was performed after extracting only two factors from the correlation matrix. This technique defines patterns which are uncorrelated with each other and uncovers distinct clusters of interrelationships among variables when they exist in the data. Table 3 presents the rotated factor loading matrix (in which a loading measures the correlation between a given variable and the individual factor). The two dimensions which are delineated account for 61.3 percent of the total variance. The first factor, accounting for 39.4 percent of the total variance, clearly demonstrates that there is a clustering of variables measuring oil industrialization. All seven variables are loaded only on this factor, even though their loadings vary somewhat in magnitude. Three generic measures of PENs' oil activities (total oil revenues, oil production, and total oil exports) have loadings higher than .84, whereas oil-related exports to Japan and the United States have loadings ranging from .76 to .46. The second factor, with 21.9 percent of the total variance, represents the level of welfare, because it exclusively involves physicians per capita (.93), GNP per capita (.80), and school enrollment ratio (.79). That these three variables have negligible correlations with the first factor serves to increase our confidence in the two-factor solution. Within the parameters of our study, therefore, we feel comfortable in stating that PENs' oil-industry development and general welfare level form statistically independent dimensions. Substantively, it means that knowing a given PEN's oil industry development at a specific time point does not help predict its level of welfare for that same time point.[11] Thus there is no statistical redundancy in investigating both dimensions.

After delineating these two dimensions, we computed factor scores in order to chart each PEN's path of development from 1960 to 1974. Though substantively meaningful, the paths for individual PENs will not be discussed here. Instead, summary scores are generated for each year by taking an average of factor scores for all fourteen PENs in our study. These yearly averages enable us to examine changes occurring in the system of fourteen PENs as a whole. The yearly score for oil industry development and the level of welfare are plotted in Figure 5. Some of the salient characteristics of this mapping follow.

Both curves show negligible increases until 1972. Not even monotone were these slight increases, indicating that a number of setbacks were experienced by the PENs. Oil-industry development registered dramatic jumps in 1973 and 1974. While these leaps can be attributed to the events following the October War, the trend toward higher oil prices can be traced to the series of negotiations between PENs and PINs

Table 3.   Orthogonally Rotated Dimensions[a]

	Factors		
Variables	1	2	h^2
REVTOT$	85		73
PRODCTBL	85		72
XPORT$	84		73
XPRTJAP$	76		59
OILUSABL	71		51
OILJAPBL	68		46
XPRTUSA$	46		24
PHYSICAP		93	86
GNPCAP		80	67
SER		79	63
Total Variance (%)	39.4	21.9	

[a]Varimax rotation of the principal axes of a product moment correlation matrix. Pairwise deletion was performed to compute correlation coefficients between variables which contained missing data. Loadings and communalities (h^2) are multiplied by 100. Loadings greater than $|.30|$ are reported.

which took place during the preceding two years. Some notable results of the negotiations were the Tehran Agreement of February 1971, which raised posted prices by 33 cents a barrel with further increases of 5 cents per barrel over the subsequent five years; the Tripoli Agreement of April 1971, which boosted posted prices by 90 cents; and the participation agreement of October 1972, which allowed the purchase by PENs of an initial 25-percent interest in the companies, eventually rising to 51 percent. The step-level increase in general welfare did not begin to show until 1974. A plausible explanation is that the spin-off from the massive revenue surpluses was slow in making impact upon PENs' spending in health, education, and welfare.

Let us examine the PENs' changing capabilities in a comparative perspective vis-à-vis Japan and the United States.

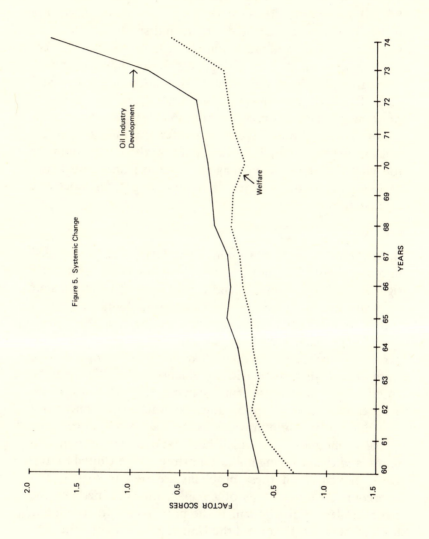

Figure 5. Systemic Change

Despite the specter of petrodollars controlling global economy, the Arab nations have a median per-capita income of less than $1,000. In contrast, Japan's GNP per capita is over $4,000, while the average income of an American is over $6,000. Moreover, the Arab world is not industrialized, has relatively scanty agricultural sectors and small and unskilled population bases, and lacks nonoil natural resources. Its economy is dependent upon a single extractive industry of non-renewable petroleum resources. If they are to modernize and diversify their economies, Middle Eastern oil-exporting nations must depend upon the technological know-how that Japan and the United States can offer. As long as their oil wells keep producing, PENs can count on these two countries for what they need. They may also benefit from competition between the two, provided that the competition does not escalate into conflict.

Conclusion

In July 1853, U.S. Navy Commodore Matthew C. Perry sailed into Edo Bay. Six months later a monumental treaty was signed, forcing the small island country which had been shut off from the rest of the world to open its doors to Western commerce. During the century and a quarter since the arrival of Perry's "black ships," Japan and the United States have passed through an incredible span of relationships ranging from deadly quarrels to friendly alliances. The 1970s may be an era of yet another shift in Japanese–U.S. relations. There is much evidence to support this observation—the emergence of a multipolar world in which Japan plays a central role, the global economic crises which have exposed Japan's vulnerability, and the changing military posture of the United States. Even though all of these problems are very important and interconnected by means of complex linkages, perhaps the most fundamental of them is the potentiality for economic friction between Japan and the United States. Economic conflict is likely to affect security ties both directly and indirectly. Indirectly, it may hamper the American design of a stronger Japanese leadership in East Asia, thus slowing United States pullout from the area. Directly, it may not only provoke Japanese hostility toward American military bases and personnel, but also provide Japan with an occasion to reshuffle its major international relations with China, the Soviet Union, and Western Europe.

It is widely accepted that there are three areas for potential economic warfare between Japan and the United States: trade, energy, and food. What is obvious is that the United States is capable of inflicting severe damages to the Japanese economy in each of these areas. Whether the United States will exercise these capabilities depends upon a multitude of domestic and international conditions. This study has examined one such condition as embodied in energy shortages. In particular, our attempt was to uncover the triangular relationships among the United States, Japan, and PENs from the perspective of the latter. Some preliminary findings are as follows:

- There is a distinct "phasing" in the timing and nature of PENs' interactions with Japan and the U.S. As PENs' oil industries develop, they tend to exhibit rising levels of resource nationalism.

- Important international events such as Arab-Israeli wars tend to have strong impacts upon PENs' oil-related behavior, indicating clearly that some economic issues could become highly politicized. Thus, their solutions will be as much political as economic.

- PENs' interactions with the U.S., when compared to those with Japan, demonstrate the clearly subordinate role Japan has played in international petroleum politics.

- Until recently, PENs' rate of economic growth has been negligible. The oil crisis of 1973 could be viewed as a manifestation of PENs' desire to "catch up" rather than to destroy the global economic structure, as many have argued.

Two conclusions can be drawn from our empirical analysis. One deals with the consistency in the behavior of PENs toward Japan and the United States. The myth of "unreliable and radical Arabs" has cultivated such a strong impression among Western scholars that any systematic study of PENs' foreign behavior is nearly impossible. It is time to abandon this myth. This study demonstrates that the growth of resource nationalism constitutes a conceptual framework that helps to delineate the underlying regularity and order in PENs' foreign-policy behavior. The other conclusion concerns the exchange of energy resources and economic development. The primary reason for their impoverishment, PENs argue, is the classic inequality inherent in the exchange of capital and technology on the one hand for natural resources on the other.

PENs are under enormous pressure from within to modernize before their energy sources are completely depleted. Cumulated over a long period, this pressure finally found outlets in the early 1970s. At present, the rules of the game in the international petroleum market are determined largely by the producers' camp. Consequently, there exists a danger of economic competition and even warfare among the consumers, especially among those who could offer attractive packages of technology to PENs in return for secure supplies of oil at "reasonable" prices. Japan and the United States are not exempt from such potential conflict, which undoubtedly will have worldwide repercussions. It is incumbent upon all the parties involved to make serious efforts to circumvent such scenarios. In particular, the United States will have to be more considerate of Japan's needs and positions, not only because the former is far less vulnerable to energy crises, but because the U.S. cannot afford to lose its most important ally in Asia.

CARD ONE:

NATION-ACTOR: COLLECTIVITY

INDIRECT   1 OPEC
(1 if Yes)   2 OAPEC
                  3 AOC
                  4 AL
                  5 Other

1   2   3
GOVERNMENTAL RANK:

4

5
SOCIAL GROUP AFFILIATION:

SOCIAL CLASS:

3 High
2 Medium
1 Low   9
0 Vague
blank None

3 Upper
2 Middle
1 Lower   10
blank unascertainable

1 Military
2 Business
3 Labor
4 Religious
5 Scientific
6 Oil Ministry, Nat. Oil Co.
7 Bureaucracy
8 Aristocracy
9 Politician
blank unascertainable

11

HOSTILITY-FRIENDLINESS SCALE:

+2 Hostile, Violent
+1 Unfriendly, Critical
 0 Neutral, Indifferent
-1 Friendly, Cordial
-2 Cooperative, Supportive, Responsive
blank Unascertainable

12   13

RESOURCES COMMITTED:	AMOUNT:	TIME:	DURATION:	CONDITIONS:
Military Manpower:	15	16	17	18
Military Goods:	20	21	22	23
Economic Resources:	25	26	27	28
Legal Resources:	30	31	32	33
Diplomatic Resources:	35	36	37	38
Symbolic Resources:	40	41	42	43
Other Resources:_____	45	46	47	48

Code:	Amount	Code:	Time (Immediacy)
1	Low	1	Unspecified by the actor
2	Medium	2	Some time in the future
3	High	3	Immediately after the event
		4	Just before or during the event
		blank	Unascertainable (from the report)

Code:	Duration of Commitment	Code:	Conditions of Commitment
1	Unspecified (by the actor)	0	Unspecified
2	Short-Term (less than 1 year)	1	Specific
3	Medium-Term (between 1 and 3 years)	2	None
4	Long-Term (more than 3 years)	blank	Unascertainable

OIL ISSUES:

Concession Area: ☐ 49

Concession Period: ☐ 50
Nationality of
Employees: ☐ 51
Exploration and
Development: ☐ 52

Investment: ☐ 53

Conservation: ☐ 54

Trade, Transport, ☐ 55
and Marketing:
Prices of Crude ☐ 56
Petroleum:
Profits of Foreign ☐ 57
Oil Companies:

Government Taxes & ☐ 58
Royalties (Revenues):
Restriction of ☐ 59
Oil Flow:
Nationalization and ☐ 60
Ownership:
Cooperation among Oil ☐ 61
Exporting Countries:

Use of Oil Revenues: ☐ 62

"The Oil Weapon": ☐ 63

Participation: ☐ 64

DATE: YEAR, MONTH, DAY

Year	Month	Day		Seq. No.	Card No.
☐ ☐	☐ ☐	☐ ☐		☐	**1**
73 74	75 76	77 78		79	80

ADDITIONAL ISSUES:

Military-Security ☐ 65
of Nation State:
Political- ☐ 66
Domestic:

Diplomatic: ☐ 67

Domestic Economic
(Development): ☐ 68
Foreign Economic
(Aid, trade, devlpt): ☐ 69

Cultural: ☐ 70

Arab-Israeli Conflict: ☐ 71

Other:_____ ☐ 72

CARD TWO:

PRIMARY TARGET: ☐ ☐ ☐
                 1   2   3

SECONDARY TARGET: ☐ ☐ ☐
                  4   5   6

NO. OF TARGETS: ☐ ☐ ☐
                7   8   9

RESULT OF THE ACTION: ☐ ☐
-2 Increase conflict   10 11
-1 Decrease conflict
 0 Neutral
+1 Decrease cooperation
+2 Increase cooperation

ACTIONS:

Grant,
Award, Reward: ☐ 12
Support,
Cooperate: ☐ 13
Agree, Accept
Consent: ☐ 14
Offer
Propose: ☐ 15
Urge, Ask,
Request: ☐ 16
Comment, In-
form, Clarify: ☐ 17

Compromise,
Accept: ☐ 18
Yield, Submit,
Surrender: ☐ 19
Dispute, Dis-
agree, Contradict: ☐ 20
Reject,
Deny, Refuse: ☐ 21
Protest,
Accuse: ☐ 22

Oppose,
Counter: ☐ 23
Demand,
Claim: ☐ 24
Threaten,
Warn: ☐ 25
Coerce, Force,
Restrict: ☐ 26
Punish, Harm,
Attack, Seize,
Invade, Damage: ☐ 27

ACTOR ID:

			Year	Month		Day	Seq. No.	Card No.
☐	☐	☐	☐ ☐	☐ ☐		☐ ☐	☐	**2**
28	29	30	73 74	75 76		77 78	79	80

APPENDIX

THE PETROLEUM EXPORTING NATIONS (PEN) CODING SHEET

NATION:_____   EVENT DATE:_____ _____ _____

EVENT DESCRIPTION:_____

_____

_____

_____

_____

_____

_____

COMMENTS:_____

_____

_____

_____

_____

EVENT BREAKDOWN

                                    PRIMARY (P)   SECONDARY (S)
ACTOR:_____ ACTION:_____ TARGET:_____

_____ _____ _____

_____ _____ _____

_____ _____ _____

SOURCE OF REPORT:_____ CODER:_____

_____

DATE OF CODING:_____

DATE CHECKED:_____

Part 3
American-Korean Relations

8

THE DYNAMICS OF AMERICAN-KOREAN RELATIONS AND PROSPECTS FOR THE FUTURE

John Chay

Professor of History, Pembroke State University

This short essay will identify and elaborate the major factors of diplomatic relations between the United States and Korea during a period of eighty-four years. The official relations between the two nations began about a century ago, in the spring of 1882, when Commodore Robert F. Shufeldt, a noted naval officer and diplomat, signed the first treaty between the two countries on the beach of Inchon Harbor. The ninety-one years from 1882 to 1973 have been divided by thirty-five years of Japanese rule, from 1910 to 1945, into two periods of equal duration. Adding another twenty-eight years from 1973 to the year 2000, this study will consider the relationship between the two nations in three periods: (1) 1882 to 1910, (2) 1945 to 1973, and (3) 1973 to 2000.

Since the study covers a long time span, it cannot be more than a sketch of the subject; the essentials for the whole period will be mapped, leaving some of the details to other chapters in the volume. This seemingly overambitious attempt is made, not because of the author's knowledge and wisdom on the subject, but partly because of his ignorance and partly because of his view of the role played by time in

international relations. Historical time seems to be much
more than a mere mass of events and is an entity in its own
right; in the arena of international relations, it allows men to
capture the national interactions in a dynamic mode which
otherwise is static, and it gives distinctive characteristics to
sets of events in a given period. Methodologically, the author's approach may be described as intuitive factor, regres-
sion, and causal analysis.

During the first fifteen years of the relationship between
the two nations, the United States was uniformly friendly
toward Korea, in accordance with a general policy of the
former nation toward the whole region of the Far East in the
nineteenth century.[1] This friendly policy toward Korea culminated in the American offer of good offices in June and
July of 1894, when the danger of a war between Japan and
China seemed imminent in Korea.[2] Japan was determined to
pursue her belligerent policy toward China, and the American
effort failed. However, even before the end of the second
Cleveland administration, as soon as Richard Olney succeeded Walter G. Gresham as secretary of state in the fall of
1895, American policy toward Korea began to shift toward a
strict neutrality, and the following four-and-one-half years of
the McKinley administration saw a period of transition from
friendly to unfriendly policies.[3] Under Theodore Roosevelt,
the United States at first maintained a position of indifference toward Korea; but as soon as Japan began to take forceful steps toward a war with Russia, the United States moved
quickly and without any hesitation to a position of virtual
desertion. When the Western powers withdrew their diplomatic missions in Seoul in the fall of 1905, the United States
was the first nation to act.[4]

What, then, were the dynamics of the American policy
toward Korea during this twenty-eight year period? For the
first half of this period, from 1882 to 1898, the major American interests in Korea were economic and cultural. Two other
factors which played an important role in American policy
were the general outlook of the major American policymakers and the nature of the international system in the Far East.
During the decade following 1898, the security interest

became the most important factor; at the same time, the American foreign policy–makers' general outlook and the Far Eastern international systemic factor remained important. Under Theodore Roosevelt, economic interests became secondary, and the role of the cultural factor, in particular the missionary interests, became almost negligible.

Even though economic interests dominated policy during the early part of the first period, American-Korean trade was small. Based on the records of the Treasury Department and on information collected by the Department of State for the years between 1894 and 1897, the estimated figure is about $.5 million.[5] Trade between the two countries increased in the mid-1900s to the level of the $3-million mark.[6] Throughout the decade between 1894 and 1904, the Korean share of American international trade was never more than a negligible .01 percent.[7] During the same period, American trade with the two other major Far Eastern countries, although not large, was substantial. American trade with China during the decade after 1894 ranged between $28 million and $42 million, while trade with Japan was a little larger, between $28 million and $72 million.[8] These two nations shared a little less than 2 percent of the total American international trade. When we compare American trade with Korea, on the one hand, and American trade with China and Japan, on the other, we find a large discrepancy.

When we turn from trade to capital investment, the picture is somewhat different. On the eve of the Russo-Japanese War, there was at least a $6-million American investment in Korea, a figure which represented about 27 percent of the total American investment in the Far East. In addition to the Unsan Gold Mine—the best gold mine in the whole region and the most profitable one in the world—railways, waterworks, electricity, streetcars, and other American enterprises in Korea were substantial.[9]

Looked at from the Korean side, the economic factor of American-Korean relations shows an entirely different picture. Korean international trade was small; during the interwar period it ranged only between $6 million and $17 million.[10] Korea's two Far Eastern neighbors took a large

portion of this small trade. Among the Western powers, however, the United States occupied a leading position, sharing
10 to 20 percent of the total Korean international trade
during the period. Especially in the area of foreign investment and concession, the American position in the Korean
economy was very significant: It almost monopolized the
field.

In summarizing the economic factor in American-Korean
relations during the first period, it should first be pointed out
that from the American viewpoint, with only .01 percent of
her total annual international trade and several million dollars of investment in a few hands, Korea was definitely not
important. However, as the leading nation among the Western
powers with regard to trading relations with the Peninsula
Kingdom and as the power almost monopolizing the capital
investment on the peninsula, the United States occupied a very
important position in Korean economic life. Also, America's
trade with Japan and China was sixty times that of her trade
with Korea.

The cultural factor played a peculiarly important role
during the early part of the first period. This area can be
dealt with in two parts: the first deals with American missionary activities in Korea, and the second with the bearing
of the cultural differences on the diplomatic styles of the two
countries. The first American missionary arrived in Korea in
1884—rather late, compared to the dates of arrival in China
and Japan. But once the nation was opened up as a new mission field, progress was rapid: On the eve of the Russo-Japanese War there were almost 200 American missionaries and
about 40,000 native Christians in Korea.[11] The Korean share
of the total American missionary activities was not large;
only 3 percent of the total number of American missionaries were in Korea, and the share of converts was only 1 percent.[12] When compared with the two other Far Eastern countries, however, the Korean mission field was not a negligible
one; in number of converts it was slightly behind China and
Japan, but, measured qualitatively, American mission work in
Korea was the most successful in the world—almost a miracle.
Without a doubt, evangelical work was the major objective of

the mission work; but the "civilizing mission" of the American mission in Korea was real and important. The contribution of American missions to Korean education, medicine, publication, and image building was truly great.

The cultural variable in international relations is still inadequately studied. In American-Korean relations, especially during the first period, cultural differences caused all kinds of tragicomic episodes and problems. The Korean mind was operating within the framework of the most orthodox moralistic and idealistic Confucian ideology in the Far East; America was a part of the rational and pragmatic Western culture. One prime example is their different interpretations of the good-office clause in the first article of the 1882 treaty. To Americans, this meant purely and simply "good offices" as that term was interpreted in the Western tradition of international law. But Koreans were inclined to read much behind the words. They believed that the strong, big-brother nation would come to the rescue of the weak, little-brother nation when the latter faced a predicament.[13]

Through the acquisition of the Philippines in 1898, the United States became a full-fledged Asian power, and suddenly the security interest came to dominate the economic and cultural interests. Whatever material and psychological value the islands had for the nation, defense of the Philippines became a real problem for the United States. The acquisition of the islands had a great impact upon American-Korean relations: When Japan demanded the peninsula in return for its pledge of nonaggression against the Philippines, the United States found Korea expendable. It is probably more accurate to say that Korea was already lost to Japan by the summer of 1905, and the United States was merely recognizing that already-established fact in the Taft-Katsura Memorandum of July 1905.[14]

The personal factor in foreign policy–making, always important, became especially so during the first period of American-Korean relations, when diplomacy was less institutionalized and, in a real sense, personal. One can select three presidents—Cleveland, McKinley, and Theodore Roosevelt—to represent the shift in foreign policy from the old-fashioned,

idealistic approach to the modern, realistic approach. Cleveland, honest and courageous, was a representative of the old
diplomacy for our period; his warm heart and moralistic outlook had much to do with the American policy toward the
Korean people during his administration. In contrast, Roosevelt was a man of new outlook who had a real appreciation of
power in international relations, and in his realistic framework Korea had absolutely no value. McKinley, a transitional
figure who came between these two men, marched forward,
facing backward.

The last, but certainly not the least important, factor in
American-Korean relations during the first period was the
nature and the condition of the international system in the
Far East. During the years through 1895 an equilibrium was
maintained among the three Far Eastern powers—China, Japan, and Russia. The United States played only a minor role
in this balance-of-power system. After a reduction in the
number of the players as a result of the Sino-Japanese War,
the balance of power remained between Japan and Russia.
During the war and the following years, the Koreans wanted
the United States to play a positive role as a balancer; but the
United States, not having sufficient interest in the region, refused to do so. Finally, after the Russo-Japanese War, a system change came about and Russia dropped out of the game,
leaving Japan alone on the stage. Therefore, when neither the
United States nor any other power would come upon the
stage against Japan, the Far Eastern international system
changed from a balance of power to one-power domination.
Korean independence—which had been sustained, unfortunately, by a delicate power equilibrium—was lost in 1905; the
United States quickly recognized the change. (Much later, in
1941, the Japanese forced the United States to the stage to
play the role of a major antagonist, which it had refused to
do in the 1890s and the 1900s.) This system change—the
only external factor, from the viewpoint of American foreign
policy–making—was probably the most important force in
regard to American-Korean relations during this period.[15]

After a break of thirty-five years, relations between the
United States and Korea were resumed in the fall of 1945.

Although there were times of uncertainty and fluctuation during the nearly three decades of this period, in general the relationship between the two nations was friendly.[16] The divided occupation of the peninsula at the end of World War II had a great and lasting effect. However, in view of the number and location of the troops of the two occupying powers and American preoccupation with military considerations for the ending of the war, it should be said that the American government did its best in the division at the 38th parallel.[17] It is true that the War Department's evaluation in 1947 that the Korean peninsula had no strategic value for American security interests, and the following series of acts and announcements of the American officials, put Korea in a very precarious position, finally leading to the outbreak of war in June 1950.[18] But the prompt, decisive, and forceful action of the United States prevented the peninsula from being dominated by communism.[19] After the end of the war, the American-Korean partnership became a very important link in the containment policy in effect during the cold war decades of the 1950s and 1960s. The Mutual Defense Treaty of 1953 and other agreements were the legal basis of the partnership, and the physical presence of some 43,000–63,000 American troops on Korean soil became a very important symbol of American commitment to Korean security.[20] In addition, the role played by $3 billion in military assistance and more than $5 billion in economic aid from the United States to Korea, during the twenty-five year period from 1945 to 1970, was certainly great.[21] With the enunciation of the Nixon Doctrine, American-Korean relations seem to have reached a turning point, which is better treated as the beginning of a new era than as the ending of the old one.

During the quarter-of-a-century after World War II, undoubtedly one of the most important factors in international relations was ideology. The whole world was in the grip of the conflict between two competing ideologies: communism and democracy. This ideological conflict was especially fierce at the points where the two forces were meeting, and Korea was one of these points. Without the ideological factor, the Koreans could have been spared the calamity of the war of

1950–53; American intervention would have been unnecessary; the postwar relationship between the two nations would have been less intimate. Only in recent years has the ideological clash lost some of its fervor, partly because of the changing value system in the world and partly because of the reaction of the world public to the Vietnam War.

The postwar concern for national security was closely related to ideology. The atmosphere of mutual distrust created by the ideological conflict caused nations, especially powerful ones like the United States, to feel very insecure. Security is mainly a matter of psychology. To combat this feeling of insecurity, the United States began, soon after the end of World War II, to build a ring around Red China and Russia through a series of collective and bilateral treaties. In this containment posture, Korea, with over a half-million troops, became one of America's most trusted and reliable allies; on the other hand, the United States, with its great strategic weapons system, became essential for Korean defense. This complementary partnership between the two countries worked out better in Korea than it did anywhere else in the world in the post–Korean War era. As in the case of ideology, the defense factor has lost some strength in recent years, a fact which can be attributed both to the lessened weight of ideology and to the new relationship between the United States and Red China which was developed under the Nixon administration.

Two other factors—probably less important than the first two but still significant—are the natures of the Far Eastern international system and of trade relations. During most of this period, Far Eastern international relations operated within the framework of bipolarity. Even though the emergence of Communist China as a colossus was the most dramatic event in the post–World War II period, the United States successfully ignored, until recently, its formal existence in international society. Japan's recovery from war-weariness after the end of the war was fast, and the world was not slow in recognizing her economic strength; however, Japan's political position in the world lagged far behind her economic strength. She was content to operate largely within the orbit of the liberal democratic nations led by the United States.

The bipolar Far Eastern international system was a part, or a subsystem, of the world international system, which had similar characteristics during the last two decades of the post–World War II period, and this bipolarity was functionally interrelated to the ideology and security factors. But, as happened to the first two factors, a change took place in the Far Eastern international system toward the end of the period: It shifted from a bipolar to a multipolar system. As a result of the rift between the Soviet Union and Communist China, which had begun earlier in this period, and the detente movement between the United States and Communist China, which became very active after the Nixon trip, China took again an independent and prominent place in the Far East and the world.

Even though Japan's political position lagged behind her economic position, and any major enhancement of her political strength and role lay in the future, no one can deny that she began to take an important position in the Far East. Together with the United States and the Soviet Union, China and Japan now formulate a four-pole multipolar international system. However, this system change has taken place only recently, and its impact on the international relations of the region in the future remains to be seen.

The trade relationship between the United States and Korea during this period was about the same as it had been during the previous period. To the United States, trade with Korea was unimportant; whereas to Korea, the United States was extremely important, even essential. The Korea share of the American trade between 1946 and 1970 ranged from $.3 million to $328 million—an annual average of .56 percent, or about at the level of .5 percent.[22] On the other hand, the American share of Korean international trade during the same period was between W.3 million and W585 million, or about 31 percent of the total Korean international trade.[23] If only the eighteen years after 1953 are considered, the American share of the Korean trade was 44 percent, almost half of the total Korean international trade.[24] China, which went through a turmoil during this period, did not do much better than Korea.[25] But Japanese trade with the United

States was markedly better than with the other Far Eastern powers; for the entire period, the Japanese share of American international trade was about 6 percent, and for the decade of the 1960s it was more than 9 percent, passing the 10 percent mark after 1968.[26] Thus, in both absolute and relative terms, Korea remained as negligible in terms of American economic interests in the third quarter of the twentieth century as it was in the later nineteenth century.

Thus far we have considered the past; we now turn to the future, the third period from 1973 to 2000. So far, the author has tried to induce or regress the underlying factors by analyzing the overt diplomatic actions between the two nations. The strategy for the third period is the reverse—trying to deduce or infer the possible future relations between the two nations from the underlying factors or constants, together with a consideration of the trends and "turning points" of an era.[27]

Herman Kahn and other modern-day prophets predict that by the year 2000 we will have a more industrialized, affluent, consumption-oriented, sensate culture.[28] They also predict that present ideology will decline or at least change, and that purpose and quality of life will become an important concern for people in the coming decades.[29] If these projections are reasonable and if the world is free from surprises during the next three decades, economics will prove most important for American-Korean relations in the third period. The systemic factor, combined with security, will continue to play an important role. Trade between the United States and Korea steadily increased during the second period, from below .5 percent to a little more than 1 percent; and this trend, in all probability, will continue in the coming decades.[30] However, no great increase can be expected; by the end of our period, the Korean share of American international trade should still be relatively small, probably at the level of about 2 percent.

Looking at the same picture from the Korean side, we can foresee a continuation of the present increase of trade with the United States, in absolute terms. But in relative terms American-Korean trade will be decreasing rather than increasing: The American share of Korean trade may fall significantly from its present level of about 35 percent.[31] This relative decrease will be caused mainly by the rapid increase of Korean trade with Japan, an increase which has already begun.[32] An important fact to be noted is that a great difference will continue to exist between the Korean share of American international trade and the American share of the Korean trade, the ratio being ten to one. Another very important fact in the trade relationship is that Korean-Japanese trade surpassed Korean-American trade in 1965 and 1966, and Japan has become again a dominant force in Korean economic life.[33] This trend will continue, at least for some years to come, and it will, without doubt, have an important impact upon the future of Korean-American as well as Korean-Japanese relations.

The Nixon Doctrine—basically the outcome of an American reassessment of her involvement in Asia and other parts of the world—had a firm ground in American defense and foreign policies, and its spirit continued to play an important role in American–East Asian relations even after Nixon's departure from the White House.[34] Because the American public's reaction to the Vietnam War was so strong that the bitter memory will last for a generation or so, U.S. administrations in the 1970s and 1980s may not be able to do much about neoisolationism. Even "judicious intervention" may not be possible for a long time to come. Since the Nixon Doctrine, as defined by the Nixon administration, did not seem to dictate immediate withdrawal of the overseas armed forces of the United States, the American commitment of a token force to Korean security will be honored, at least in the foreseeable future; but the burden of the defense of the peninsula will be gradually shifted to Korean shoulders.[35] This will certainly become an important factor for the future of American-Korean diplomatic relations. The slowly but steadily growing role of the Japanese defense force in the Far East will also become important to Korean-American as well as Korean-Japanese diplomatic relations. Nuclear proliferation in the region—specifically, the Japanese possession of nuclear weapons and the possible emergence of some more formidable weapons system in the future—will undoubtedly add a new dimension to Korean defense and to American-Korean relations.[36]

The third continuing, and probably most important, factor for American-Korean relations for this last period may prove to be the structure of the international system. One projection that can easily be made for most of the period is that the world international system will remain multipolar. Beyond 1990, however, its form is harder to predict; *la belle époque* may continue for one or two more decades, or a turning point may come at the turn of the century, and the 1990s may prove less quiet than the preceding decades.[37]

The Far Eastern multipolar system has just begun, and the system may remain for a few more decades. It is true that this subsystem will share the general characteristics of the overall world international system, but it should be pointed out that as a subsystem it may also have its own peculiarities. In the Far East, one of the dominant forces in the coming decades will be the reemergence of Japan as a colossus. The power of China will be even greater.[38]

Coupled with this supposition, another crucial aspect is the position and role of the two Western powers—the United States and the Soviet Union—in the Far East. These two powers, at least in the near future, may remain concerned about and involved to a certain extent in Far Eastern affairs, thus sustaining a kind of multipolar system. A less moderate course is certainly possible, especially from the late 1980s onward. One possibility is that the U.S. and the USSR will be very active in the Far East, and that the multipolar system will remain in effect during the coming decades. If the present trend of lessening the relative strength and interests of the two Western powers in the Far East and of increasing the strength and will of the two indigenous powers continues, however, another possibility exists. Before too long, probably by the 1980s or early 1990s, the Far Eastern international system may move to a hierarchical multipolar arrangement, in which two poles will be much larger than the two other poles, or even to a bipolar system. In view of the continuing Sino-Soviet rivalry, the impact of the Vietnam War on American and world public opinion, and the changing value system in American society, the bipolar system seems to have more probability. Of course, for the stability of Far Eastern international relations, the second course—maintenance of a genuine multipolar system—is most desirable. If the third course takes place, developments in the Far East toward the end of the century may not be much different from what they were exactly a century ago—reduction of the players and a shift from a multipolar to a bipolar system, with a further shift to a one-power domination system. Of course, some conditions in the late twentieth century will differ from those of a century ago: China will be much more vigorous, and Korea will be more awake and self-conscious. If imperialism has not disappeared completely, it will exist in a more subtle form because nations now know how to milk cows without owning them. Whichever course the Far Eastern international system takes will be extremely important for American-Korean relations.

In summary, during the coming two to three decades American economic interests in Korea will be reduced, in relative terms; her security interests in the peninsula may remain but will be much smaller in size; and a multipolar international system may remain in the Far East, although there is more probability of a change to a bipolar system toward the end of the century. Given these major factors, what, then, would be the diplomatic relations between the United States and Korea during the coming three decades?

It is not difficult to foresee that congenial and friendly American-Korean relations will continue in the near future— the 1970s and part of the following decade. But the two nations' relationship during the latter half of the period is uncertain. The friendly relationship may well remain; certainly this is a possibility. However, as our survey of the three major factors indicates, this prediction lacks a realistic basis. Of course, foreign policies are often made irrationally, without sufficient basis. But if the projected lessening of the economic and security interests of the United States and, even more probable, undesirable systemic factors have some impact upon the future of American-Korean relations, there is an even stronger probability of a gradual deterioration of the two nations' relationship in the latter part of the third period—from intimacy to cordiality and from cordiality to indifference, as happened a century ago.

In conclusion, it can be said first that in general Americans and Koreans have been more friendly than hostile to one another; there have been more pleasant years than unpleasant years during the past sixty years of the two nations' relationship. The relationship between the two nations during the first fifteen years and during the two decades in the post–Korean War period were certainly congenial. It should also be pointed out, however, that the friendship lacks a firm basis. In the late nineteenth century, the general outlook and predisposition of American foreign policy–makers was most important to U.S.–Korean relations; later, in the post–World War II years, the cold war environment, with its extreme emphasis on ideological conflict, became significant.

Although it is true that circumstantial factors, irrationality, and aberration play significant roles in any diplomatic relationship, the future foreign policy–makers of the two nations will have to look more realistically at the cold facts underlying the two nations' relationship. The process of realistic reassessment and readjustment that took place in the United States as a result of the Nixon Doctrine has made the Koreans more keenly aware that they have to stand on their own feet. The clear realization that there is a great discrepancy between the two nations' needs for and interest in each other should form the starting point both for policy-making and for a real understanding of the two-nation relationship: The United States has always been very important to the Koreans, but Korea has never been significant to the United States. Last, it should be pointed out that a significant degree of Korean independence will be very important and decisive during the coming decades in the Far East as well as in American-Korean relations. By the turn of the last century, the Koreans had had two decades of opportunity for independence but had failed to use this opportunity successfully; it does not require a prophet to see that the Koreans now, exactly a century later, face another twenty years of opportunity. The 1990s may not be as smooth as the preceding two decades; but if the Koreans use this opportunity effectively, they should be able to pull their nation safely through the possibly rough decades at the turn of the century.

Korean independence is important for the sake of the peace and stability of the whole region; if Korea becomes one nation again and even plays the role of a pole in the Far Eastern international system, the region, with five poles, would be much more stable. One of the most fundamental assumptions of the Nixon Doctrine and of the policies of the Ford administration has been that of the desirability of more independent roles for the Far Eastern nations, including Korea.[39] If the Koreans become more independent and self-reliant, and base their relationship with the Americans on a more realistic foundation, the two-nation relationship in the coming decades should be satisfactory; otherwise, the unpleasant developments at the turn of the century may be repeated.[40]

9

AMERICAN-KOREAN SECURITY RELATIONS: SOURCES OF MISUNDERSTANDING

John P. Lovell

Professor of Political Science, Indiana University

Every informed observer of the relations between the United States and the Republic of Korea (ROK) recognizes that the two countries have experienced frustrations and misunderstandings in their efforts to satisfy their respective security interests over the years. That such frustrations and misunderstandings have increased in recent years also is widely recognized. The simplest explanation of the strain in the relationship is that the interests of each state are different. Such an explanation is a mere truism, however, if nothing more is meant than the observation that no two nation-states have identical interest, and that they therefore are likely to experience periodic strains in their mutual relations. Or the explanation may be tautological. For instance, if one points to changing U.S. interests to explain tensions between the U.S. and ROK in the aftermath of President Nixon's visit to Peking, the danger of tautology looms large: How does one know that U.S. interests have changed? Because President Nixon visited China.

In order to go beyond truism and tautology in analyzing the problems (and opportunities) associated with the security relations between nation-states, one must come to grips with the subjective nature of determinations of national security requirements and with the plurality of goal-values that complicate the assessment of security interests. Because national security interests cannot be determined by a purely objective process and can only rarely be determined with reference to a single, coherent set of goal-values, ambiguities and internal contradictions tend to be the rule rather than the exception in the national-security policies of a state.

When, in turn, the policymakers of one state attempt to coordinate their own policies with those of an ally, ambiguities and contradictions become magnified. The problems of misunderstanding that arise between nation-states are analogous to a degree to misunderstandings between individuals; the problems can be described in terms of the selectivity that is inherent in information gathering, processing, and interpretation, whether by individuals or by governments. No individual nor any government can keep track fully of what is happening in the world, nor interpret with complete accuracy the events and behavior that are experienced. Instead, individuals and governments are selectively exposed and are selectively attentive to their environment—aware of some aspects, oblivious to others. Individuals and governments perceive their experiences through lenses shaped according to preexisting biases and beliefs. The past is mobilized by individuals and by governments as an aid to interpretation of present reality, but the past is recalled selectively.

The concepts of selective exposure and attention, selective perception, and selective recall are broad rubrics within which one can identify a number of more specific barriers that have impeded understanding in security relations between the United States and the Republic of Korea.

Selective Exposure and Attention

Writing in the *Dong-a Ilbo* in early 1948, a Korean intellectual who subsequently became foreign minister and later prime minister of the Republic of Korea observed plaintively:

America failed us at Portsmouth and at Yalta,

which inspires us with anything but confidence. Who knows but that she will fail us again this time? This is a question that racks Korean minds at the present time. . . . So far the USA State Department has behaved as if it did not know its own mind.[1]

Doubts about whether the American government knew what their own interests were in Korea in 1948 were well founded. Numerous factors might be cited in explanation of the lack of clarity and decisiveness in American policy in the early post–World War II period. However, the salient point here is that American policymakers had been almost totally inattentive to Korea until they found themselves in a position of having to formulate a Korean policy. With the exception of fifty officers who had been given some civil-affairs training, the first American soldiers to assume responsibility for the occupation of Korea south of the 38th parallel beginning in September 1945 were tactical troops. They had had virtually no preparation for any military-government role, much less for the government of Korea. Of the better-prepared group of fifty officers, none spoke a sentence of Korean. Only two had previously seen the land they were to govern.[2]

Only five weeks later did a sizable contingent of specially trained civil-affairs personnel arrive. Mostly these were men who had been trained for occupation duties in Japan, only to be reassigned at the last moment. Few had more than a sketchy idea of Korean history, culture, economics, and politics. An officer who was a part of this contingent reported that, in a year of preparation for military-government duties, his total instruction on Korea had consisted of a single one-hour lecture.[3]

No clear American policy had been formulated and transmitted to those responsible for setting up a government south of the 38th parallel in Korea, and no separation of command had been established between the Korean and Japanese occupations. Both were under the authority of General MacArthur, the supreme commander of the Allied powers (SCAP). As E. Grant Meade has pointed out, Korean problems received a low priority as a result of this organizational structure, since MacArthur's headquarters was concerned first with Japan. Furthermore, the filtering of policy from Washington through Japan conditioned the attitudes of the American military toward the Koreans whom they governed.[4]

A related point is that when, after the initial maladroit order to retain Japanese officials in their colonial positions in Korea had been rescinded, thereby removing the Japanese officials, USAFIK (U.S. Armed Forces in Korea) became heavily dependent upon the advice and assistance of its translators and interpreters—that is, upon the small fraction of Korean society that spoke English. (Koreans were heard to quip that USAFIK provided "a government of, for, and by interpreters.")

By 1948, American policy at least had become more informed on the basis of on-the-job training. Some clarification of U.S. policy was attained with the abandonment of hope that a reconciliation with the Soviets would be reached on the Korean question. Tacit recognition of the reality of a divided Korea was apparent in American policy, as was sponsorship of the newly founded Republic of Korea. The extent of the American commitment to the new ROK government was extremely unclear, however, as subsequent events were to demonstrate.

Attention as a Function of Structure

The preceding discussion of U.S. relations with Korea in the 1945–50 period placed emphasis on the lack of prior exposure and attentiveness by Americans to Korean affairs, with resultant dependence upon selected sources of information, and numerous miscalculations and misunderstandings. Still another facet of the problem of selective attention is the complexity of the international subsystem relevant to the policy decisions at hand. When the relevant subsystem is quite simple, as it was in Korea throughout the 1950s, security calculations can be made within a narrow focus, thereby keeping to a minimum the issues to be resolved among allies. As the relevant subsystem becomes more complex, however, as it had become in U.S.–Korean security relations by the late 1960s and the early 1970s, it becomes more difficult for each ally to remain fully attentive to the multiple (and sometimes contradictory) goal-values at stake for the other; the probability of misunderstanding and friction is thereby increased. These points—which should be viewed as hypotheses—can be illustrated briefly.

Prior to the outbreak of the Korean War, there was considerable ambivalence in the containment policy of the Truman administration generally, with its belligerent verbal posture, but a continued demobilization and imposition of a $15-billion ceiling on defense expenditures. The ambivalence was even more striking in Asia than it was in Europe—as the ambiguity of the defense-perimeter speeches of MacArthur and Acheson, in 1949 and early 1950 respectively, suggests. The culmination of Mao's victory in China in 1949, followed by the Sino-Soviet pact and then the North Korean attack across the 38th parallel, had the effect of forcing policy clarification upon the American government. The events also thrust the new ROK government into a position of virtually complete dependence upon the United States.

In these circumstances, whatever pain and anguish were associated with the relationship, "security" for each of the two nation-states could be defined in relatively simple terms. That is, it seemed obvious in the 1950s in the United States as well as in the Republic of Korea that, as a minimum, security required containment of Communist expansion (with agreement that communism was a monolithic force, headquartered in the Kremlin). Some important differences arose within the United States government as well as between the U.S. and the government of Syngman Rhee regarding the optimum goal of achieving non-Communist rule for all Korea; differences also arose regarding methods of governance in the Republic of Korea. But in general the structures of the politico-military situation in Korea in the 1950s represented in microcosm the relatively simple bipolar structure that prevailed in international politics throughout most of the world.

That a bipolar structure at least has the virtue of simplifying policy analysis can be recognized if one compares the power structure that prevailed on the Korean peninsula in the 1950s with the one ascertainable a half-century earlier—especially in the final decade of the nineteenth century, with imperial competition for dominance or influence in Korea raging among China, Japan (eventually supported by Great Britain), Russia (with French financing), and, to a lesser extent, the United States.

Likewise, the simple power structure of the 1950s contrasts sharply with the power structure that prevails currently. A bipolar world has given way to a multipolar one. The international subsystem that exerts influence over the fortunes of the two Koreas (and thus over U.S.-ROK security relations) also has become multipolar rather than bipolar. Relationships that had been definable almost totally in terms of mutual hostility and threat now contain elements of bargaining and cooperation (U.S.-PRC, U.S.-USSR, ROK-DPRK). Conversely, relationships that had been built upon the premise of full collaboration to meet a common threat have been or now are being redefined (USSR-PRC, USSR-DPRK, PRC-DPRK, U.S.-ROK). Japan, the security of which was an important factor in U.S. policies toward Korea in the early post–World War II period but which had exerted little independent influence on U.S.-Korean relations, has become a major actor in the international subsystem (especially since the ROK-Japan treaty of 1965).

In short, a simple bipolar subsystem has given way in Korea to a relatively complex subsystem of six major actors, and even more minor ones. (If one includes the United Nations and the various competing political factions in each of the major states involved, the full complexity of the situation becomes apparent.) The consequence for U.S.-ROK security relations is that the policy calculations that define the relationship have become more complicated. In formulating its own security policies, no longer can the ROK government settle simply for an answer to the question of the magnitude of the American commitment to the defense of South Korea for the immediate future. Rather, the (ultimately unanswerable) question of the importance of the U.S. commitment to Korea, relative to the maintenance of the initiative toward detente with China and with the Soviet Union and to readjustments in the U.S. relationship to Japan, must be considered. If the rumor is true, it is small wonder that Park Chung

Hee had difficulty sleeping at night during the Nixon visit to China; future American policies in Korea had become highly unpredictable. Likewise, the United States no longer can assume a simple patron-client relationship with the ROK government. The Park government has demonstrated its intention and capacity to pursue interests independent of those defined by U.S. policy goal-values.

Selective Perception

One might well note, as further evidence of the selectivity of the exposure of Americans to Korea and of Koreans to the United States, the dearth of American press coverage of Korean events and the biases and distortions in the depiction of American life and politics in the Korean mass media. Michael Armacost has made a similar observation regarding the "attention gap" that plagues U.S.–Japanese relations.[5] As Armacost notes in his analysis, however, the problem of communication across cultures is manifested in ignorance and distortions attributable, not only to selective exposure and attention to one another's customs, values, and beliefs, but also to the selectivity of perception that is evident in interpretations that are made of the actions and statements of one another.

When the behavior of persons from another culture is interpreted in the light of the norms and practices of one's own culture, the resulting distortions can range from highly romanticized views to unduly pejorative ones. John Fairbank has noted that over a period of decades American folklore and popular writings on China have varied from an exotic image of Chinese behavior, stressing the apparent mystery and paradox, to idealized images that have revered Eastern wisdom and culture, to disillusioned pictures of China which have reflected annoyance with the seeming failure of Chinese to conform to American standards of behavior.[6] Clearly, similar fluctuations in the attitudes of Americans toward Korea and Koreans are evident over the years. Just as clearly, dramatic shifts in (popular and governmental) Korean attitudes toward America and Americans, ranging from uncritical adulation to bitter contempt, reflect misperceptions rooted in cultural differences.

Misperceptions between the U.S. and ROK governments in their security relations stem not only from cultural differences, however, but also from a failure to acknowledge the intrinsically subjective nature of security calculations. Policymakers and politicians (Korean and American) typically advance their own views regarding national security as if security were a precisely measurable commodity and as if they had completed the exacting measurement necessary to provide definitively the requirements to attain it. Of course, any such claim is balderdash.

"To be sane in a world of madmen," Jean-Jacques Rousseau once observed, commenting on the inherent absurdity of the nation-state system, "is in itself a kind of madness."[7] The search for national "security" in the world of nation-states is necessarily problematical, and the results are necessarily ephemeral. So it is in the security relations between nation-states. Security may be discussed by two allies in common terms that have concrete referents: the state of training of soldiers, the sophistication of military hardware, the number of divisions deployed, the structure of command and communications systems. But in the final analysis, whether each of the allies decides that the calculations add up to "security" is a matter of subjective judgment, which can differ from one party to the next in spite of agreement on the relevant "facts," or which can differ from one year to the next within a single government because of changing perceptions of what constitutes a "threat" or what strategies will effectively deter an adversary.

Not only politicians but all of us sometimes fall into the trap of thinking of "national security" requirements as totally objectifiable, probably because of the prevalence of the habit of reifying the nation-state in policy discussions. We speak of "Korean policies" explicable in terms of underlying "Korean interests," rather than in terms of Park Chung Hee's personal interests or those of his entourage. Likewise, we speak of "American interests in East Asia," often ready, along with the late Charles E. Wilson, to assume that what is good for General Motors (or Rotary International, or the U.S. Army, or the Presbyterian church) is good for America—

and perhaps good for Korea as well. Such gross misconceptions can serve to sustain as well as to launch ruinous or divisive policies.

Selective Recall

In designing military strategy, policymakers almost always attempt to draw upon relevant prior experience. The question, of course, is: What experience is relevant? Moreover, a less obvious but equally troublesome question is: Which facets of relevant prior experience are isomorphic to present needs? The American and ROK governments both have drawn upon the experiences of the Korean War and the war in Southeast Asia in formulating strategies for the 1970s in Korea. Whether the "lessons" of the past which are being applied are appropriate to present needs is highly debatable—the old saw about generals always being prepared to fight the last war appears to have substance. (Indeed, the maxim may be expanded to include civilian as well as military strategists.) One may expect differing interpretations of the "lessons of the past" to contribute to increasing frictions between the U.S. and ROK governments in the future.

For example, what military "lessons" from the Korean War are applicable to present ROK security needs? The conventional wisdom is that the weakness of the ROK military establishment, from the founding of the republic in 1948 to 1950, was a major inducement to the North Koreans to launch an attack, with the expectation of quick success. The "lesson" to be drawn, one that seems to have been accepted both by the Park Chung Hee government for many years and (with growing reservations) by the American government, is that only the maintenance of an imposing military force south of the 38th parallel will deter a future attack. Like the Munich analogy, however (which seems to have been so seductive to Lyndon Johnson, Dean Rusk, and others responsible for the escalation of American involvement in Vietnam), the preconditions of the June 1950 attack highlight only the general risks of major imbalances of military forces; the experience provides no clear guidance as to the specific force levels required. Contrary to the argument that every added increment of military force purchases more security, one might well argue that at some point (which cannot be specified with precision, but which involves defense expenditures per capita and the ratio of military manpower to the total population), increases in the size of armed forces make a nation-state *less* secure.

Discussion of selective recall of the Korean War also must include mention of the MacArthur myth, which has mesmerized some Korean as well as some American strategists. The "never again" school of American military men, who believed essentially that MacArthur was right in substance if not in procedure in the Truman-MacArthur controversy, attempted to translate the "lessons" of Korea into "victory" in Vietnam. The view also may be found in some discussions of how a future war in Korea should be fought. Especially evident is MacArthur's notion that Chinese continuation in the Korean War could have been terminated by bombing the Chinese mainland and sealing off the Sino-Korean border with nuclear weapons. Conveniently forgotten by MacArthur idolators frequently is the belatedness of MacArthur's advice regarding keeping China out of the war (having assured President Truman at Wake Island in October 1950 that the Chinese would not enter the war). However, the salient point here is related, not to MacArthur's failings or successes as a military strategist, but rather to the selective application of an experience of twenty-odd years ago to current planning, which the continued influence of his ideas represents.

Not surprisingly, the experience of the war in Southeast Asia, as well as of that in Korea from 1950 to 1953, has had an effect upon current strategic planning by the ROK and American governments. The Park government seems especially concerned about the threat of a "war of national liberation," à la Vietnam, with pockets of insurgency within South Korea generated by North Korean agents. The exposed position of Seoul and its extraordinary importance as the heart and nerve center of South Korea have made the threat of encirclement, through an insurgent or commando attack combined with a thrust from the north, a source of considerable anxiety. The failure of ROK military intelligence to provide advance warning of the approach to Seoul of a mutinous group of ROK airmen in August 1971 seems to have stimulated additional concern for such a contingency. The imposition of martial law by Park Chung Hee in October 1972 and the accompanying suppression of dissent and proclamation of a new constitution increasing the power of the president were rationalized in part on the grounds of the threat to national security posed by internal disorder (as well as on the need for unity in negotiations with the North Korean regime).

However, the selective application of historical experience other than the war in Vietnam may be read into Park's actions. As Gregory Henderson has noted perceptively, the emphasis in the newly imposed ROK constitution on "restoration" and "self-reliance" had strong overtones of rebellion against American institutions in favor of a reversion to a pre–World War II Japanese model.[8] One may note also that Park's imposition of martial law in South Korea on October 17 followed by less than a month the imposition of martial law in the Philippines by President Marcos. One may surmise that the facts that the official American reaction to the Marcos move was muted and that popular American reaction was negligible were at least of as much interest to Park Chung Hee as was the example of techniques to be employed in coping with political opposition.

For the American government, that is, for the Ford administration, the salient lesson of the drawn-out war in Southeast Asia seems to focus less on the insurgency threat that concerns Park Chung Hee than on the importance of avoiding another prolonged (and eventually unpopular) American military involvement. The search for an option that would be "decisive" in the event of renewed fighting in Korea has led American officials to talk ominously, if ambiguously, of the possible use of nuclear weapons. In mid-1975, an interviewer from *U.S. News and World Report* asked Secretary of Defense James Schlesinger, "Are you saying that the U.S. would resort to drastic action if South Korea were invaded?" Schlesinger replied that "one of the lessons of the Vietnamese conflict is that rather than simply counter your opponent's thrusts, it is necessary to go for the heart of the opponent's power: Destroy his military forces rather than simply being involved endlessly in ancillary military operations."[9] A few weeks later (July 6), appearing on "Issues and Answers" (ABC-TV), Schlesinger reiterated the determination of the United States to defend Korea, and acknowledged that this might require the use of nuclear weapons—although he attempted to convince the panel of questioners that this was a most unlikely event.

One cannot be sure which of the "lessons of history" recalled selectively by policymakers are now actually being incorporated into strategic plans, because all governments endeavor to keep potential adversaries guessing with declarations of what they *might* do—declarations that may be at variance with their actual plan for responding to a particular contingency. However, there are at least two important risks associated with tough-minded bluffs (if they are that) such as those threatening the use of nuclear weapons. The first is that the adversary will call the bluff and that one will be tempted to make good the threat, having repeated it many times, regardless of plans to the contrary. The second risk is that even if the adversary is deterred by the threat, one's ally (the Park Chung Hee regime, in this case) will be so emboldened by the pledge that he will provoke the very confrontation with the adversary that one wished to avoid.

Conclusions

What policies and actions will best ensure "security" on the Korean peninsula? The American and ROK governments are likely to express increasingly discordant views on this question in coming months and years. The Park regime will continue to pursue a course that resists the dictates of the United States, even as Park seeks to postpone for as long as possible the inevitable withdrawal of American forces from the Korean peninsula. The Ford administration, in turn, will continue to experience pressures for removal of American forces stationed abroad and for reduction of expenditures for military assistance to the Park regime (the Ford-professed adherence to the Nixon Doctrine notwithstanding). At the same time, the importance of Korean affairs in international politics is likely to continue to grow, thereby heightening the intensity with which disagreements between the U.S. and ROK governments are expressed and felt.

Disagreement is not necessarily undesirable, however, and may be preferable in the long run to the maintenance of harmonious but obsolete policies. Indeed, a mutual reappraisal of U.S.–ROK security policies is overdue. One hopes that as the reappraisal occurs, issues will not be debated within a sterile framework that assumes that "security" can be calculated exclusively in terms of an objectifiable set of military data. The Korean peninsula currently is the most heavily armed territory of comparable size in the world. If security were assured by guns and missiles, certainly the Republic of Korea would be justified in continuing to maintain an armed force of 645,000 (the sixth-largest in the world), and the United States would be justified in continuing to provide extensive military assistance and 43,000 American troops. But, hopefully, those who debate the issues in the United States and in Korea will ask: *Whose* security is being sought (Park Chung Hee's or that of the Korean people generally, for example)?—and at what cost to other values?

10

UNITED STATES–KOREAN ECONOMIC RELATIONS AND THEIR IMPACT ON KOREAN ECONOMIC DEVELOPMENT

Pong S. Lee

Associate Professor of Economics,
State University of New York at Albany

The victory of the Allied powers that ended the Pacific war in August 1945 also brought the liberation of Korea from thirty-six years of Japanese colonialism. The Korean liberation at the same time meant a partition of the country into two parts, North and South, and marked the beginning of what turned out to be a long American involvement in virtually every aspect of South Korean affairs, including military, political, and economic interrelations of the two countries.

The purpose of this brief study is to examine the economic relations of the two countries, and especially to trace the process by which these relations affected the Korean economy so as to radically transform a stagnant and underdeveloped country into one with a dynamic and industrialized economy by the middle of the 1970s. We shall not attempt any rigorous analysis of the subject. Instead, we shall set up a number of broad criteria by which to hypothesize the impact of American economic aid, loans, and trade partnership on Korean economic development.

In general, in order for any economy to develop and grow

it must increase its capacity to produce goods and services. The productive capacity of the economy, in turn, depends upon availability of natural resources, capital, labor, and other human resources. Perhaps even more crucial for productive capacity is the technological know-how of the economy as manifested in certain qualities of capital and labor: skills, managerial and entrepreneurial talents, and the ability of the whole economy to organize efficiently and allocate the productive resources. On the other hand, an increasing productive capacity of the economy, particularly in a capitalistic system, must be accompanied by a more or less proportional increase in domestic and international demand for the output of the economy.

In our evaluation of American-Korean economic relations, therefore, our primary concern will be to examine how these relations may have contributed to mobilizing hitherto underutilized natural and human resources and to increasing the supply of savings and the level of capital accumulation that are essential to the sustained growth of the economy. We shall also focus on technological progress as indicated by an increased supply of skilled manpower, managerial and entrepreneurial ability, and improvement in the efficiency of allocating productive resources.

Somewhat arbitrarily, we shall divide the period under study into two equal parts: the first from 1945 to 1960, and the second from 1961 to the present. During the first fifteen years, the massive scale of American aid to Korea does not appear to have resulted in major success, judging from actual performances and achievements of the Korean economy. Nevertheless, this was the period when most of the essential groundwork was laid for the spectacular economic development achieved in subsequent periods.

Period of Dependency, 1945–60

The fifteen years that followed the liberation can be divided into three somewhat distinctive economic periods: post–World War II dislocation, Korean War devastation, and post–Korean War reconstruction.

The end of World War II, which caused the political

liberation of Korea from Japan, resulted in a major break-down of the Korean economy. A sudden and total with-drawal of Japanese population from Korea meant a retreat of approximately 80 percent of the technically skilled man-power in all phases of the Korean economy. Because the Ko-rean economy had been an integral part of the Japanese econ-omy prior to 1945, by design of the Japanese rulers, the liberation inevitably suspended almost all productive activi-ties because of the lack of Japanese materials and the loss of the Japanese market. The partition of the country into two politically opposing camps created an additional and drastic economic dislocation in both parts. For South Korea, the division meant a loss of natural resources and of complemen-tary industrial sectors, such as electrical, chemical, coal, metal, and other heavy industries, which are located primar-ily in the northern half.[1] At the time of liberation, two-thirds of the total Korean population of about 25 million was living in South Korea. To make the matter worse, the end of the war and the partition of the country set in motion a large-scale migration of refugees from the North and the repatria-tion of Koreans from Japan, Manchuria, and China.[2]

Aggravating these problems was the fact that both the United States military government and the South Korean government that succeeded it were totally unprepared for and incapable of coping with the complexity of the situation that then existed. For instance, the total money supply ra-pidly expanded about 15 times, causing an increase in the price index of about 123 percent during the first four years, despite a massive influx of United States economic aid and relief goods during the period.[3]

The outbreak of the Korean War in 1950 and its devastat-ing effect on the country in general completely wiped out the potential for economic gains that had slowly and gradually been developed. For example, the war damages to economic facilities alone are estimated to have been $3 billion, a figure approximately equal to the gross national product of 1953.[4] The extensive destruction of the war forced Korea to start the difficult task of postwar reconstruction virtually from scratch. What facilitated the recovery process and enabled the economy to achieve a respectable gain, at least until 1958, was again the unparalleled economic aid from the United States and other allies. In other words, the Korean War and the desperate need of postwar reconstruction further heightened Korean dependence on United States economic aid. We shall now examine the extent to which Korea was dependent upon U.S. aid during the period.

Table 1 is a summary of exports and imports and of the composition of imports by sources of funds between 1952 and 1974. Although not shown in Table 1, the total Korean export was $197 million, while import was $260 million, between 1945 and 1949. During the same period, official American aid, mostly through Government and Relief in Occupied Area (GARIOA), amounted to $526 million and was comprised largely of food products, clothing, and medical supplies.[5] We note from Table 1 that foreign-aid imports amounted to 71 percent of the trade deficit in the 1952–55 period ($1,035 million) and 76 percent of the trade deficit in the 1956–61 period ($2,013 million).

A summary of total foreign economic aid and foreign loans received between 1945 and 1974 is shown in Table 2. The aid under the program of Economic Cooperation Administration (ECA) and Supplies, Economic Cooperation (SEC) was primarily for long-range economic recovery, and was initiated after the South Korean government was established in 1948. Accordingly, the major components of ECA and SEC were industrial raw materials, fertilizers, machinery, and transportation equipment.

During and immediately after the Korean War, most economic aid was carried out ostensibly under the auspices of two United Nations organizations, Civil Relief in Korea (CRIK) and the United Nations Reconstruction Agency (UNKRA). The former, funded largely by the United States, was primarily concerned with the pressing need for food, clothing, medical and other relief goods, whereas the latter supplied necessary materials, equipment, and technology to rebuild and expand basic industrial and mining sectors of the economy. UNKRA aid, with more than two-thirds of its funding from the United States, was responsible for the

Table 2. Summary of Foreign Economic Aid and Loans, 1945-1974
(In millions of U.S. dollars)

| | Foreign Aid[a] | | | | | | | Foreign Loans[b] |
| | | U. S. A. | | | | | | |
	Total	GARIOA	ECA&SEC	PL480	AID	CRIK	UNKRA	Total
1945-1950	584.6 (97.4)	511.5 (85.3)	73.1 (12.2)			9.4		
1951-1953	462.0 (154.0)		36.0 (12.0)		5.6	388.8 (129.6)	31.7 (10.6)	
1954-1960	1,889.1 (269.9)			157.7 (22.5)	1,581.7 (226.0)	59.2	90.4 (12.9)	
1962	232.3			67.3	165.0			78.4
1964	149.3			61.0	88.3			100.5
1966	103.3			38.0	65.3			261.7
1968	105.9			55.9	49.9			357.8
1970	82.6			61.7	20.9			548.1
1972	5.1				5.1			729.6
1974	1.0				1.0			1,056.7

Sources: a   The Bank of Korea, *Economics Statistics Yearbook*, 1961, p. 192; 1975, p. 218. Figures in parentheses indicate an annual average.

b   The Bank of Korea, *Review of Korean Economy*, 1969, p. 146; Yoncha Boko So (Annual Report), 1965, pp. 128-129; 1972, pp. 125-127; 1974, pp. 110-115.

Table 1. Summary of Korean Exports and Imports, 1952-1974
(In millions of U.S. dollars)

| | Exports | Imports | | | | | Trade Balance |
		Total	Commercial	Foreign Loans	Official Aid	Relief & Others	
1952	27.7	214.2	53.6		160.5		-186.5
1954	24.2	243.3	93.9		149.4		-219.1
1956	24.6	386.1	66.2		319.9		-361.5
1958	16.5	378.2	48.7		311.0	18.5	-361.7
1960	32.8	343.5	97.2		231.9	14.4	-310.7
1962	54.8	421.8	179.0	4.5	218.5	19.7	-367.0
1964	119.1	404.4	184.5	34.6	142.6	42.6	-285.3
1966	250.3	716.4	401.9	108.4	143.6	62.5	-466.1
1968	455.4	1,462.9	964.4	299.6	125.7	73.1	-1,007.5
1970	835.2	1,984.0	1,256.3	400.2	161.2	166.4	-1,148.8
1972	1,624.1	2,522.0	1,702.2	628.6	21.7	169.4	-.897.9
1974	44,460.4	6,851.8	5,554.5	638.8	-	658.5	-2,391.5

Source: The Bank of Korea, Economic Statistic Yearbook, 1973, p. 3; 1975, pp. 3, 185.

construction of various industrial plants, including cement, plate-glass, iron, and steel factories, and of modern paper and textile mills during this period. The well-known PL480 program consisted of aid money derived from sales of American surplus agricultural commodities, mostly wheat and cotton. Perhaps more than any other aid program, the Agency for International Development (AID), which replaced the International Cooperation Administration (ICA) in 1961, made a direct contribution to post–Korean War reconstruction by providing capital equipment, industrial raw materials, and wide-ranging forms of technical-assistance programs.[6]

From the beginning, Korea was also heavily dependent upon the United States for its international trade. In 1956, for instance, 44.4 percent of Korean exports went to the United States, followed by 33.1 percent to Japan, while 22.5 percent of her imports came from the United States and about 5.4 percent from Japan.[7]

This massive and unprecedented economic aid, totaling nearly $3 billion, in what appeared to be a semipermanent ward relationship between the two countries during this period no doubt generated a far-reaching impact on the Korean economy, especially on its potential for development. First, it appears that the aid, because of its emphasis on consumption and short-term stabilization, resulted in increases in public and private consumption levels rather than in the speedy mobilization of domestic savings and the increase of capital formation which are essential for self-sustained growth. One estimate shows that between 1953 and 1961, for example, domestic savings never exceeded 4 percent of GNP. In effect, on the average, domestic savings had been less than 1 percent of GNP, while gross investments averaged 9.1 percent of GNP during the same period—a clear indication that Korea had been persistently dependent upon foreign aid to finance the investment.[8]

It also appears that the large-scale imports of American agricultural surpluses under PL480 depressed prices of rice and other grains and thus distorted the overall distribution of income in favor of the nonfarm sector to some extent, providing a disincentive to domestic agricultural production.

There existed, however, a widespread distortion in the pricing system of the economy in such areas as foreign exchange and interest rates during this period. These distortions are, of course, attributable more to inept government policies than to foreign economic aid.

On the other hand, American economic aid was the key factor that contributed to the relative stability of this period against the overwhelming odds of an economy in complete disarray brought about by the liberation, war, and rapidly increasing consumption by an ever-increasing population. In view of the fact that the Seoul consumer price index increased 68 percent in 1954 and about 23 percent in both 1955 and 1956 despite the massive inflow of aid, it is not difficult to conjecture how explosive the situation could have been in the post–Korean War period without U.S. economic aid.

Detailed statistics on GNP and industrial production are not available for the period before 1953 for an analysis of the impact of economic aid on actual economic performances. Judging from the limited series of commodities produced, it seems that the industrial output had been steadily recovering from 1946 to 1950 and again during the Korean War period. According to one estimate, however, the 1953 industrial level was only about one-third of the 1940 level.[9] Economic recovery after the war was relatively rapid until 1958, with an average annual increase in GNP of 4.8 percent, and then began to slow down, reaching 3.5 percent in 1961. The annual rate of increase in the mining and manufacturing sectors was an impressive 13.4 percent in the 1954–58 period, decreasing to about 8 percent from 1959 to 1961. Output in the agricultural sector fluctuated rather severely, averaging a 3.5 percent annual increase during the 1953–61 period.[10]

At least on the surface, it appears that the contribution of massive economic aid to the overall economic achievements of Korea was less than impressive during the period, as, for example, we witness the low level of $83 per capita GNP as late as 1961.[11] From a long-range perspective, however, many important transitions in social and economic conditions were rapidly taking place during this period. There is no doubt that the large-scale and continued inflow of economic aid was primarily responsible for a phenomenal rise in the educational level of the population as a whole, a steady increase in the supply of managerial and entrepreneurial talents, and a rapid formation of social infrastructure. We shall now examine the period when a spectacular growth in the economy took place.

Period of Rapid Growth, 1962–74

In many ways, the military coup of May 1961 was a major turning point in terms of the economic development as well as the political development of Korea. From the outset, the new leadership not only made the economic improvement of the country one of the top priorities but also quickly formulated and implemented various new policies conducive to rapid economic development.[12] Among the reformulations of policies which had direct bearing on United States–Korean economic relations were foreign-exchange rate reforms and a combination of various policies to accelerate inflow of foreign loans.

During the 1950s, along with a complex tariff system, an elaborate mechanism of multiple exchange rates was employed in order to control the allocation of scarce foreign exchange by restricting imports and encouraging exports. With the exception of a brief experimentation with multiple rates reinstated in 1963, a uniform exchange rate and a unitary fluctuating exchange rate system were adopted in the 1960s. Since the major devaluation in May 1964, a considerable liberalization of import policy was implemented, in large measure because of an improvement in the balance of payments. At the same time, the form of incentive to promote export was somewhat changed from direct subsidies to more implicit forms. For example, there was developed a variety of preferential loans for export industries.[13]

Perhaps so-called normalization of the interest-rate policy, which raised the ceiling on commercial bank lending rates from 16 percent to 26 percent, provided one of the strong incentives to import foreign credit by creating substantial divergence in the domestic and foreign interest rates. In any case, improvement in domestic economic conditions, in general, and a number of government policies to promote foreign capital inflow, in particular, cannot be ignored.[14]

The policies that had important, though somewhat indirect, bearings on economic relations between the United States and Korea were the normalization of relations with Japan and the implementation for the first time of a series of five-year economic development plans. We shall now briefly review the consequences of these policies as reflected in structural changes in Korea's international trade and in other principal economic indicators.

From Table 1, we note continual and sharp increases in trade activities after 1962. For instance, while in 1974 the value of imports had increased to 16 times their value in 1962, export values rose by a factor of 81 during the same period. The deficit in trade balance, however, continuously expanded also—about 6.5 times—during the same span of time. One significant change for this period was in the method of financing the trade deficit. Official aid, for example, gradually declined, reaching zero in 1973, and a dramatically increasing inflow of foreign loans replaced the aid.

We observe essentially the same trend in Table 2, which shows that the dwindling amount of total economic aid was more than offset by a sharp rise in total foreign loans. Whereas in 1962 total economic aid was $232.3 million, more than 10 percent of Korea's GNP, it had decreased to $82.6 million—about 1 percent of an ever-expanding GNP—by 1970. On the other hand, loans, which were almost insignificant until 1962, rapidly climbed to exceed the $1 billion mark in 1974. In 1966 and thereafter, the ratio of foreign loans to rising GNP remained at a little more than the 7 percent level.[15]

Table 3 lists a summary of foreign loans by types of borrowing, by countries, and by repayment obligation for selected years. The sharp increase in the total of foreign loans, in effect was due largely to a dramatic increase in the influx of private commercial loans and direct investment, rather than to a rise in government loans. This change was a sign that the Korean economy by then was clearly over the

Table 3. Summary of Foreign Loans, 1962, 1968, 1974
(In millions of U.S. dollars)

	1962	1968	1974
Total Foreign Loans	78.4	357.8	1,056.7
By Types of Borrowing			
Government loans	73.4	70.2	316.6
Commercial loans	1.8	268.4	616.0
Foreigners' investment	3.6	19.2	124.1
By Countries			
U.S.A.	n.a.	151.7	345.9
Japan	n.a.	122.5	337.7
W. Germany	n.a.	38.7	32.2
Others	n.a.	44.9	340.9
Repayment	1.1	60.4	548.3
(Of Which Interest)	-	16.2	210.2

Sources: The Bank of Korea, Yoncha Boko So (Annual Report),
1965, pp. 128-129; 1972, pp. 125-127; 1974, pp. 110-
115.

threshold of development and thus able to attract a large sum
of foreign private capital—provided, of course, that government policies were geared toward the strong inducement of
foreign credits. Examining the countries which supplied the
foreign capital, we see that the relative importance of the
United States steadily declined to less than a third of the
total loans supplied, whereas Japan and the rest of the world
increased their shares to a third each in 1974.

Korea's exports and imports are shown by selected countries in Table 4. Approximately two-thirds of the volume of
Korean international trade has been with two countries, the
United States and Japan. On the export side, the United
States and Japan alternated as the primary buyers of Korean
exports throughout the period under study. On the other
hand, Japan has clearly dominated the United States as the
major supplier for Korean import needs since 1966. The

Table 4.   Exports and Imports by Countries

	1963	1966	1972	1974
Exports				
In millions of U.S. dollars	86.8	250.3	1,624,1	4.460.4
Shares by country, in %				
U.S.A.	28.0	38.3	46.7	33.5
Japan	28.6	26.5	25.1	30.9
Others	43.4	35.2	28.2	35.6
Imports				
In millions of U.S. dollars	560.3	716.4	2,522.0	6851.8
Shares by country, in %				
U.S.A.	50.7	35.4	25.7	24.8
Japan	28.4	41.0	40.9	38.2
Others	20.9	23.6	33.5	36.9

Source: The Bank of Korea, Economic Statistics Yearbook, 1967,
          pp. 262-263; 1975, pp. 188-195.

increasing share of Japan in Korea's imports represents not only an advantage arising from geographical proximity but also a substantial sum of payments made by Japan as a property claims settlement agreed upon by the two countries in April 1965.[16]

The rapid expansion in trade volume was accompanied by equally drastic changes in the commodities composition of exports, 49.7 percent consisted of crude materials, followed by 31.9 percent in food and beverages. In 1974, however, exports of food, beverages, and crude materials together was only 12 percent, while manufactured goods, including machinery and transport equipment, made up 83 percent of the $4,460 million exported.[17] On the import side, between 1962 and 1973 shares of imports in both consumer and producer goods increased, respectively, by 6.4 and 8.9 percentage points, a rise which was offset by a decrease in shares of raw materials imports of 15.3 percentage points. In absolute value, however, the raw materials total increased by about 7.6 times during the same period.[18]

This radical change in the structure of international trade is intimately related to the particular pattern of economic development that Korea pursued. In Table 5, average annual growth rates in selected economic indicators are shown. Compared to the 1956-61 period, the rate of increase in population visibly tapered off; the result was a respectable rate of increase in per-capita real GNP. Real GNP per capita in 1974 was about 2.5 times the 1960 level, while in current dollar terms it increased from $83 in 1962 to $376 in 1973.[19]

Table 5

Average Annual Growth Rate in Principal Economic Indicators

	1956-61	1962-66	1967-71	1972-74
Real GNP	4.0	7.8	10.5	10.6
Population	3.0	2.6	1.9	1.7
Per capita real GNP	1.0	5.2	8.6	8.9
Agriculture, forestry, and fishery	3.2	5.3	2.5	4.7
Mining and manufacturing	9.6	14.2	20.3	20.5
Social overhead and other services	3.7	8.4	12.3	8.2
Consumer price index	10.5	15.9	11.4	12.8
Exports	18.6	43.9	33.8	63.0
Imports	-0.3	21.5	28.0	45.0
Gross domestic capital formation	4.7	21.1	18.7	15.7

Source: The Bank of Korea, Economic Statistics Yearbook, 1975, pp. 3-4, 6, 268-269, 282-283; Korea Development Institute, Korea's Economy, Past and Present (Seoul, 1975), pp. 342-343.

It is evident from Table 5 that the rapid growth in GNP was attributable to the growth in the mining and manufacturing sectors, which averaged an unprecedented growth rate of

more than 20 percent a year. Social overhead and other
service sectors also attained rapid growth rates—8.4 percent
in 1962-66, 12.3 percent in 1967-71, and 8.2 percent in
1972-74. The growth rates in the agriculture, forestry, and
fishing sectors, though they fluctuated between a minimum
of 1.7 percent in 1972 and a maximum of 6.9 percent in
1974, retained a significant 5 percent average level per year.

In summarizing the period between 1962 and 1974, there
is no question that the growth of the Korean economy has been
most impressive indeed. Among the numerous factors that
contributed to the growth were the strong commitment of
the government to develop the economy rapidly and the
proper mix of government policies to utilize the full potential
of the economy that had been gradually nurtured during the
period prior to 1962. Some of the manifestations of the policies that are relevant to the present study include a tremendous inflow of foreign capital and a phenomenal rate of increase in exports, which was facilitated by an unparalleled
spurt of industrialization. This economic growth does not
mean, however, that there have been no problems associated
with this particular pattern of development. In the following
section, we shall attempt to evaluate United States–Korean
economic relations and their impact on the particular strategy that the Korean economy has adopted.

Conclusion

In our introductory section we pointed out that in order for
an economy to develop successfully it must satisfy crucial requirements from two sides. On the supply side, it is essential
to have continuous increases in productive resources; namely,
in natural resources, capital, the labor force, and innovation
in technology. On the other side, the expanding supply capacity of the economy must be accompanied by a somewhat
proportional and sustained increase in the aggregate demand
for the produced goods and services from home and abroad.

South Korea has had very scarce natural resources and
little ability to accumulate domestically the required capital,
but an abundant labor force, which represents both a liability
and an asset to the economy. This labor force is a liability

because of the huge consumption needs of an expanding population. Even when total output increases, per-capita consumption may not be increasing fast enough. Korea's labor force could be an asset if, for instance, the economy is able to carry out a massive mobilization of every idle human resource into requisite domestic capital formation. Such a method, however, would necessitate a highly centralized command-type economy and at the same time a reduction in the already meager consumption level of the population. Since Korea was desperately poor in the 1940s and 1950s, the accumulation of capital through mobilization of her labor force and the simultaneous reduction in consumption would have certainly meant immeasurable human suffering and sacrifices.

United States–Korean economic relations, which included aid, loans, and expanding trade, therefore provided Korea with the least painful economic alternative for her rapid development in a number of different ways. First, the relations alleviated natural-resource bottlenecks, enabling Korea to import necessary industrial raw materials and other natural resources that were not available at home. At the same time, rapid development of certain mineral resources, such as tungsten ores, was possible largely because modern mining facilities were available abroad as well as a ready market for the product.

Second, the process of capital formation in Korea initially was entirely dependent upon the United States. As foreign aid began to decrease and foreign credits began to flow in large volume, domestic sources of capital formation rapidly increased in the late 1960s and 1970s. For example, domestic savings averaged only about 3 percent of GNP in the 1953–63 period, but had increased to about 11.7 percent of GNP by 1966. Coupled with steadily rising domestic savings, the flow of foreign loans accelerated gross domestic capital formation, which reached nearly 30 percent of GNP in 1974.[20] Moreover, the aid, loans, and trade relations not only increased the pace of capital accumulation but also were the primary contributing factor in upgrading the quality and the modernization of capital goods in Korea.

Third, her economic relations with the United States enabled Korea to mitigate the acute problems caused by the consumption needs of her population during these turbulent periods, and thus greatly contributed to transforming the whole population into a highly educated, well-trained, and productive labor force that included managerial and entrepreneurial talents both in the private and public sectors of the economy. When domestic productive capacity was limited, the economic relations with the United States served as the major economic stabilizer; when, conversely, that capacity rapidly expanded, the consumption-oriented economy that had been nurtured by these economic relations proved to be a ready and strong domestic market for the output of goods and services. The existence of such potential domestic as well as foreign markets, of course, offered great incentives for investment opportunities.

In conclusion, the path of economic development of South Korea which followed strong economic ties with the United States and later with Japan proved to be, unquestionably, a successful one. Nevertheless, the very factors that promoted its success may possibly contribute also to a number of closely interrelated problems. These include a gap between investment and domestic savings, forcing a continued reliance on foreign capital; a decreasing export market; an increasing requirement for raw-material imports; and a deterioration in terms of trade. Related to these are problems of imbalance between agriculture and industry, inflation, and an inequitable distribution of income. Most of these problems will culminate in complex balance-of-payment problems or in a problem of debt-service payments—which, as we have shown in Table 3, were $548.3 million by 1974. There are strong evidences that Korea by now has developed the excellent administrative and managerial capacity to cope successfully with these problems.

Notes

Notes to Chapter 1

1. Ernest R. May and James C. Thompson, Jr., eds., *American–East Asian Relations: A Survey* (Cambridge, 1972).

2. JIS 80/9, Oct. 26, 1945, Joint Chiefs of Staff Papers, National Archives.

3. Clark Clifford, "American Relations with the Soviet Union," Sept. 24, 1946, Harry S. Truman Library.

4. NSC 7, Mar. 30, 1948, National Security Council Papers, National Archives.

5. NSC 6, Mar. 26, 1948.

6. JIS 80/5/M, Oct. 22, 1945.

7. NSC 37, Dec. 1, 1948.

8. *Foreign Relations of the United States 1947* 1, p. 745.

9. NSC 13/2, Oct. 7, 1948.

10. NSC 51, July 1, 1949.

11. *Foreign Relations of the United States 1947* 1, p. 737.

12. NSC 6.

13. NSC 34/1, Jan. 11, 1949.

14. NSC 37.

15. NSC 37/3, Feb. 11, 1949.

16. NSC 37/1, Jan. 19, 1949.

17. NSC 8, Apr. 2, 1948.

18. NSC 49, June 15, 1949.

19. NSC 49/1, Oct. 4, 1949.

20. NSC 51.

21. See Akira Iriye, "Japan and the Cold War," paper presented at the Symposium on the International Environment in Postwar Asia, Kyoto, November 1975.

22. Hornbeck to Berle, Feb. 20, 1943, Stanley K. Hornbeck Papers, Hoover Institution on War, Revolution, and Peace.

23. P. 236, July 2, 1943, Harley Notter Papers, National Archives.

24. See Roger Louis, *The United States and the Decolonization of the British Empire*, forthcoming.

25. Sterndale Bennett memo, May 9, 1945, F 2444/364/G 23, Foreign Office Archives.

26. JIS 1888/2, Apr. 13, 1950.

Notes to Chapter 3

1. U.S. State Department, *United States Relations with China* (Washington, 1949), pp. 14–15. Viewing the Chinese upheaval as an indigenous conflict, the administration was prepared to accept the extension of Communist authority to Formosa, where the Nationalists were establishing themselves.

2. Mao Tse-tung, *On People's Democratic Dictatorship* (Peking, 1952), p. 10.

3. Acheson to Jessup, July 18, 1949. Committee on Foreign Relations, *Hearings on the Nomination of Philip Jessup to Be U.S. Representative to the Sixth General Assembly of the United Nations*, 82nd Cong., 1st Sess., 1951, p. 603.

4. See Acheson's comments on the White Paper in *Department of State Bulletin* (hereinafter referred to as *State Bulletin*) 21 (Aug. 15, 1949), p. 236.

5. Ibid. (Sept. 5, 1949), p. 324.

6. *Congressional Record*, vol. 95, pt. 15, 81st Cong., 1st Sess. (Aug. 22, 1949), pp. A5451–53.

7. Ibid., (Sept. 9, 1949), pp. 12755, 12758.

8. *State Bulletin* 21 (Nov. 28, 1949), p. 826.

9. Karl Lott Rankin, *China Assignment* (Seattle, 1964), pp. 35–36.

10. *State Bulletin* 22 (Jan. 23, 1950), pp. 113–14.

11. Ibid., p. 115.

12. Ibid. (Mar. 27, 1950), p. 468.

13. There was little in the treaty to suggest any real or imagined Chinese subservience. The mutual defense arrangements for the Far East

favored the Chinese, whose enemy resided on Formosa. There was no danger of a Japanese attack on Russian Siberia.

14. *State Bulletin* 22 (Mar. 27, 1950), pp. 469–72; see also Dean Acheson, "New Era in Asia," *Vital Speeches of the Day* 16 (Apr. 10, 1950), pp. 356–57.

15. *State Bulletin* 22 (Apr. 10, 1950), p. 562.

16. Ibid. (Apr. 24. 1950), p. 627.

17. *State Bulletin* (July 31, 1950), p. 165.

18. Interview, July 1, 1950. Ibid. (July 10, 1950), p. 49.

19. Ibid. (Sept. 18, 1950), p 463.

20. *New York Times*, Nov. 30, 1950; *Public Papers of the Presidents: Harry S. Truman, 1950* (Washington, 1965), p. 725.

21. Stanley K. Hornbeck, "The United States and China," *Vital Speeches* 16 (Oct. 1, 1950), pp. 745–46.

22. *State Bulletin* 24 (Jan. 22, 1951), p. 123.

23. Ibid. (May 28, 1951), p. 844.

24. Ibid. (Mar. 26, 1951), p. 484.

25. Ibid. (May 28, 1951), p. 847. For Dulles' statement on nonrecognition see p. 844.

26. *State Bulletin* 28 (Feb. 9, 1953), pp. 212–13.

27. Rankin, *China Assignment*, p. 173.

28. *State Bulletin* 39 (Sept. 8, 1958), pp. 388–89.

29. *State Bulletin* 41 (June 8, 1959), p. 661.

30. Ibid. (July 15, 1959), p. 91.

31. Ibid. (Sept. 2, 1957), p. 389.

32. *State Bulletin* 40 (Apr. 6, 1959), p. 475.

33. *State Bulletin* 45 (July 31, 1961), p. 179.

34. *State Bulletin* 48 (Feb. 4, 1963), p. 162. For Rusk's statement see ibid. (Apr. 29, 1963), p. 644.

35. Ibid. (Feb. 25, 1963), p. 274.

36. *State Bulletin* 49 (July 8, 1963), p. 44.

37. See, for example, *Public Papers of the Presidents: John F. Kennedy, 1963* (Washington, 1964), p. 349.

38. Roger Hilsman, "Orchestrating the Instrumentalities: The Case of Southeast Asia," in *Foreign Policy in the Sixties: The Issues and the Instruments*, ed. Roger Hilsman and Robert C. Good (Baltimore, 1965).

39. *State Bulletin* 46 (Jan. 15, 1962), p. 109.

40. Ibid., p. 112.

41. *State Bulletin* 50 (Jan. 6, 1964), pp. 11–17.

42. *State Bulletin* 53 (Dec. 13, 1965), pp. 941–43.

43. Lin Piao, "Long Live the People's War," *Peking Review* 8 (Sept. 3, 1965).

44. Rusk quoted in New York Times, Apr. 17, 1966.

45. Quoted in Paul S. Holbo, *United States Policies toward China* (New York, 1969), p. 100.

46. Congressional Quarterly Service, *China and U.S. Far East Policy, 1945–66* (Washington, 1967), p. 3.

47. Walter Lippmann in *Washington Post*, Oct. 10, 1971.

48. William Pfaff, "Reflections: That Statesman and the Conqueror," *New Yorker*, June 3, 1972, p. 79.

49. James Chace, "The Five-Power World of Richard Nixon," *New York Times Magazine*, Feb. 20, 1972, pp. 42–43.

Notes to Chapter 4

1. See *Milwaukee Journal*, Dec. 4, 1975; also *China News* (Taipei), Oct. 28, 1975, and *Japan Times* (Tokyo), Oct. 15, 1975, for reports of Nationalist opposition to the Ford trip. Ford had made his first trip to China as House minority leader and later criticized the PRC in a University of Michigan talk, but most Washington newsmen believe that he relies wholly on Secretary Kissinger for foreign-policy decisions.

2. See Douglas H. Mendel, Jr., "Japanese Public Views of Taiwan's Future," *Asian Survey*, Mar. 1975, pp. 215–20.

3. *Japan Times*, July 10, 1974. Taipei and overseas Chinese groups all attacked Jackson's proposal. Senators Mansfield and Fulbright favored it, while most members of Congress and labor leader George Meany of the AFL–CIO did not.

4. See John S. Service, *Lost Chance in China* (New York, 1974); John F. Melby, *The Mandate of Heaven* (New York, 1971); and Barbara Tuchman, *Stillwell and the American Experience in China, 1941–45*

(New York, 1971). The Melby book is the most objective, whereas Tuchman and Service have been widely criticized by the Taipei government and press. See Ray Cline's ranking of ROC as twenty-seventh among world powers in *China News*, Sept. 20, 1975.

5. See Peter Calvocoressi, *Survey of International Affairs 1953* (London and New York, 1956), pp. 244–30.

6. See the annual *China Yearbook* (Taipei), 1974 and later, and issues of the *Free China Review* for economic and military statistics.

7. *United Nations Treaty Series*, vol. 248, pp. 226–28, reprinted in Hungdah Chiu, ed., *China and the Question of Taiwan: Documents and Analysis* (New York, 1973), pp 252–53.

8. Arthur Schlesinger, Jr., *A Thousand Days* (Boston, 1965), pp. 483-486.

9. Kenneth Young, "American Dealings with Peking," *Foreign Affairs* 45 (Oct. 1966), pp. 81–82.

10. *Japan Times*, Sept. 19, 1975.

11. See Mendel, "The Role of Violence in Liberation Movements," *Independent Formosa*, Summer 1970, pp. 12–13; also "Taiwan on the Horns of a Dilemma," *Understanding China* 9 (May–June 1973), and "Selling out Taiwan for Peace with Peking?," *Journal of International Affairs* 26 (1972), pp. 216–20.

12. See William Bueler, *U.S. China Policy and the Problem of Taiwan* (Boulder, Colo., 1971), for an ex–CIA man's pro-Taiwanese views.

13. Kunming Military District Papers, published in translation by Chinese Information Service (New York, 1973). Also reported in *New York Times*, Apr. 10, 1974, p. 4. Whole set of documents was reprinted with English translation in *Chinese Communist Internal Politics and Foreign Policy* (Taipei, 1974). Joseph Lelyveld is a *Times* man in Hong Kong who often writes excellent reports from Taipei, as did Fox Butterfield, a former Fulbright graduate student in Taipei in 1961-62 who revisited Taiwan in 1975 to report on major reforms and changes. (See *New York Times*, Oct. 14, 1975.)

14. U.S. State Department, Dec. 7, 1975. In April 1973, the Harvard University Kennedy School of Government published a discussion paper by Graham Allison which stated: "In its quest for a generation of peace at any price, the U.S. government is certainly capable of flipflopping from the myth that China did not exist to the myth that Taiwan and the Taiwanese do not exist. But are there no consequences to a betrayal of Taiwan?"

15. See State Department pamphlet on changes in U.S. China policy, Aug. 1972.

16. "Coming to Grips with the Two Chinas," *Far Eastern Economic Review*, Jan. 24, 1976, pp. 22–24. Taiwan trade totals were given for 1974 as $3.6 billion imports and $3 billion exports, whereas Department of State and ROC figures were less. See also *United States Trade with the People's Republic of China*, State Department pamphlet no. 8818, June 1975.

17. *Business Week*, Dec. 15, 1975, pp. 40–44; see also *China News*, Dec. 16, 1975.

18. *China News*, Oct. 17, 1975 (reprinted from *New York Times* article of Oct. 14).

19. *China News*, Sept. 18, 1974.

20. *China News*, Nov. 1, 1974. Senate majority leader Mike Mansfield urged Washington to encourage Taipei to negotiate a settlement with Peking, as he thought mainland patience might give out after Mao's death, but he opposed breaking off diplomatic relations or the security treaty with Taipei. (See *Japan Times*, Feb. 24, 1975.)

21. *China News*, Oct. 18, 1974; see also William Glenn, "Defence: Taiwan's New Objectives," in *Far Eastern Economic Review*, May 23, 1975. Glenn, a veteran observer of Taipei affairs, reported that Vice-President Rockefeller spent forty-five minutes with Premier Chiang and reaffirmed the U.S. commitment. Glenn observed, "Taiwan is a low-cost asset for America: no economic aid, no military grants, and the U.S. presence of a mere 4,500 men [now about 2,000]. The Nationalists have nowhere else to go; neutralism is impossible. They cannot make a deal with the Chinese Communists nor go over to the Soviet Communists. For better or worse, they are wed to the Americans."

22. *Japan Times*, Aug. 13, 1974.

23. *Japan Times*, June 5, 1974.

24. *China News*, Apr. 28, 1975. This was the third visit of a Congressional group since U.S.–Peking relations began to thaw in 1971.

25. *China News*, Aug. 27, 1975. Javits was joined by many other senators with the same view.

26. Ibid.

27. *Japan Times*, July 10, 1974.

28. *China News*, Feb. 8, 1975. The full results are in *A Gallup Study of Public Attitudes toward Nations of the World* (Princeton, N.J., 1974).

29. *Gallup Study* (Princeton, N.J., 1975).

30. See "Seeing is Believing," a pamphlet published in 1974 by the Taipei government which included articles by Edward O'Brien of the *St. Louis Globe-Democrat* and Ralph de Toledano of the Copley News Service. Jenkins told audiences in Taiwan and the U.S. after leaving Peking that Americans were highly restricted in their mainland activities. Pritam Singh, an Indian representative of a clothier in Hong Kong, told Taipei reporters he much preferred Taiwan to the mainland (*China News*, Dec. 23, 1974). See also William Armbruster, "A Gust of Liberalism," *Far Eastern Economic Review*, Oct. 17, 1975; and "Taiwan After Chiang Kai-shek," *Wall Street Journal*, Apr. 17, 1975.

31. The quotes from Ford and Schlesinger are from a press release, dated May 9, 1975, issued by Hugh C. Newton and Associates, Alexandria, Va., an agent of the Chinese Information Service in New York.

32. *China Report*, published by the Committee for a Free China, October 1975. The same issue contains the House resolution on Free China, ex–Defense Secretary Melvin Laird's statement of opposition to normalization with Peking, and comments by Winberg Chai, head of the Asian studies department at the City University of New York, who was surprised by the great changes in Taiwan politics and asked: "If a person like me has these misperceptions about his own fatherland, what would the non-Chinese have thought about Taiwan?" Chai has not visited Taiwan for twenty-two years.

33. *Mainichi Daily News*, July 6, 1975. See also *China and U.S. Foreign Policy* (Washington, 1971) for data on pre-1971 relations.

34. *China News*, Dec. 17, 1975. Chien is one of the brightest young diplomats in the ROC.

35. *Asian Survey*, Aug. 1974, pp. 679–99.

36. *China News*, Oct. 11, 1975. Leo Newman, chief of the Grand Canyon State Travelers' Association, has visited Taiwan fifteen times in the past ten years.

Notes to Chapter 5

1. See U.S. Ambassador to Japan Hodgson's comments in *Japan Times Weekly*, Sept. 20, 1975.

2. The dire predictions made regarding the effect on the Japanese economy of the Arab oil boycott of 1973 are a case in point. See *Japan Times Weekly*, Nov. 24, 1973.

3. Robert Scalapino, *American-Japanese Relations in a Changing Era* (New York, 1972), p. 25.

4. Donald Hellmann, *Japan and East Asia* (New York, 1972), ch. 5.

5. Scalapino, *American-Japanese Relations*, pp. 28-30.

6. Hellmann, *Japan and East Asia*, p. 9.

7. With the exception of some technologically sophisticated artificial fibers.

8. Scalapino, *American-Japanese Relations*, p. 28.

9. This discrepancy has also facilitated the evolution of economic conflict into emotional, irrational confrontation, as discussed by Fuji Kamiya in Gerald Curtis, *Japanese-American Relations in the 1970s* (Washington, 1970), p. 2.

10. Gerald Curtis sees the treaty as the most important problem involving the two nations. *Relations in the 1970s*, p. 177.

11. Such behavior may be a sign of domestic American problems as much as of real security concerns. Ibid., p. 4.

12. Martin Weinstein, *Japan's Postwar Defense Policy* (New York, 1971), p. 2. Japan's consternation and temporizing over China's demands for an "antihegemony" clause (directed against the USSR) in the proposed Sino-Japanese Treaty of Peace and Amity is an example of this.

13. Ibid., ch. 2.

14. Hellmann, *Japan and East Asia*, p. 115.

15. For a corroborative argument, see William Overholt, "Japan's Emerging World Role," *Orbis*, Summer 1975.

16. *Japan Times Weekly*, Sept. 6, 1976.

17. Ibid.

18. The response of the Arabs to Japan's Middle East policies in late 1973 is a case in point.

19. See James W. White, "Report on the Conference on the State of Japanese Domestic Politics," Washington, U.S. State Department, April 1974.

20. Fuji Kamiya has even suggested that the real sources of Japanese-American friction are psychological, not economic, thus increasing the potential for hostility even if solutions to outstanding economic problems are found. See Curtis, *Relations in the 1970s*, pp. 11-12.

21. White, "Tradition in Studies of Contemporary Japanese Politics," *World Politics*, April 1974.

22. Zbigniew Brzezinski, *The Fragile Blossom* (New York, 1972), p. 111. It must also be noted that Japanese self-assertion will inevitably be most significant as exercised vis-à-vis the United States. See Curtis, *Relations in the 1970s*, p. 22.

23. Scalapino, *American-Japanese Relations*, p. 42; Curtis, *Relations in the 1970s*, pp. 157–58.

24. Scalapino, *American-Japanese Relations*, pp. 36–37.

25. Ibid., p. 76.

26. *Japan Times Weekly*, Sept. 6, 1975.

27. Hellmann, *Japan and East Asia*, p. 6.

28. Herman Kahn, *The Emerging Japanese Superstate* (Englewood Cliffs, N.J., 1970), ch. 1, p. 153.

29. Hellmann, *Japan and East Asia*, chs. 5, 8.

30. Curtis, *Relations in the 1970s*, pp. 28–29.

31. Japanese prosperity will contribute to the rest of Asia also, in that as Japan becomes more affluent she will price herself out of certain markets (e.g., textiles and simple electronic manufactures) in which the other countries of Asia may then enjoy a comparative advantage. Increasing Japanese wage levels in general makes it easier for these countries to compete with her. Curtis, *Relations in the 1970s*, pp. 106–107, 166.

Notes to Chapter 6

1. A technical point worthy of notice is that Japanese statistics report exports FOB and imports CIF, while American statistics give both exports and imports FOB. CIF figures are higher than FOB figures because of the value of freight and insurance—which constitute 10 to 15 percent of the latter. This point should be kept in mind when comparing American and Japanese trade data.

2. Exports of manufactures are less important in the United States than in Japan. As a proportion of the total value of production, they were 0.7 percent in the U.S. and 9.5 percent in Japan in 1969.

3. It is estimated that differentials in the physical productivity of labor in manufacturing had been considerably narrowed by 1970, when the U.S./Japan ratio was at most 1:5.

4. In Table 4, Japan's trade figures are those of customs clearance with exports FOB and imports CIF. In the standard IMF statistics, the trade balance was $90 billion in 1972 instead of $51 billion, as reported in the table.

Notes to Chapter 7

1. James C. Abegglen, "Materials and Energy: Japan's Problems and Policies," in Study Group Sponsored by the Chicago Council on Foreign Relations and the Japan Trade Center of Chicago, *U.S.-Japanese Relations: Options in the Multipolar World* (Chicago, 1974).

2. For a detailed discussion of oil events initiated by each of our sample nations, see Tong-Whan Park, Farid Abolfathi, and Michael Ward, "Resource Nationalism in the Foreign Policy Behavior of Oil Exporting Countries: 1947–1974," paper presented at the annual meeting of the American Political Science Association in Chicago, 1974 (forthcoming in *International Interactions*).

3. James A. Bill and Robert W. Stookey, *Politics and Petroleum: The Middle East and the United States* (Brunswick, Ohio, 1975).

4. M. Y. Yoshino, "Japanese Foreign Direct Investment," in Isaiah Frank, ed., *The Japanese Economy in International Perspective* (Baltimore, 1975).

5. Because of the problem of ensuring security of oil supplies at reasonable prices, Japanese resource industries have concentrated on the expansion of processing capacities. The advantage of this strategy is that the Japanese could thus avoid the high risks and capital requirements necessary for extractive activities. With this burden assumed by others, Japan could put its limited capital to maximum possible utilization by investing in refineries.

6. Gerard C. Smith, "The Vital Triangle," in *U.S.-Japanese Relations*, vol. 7.

7. M. Ignotus, "Seizing Arab Oil," *Harper's*, March 1975, pp. 45–62; R. Tucker, "American Force: The Missing Link in the Oil Crisis," *Washington Post*, Jan. 5, 1975.

8. Ragaei El Mallakh, "The Energy Relationship between the Arab World and the United States: Conflict or Cooperation?," in M. Cherif Bassiouni, ed., *Issues in the Mediterranean* (Chicago, 1975).

9. IEP has been investigating the problems in international energy flows utilizing the framework of resource nationalism. It has established a data bank which includes event/interactions of major actors in interna-

tional petroleum as well as basic indicators of their attributes. Attribute data used in this section and the events data referred to in the previous section have been drawn from this bank.

10. For a methodological exposition of this particular form of factor analysis, see Tong-Whan Park, "Measuring the Dynamic Patterns of Development: The Case of Asia, 1949–1968," *Multivariate Behavioral Research* 8 (April, 1973), pp. 227–251.

Notes to Chapter 8

1. Tyler Dennett, *Americans in East Asia: A Critical Study of United States Policy in the Far East in the Nineteenth Century*, reprint ed. (New York, 1963), p. viii.

2. Uhl to Sill, June 23, 1894, Instruction, Korea, File Microcopies of Records in the National Archives (hereinafter cited as Microfilm NA), no. 77, reel 109; Sill to Uhl, June 25, 1894, Despatches, Korea, Microfilm NA, no. 134, reel 11; Gresham to Dunn, July 7, 1894, Instructions, Japan, Microfilm NA, no. 77, reel 107; Dunn to Mutsu, July 8, 1894, *Nihon Gaikobunsho* [Japanese Diplomatic Documents] (hereinafter cited as *NGB*) (Tokyo, 1936), vol. 27, pt. 2, p. 296.

3. Olney to Sill, Nov. 20 and Dec. 2, 1895, Instructions, Korea, Microfilm NA, no. 77, reel 109; Kurino to Saionji, Oct. 22, 1895, *NGB*, vol. 28, pt. 1, p. 522.

4. Root to Morgan, Nov. 24, 1905, Instructions, Korea, Microfilm NA, no. 77, reel 109; Root to Griscom, Nov. 24, 1905, Instructions, Japan, Microfilm NA, no. 77, reel 109.

5. U.S. Treasury Department, *The Foreign Commerce and Navigation of the United States, 1894-95* (Washington, 1896), p. xxxviii; U.S. State Department, *Commercial Relations of the United States, 1895–96* (Washington, 1897), p. 862; Allen to Hay, Feb. 2, 1902, Despatches, Korea, Microfilm NA, no. 134, reel 17; U.S. State Department, *Commercial Relations, 1896–97*, vol. 1, p. 1086.

6. U.S. Treasury Department, *Foreign Commerce and Navigation, 1903–04*, p. 140.

7. U.S. Treasury Department, *Foreign Commerce and Navigation, 1894–95*, p. xxxiii; U.S. Treasury Department, *Foreign Commerce and Navigation, 1903–04*, p. 140–142.

8. U.S. Treasury Department, *Foreign Commerce and Navigation, 1894–95*, p. xxxviii; U.S. Treasury Department, *Foreign Commerce and Navigation, 1903–04*, p. 140.

9. Edward C. Kirkland, *Industry Comes of Age: Business, Labor, and Public Policy, 1860-97*, The Economic History of the United States, vol. 6 (New York, 1961), p. 81; Sill to Olney, Apr. 16 and Aug. 5, 1896, Despatches, Korea, Microfilm NA, no. 134, reel 12; Allen to Sherman, Feb. 15, 1898, ibid., reel 14; Allen to Hay, Nov. 18, 1899, ibid., reel 15; Allen to Rockhill, Jan. 30, 1898, William R. Rockhill Manuscripts, Houghton Library, Harvard University, Cambridge, Mass.

10. "Report on the Trade of Korea for the Year 1904 and Abstracts for the Years 1895-1905," Horace N. Allen Manuscripts, New York Public Library, New York.

11. Allen to Hay, Sept. 15, 1900, Despatches, Korea, Microfilm NA, no. 134, reel 16; *Missionary Review of the World* 11 (1898), p. 958; ibid. 16 (1903), p. 687; Horace G. Underwood, "Twenty Years Missionary Work in Korea," in ibid. 19 (1906), p. 375.

12. *Missionary Review of the World* 12 (1899), pp. 72-73; ibid. 14 (1901), pp. 66-67; *Boston Transcript*, Dec. 13, 1905.

13. Uhl to Ye, June 22, 1894, Notes to Korean Legation, Microfilm NA, no. 99, reel 68; The Palace [Korean king] to Ye, June 28, 1894, Notes from Korean Legation, Microfilm NA, no. 166.

14. For different interpretations of the memorandum see A. Whitney Griswold, *The Far Eastern Policy of the United States*, reprint ed. (New Haven, 1962), pp. 125-126; Raymond A. Esthus, "The Taft-Katsura Memorandum Reconsidered," *Pacific Historical Review* 37 (1968), pp. 321-6.

15. Hans J. Morgenthau treats the Korean case as one of the prime examples of the balance of power in operation in *Politics among the Nations: The Struggle for Power and Peace*, 4th ed. (New York, 1967), p. 171.

16. See Dean Rusk's recollection in *Foreign Relations of the United States, 1945*, vol. 6 (Washington, 1969), p. 1039.

17. See "Memorandum by the Special Interdepartmental Committee on Korea," dated Feb. 24, 1947, in *Foreign Relations of the United States, 1947*, vol. 6 (Washington, 1972), pp. 608-18; Patterson (secretary of war) to Acheson (acting secretary of state), Apr. 4, 1947, ibid., pp. 625-28; State-War-Navy Coordinating Committee to Secretary, Joint Chiefs of Staff, Sept. 15, 1947, ibid., p. 789; Forrestal (secretary of defense) to Marshall (secretary of state), Sept. 26 [29], 1947, ibid., pp. 817-18. For Dean Acheson's Jan. 12, 1950, speech to the National Press Club, see State Department Bulletin 32 (Jan. 23, 1950), pp. 111-

16; Soon Sung Cho, *Korea in World Politics, 1940-50* (Berkeley and Los Angeles, 1967), pp. 259-61.

18. For the American decision to intervene, see Glenn D. Paige, *The Korean Decision, June 24-30, 1950* (New York, 1968); Richard C. Snyder and Glenn D. Paige, "The United States Decision to Resist Aggression in Korea: The Application of an Analytical Scheme," *Administrative Science Quarterly* 3 (1958), pp. 341-78; David S. McLellan, "Dean Acheson and the Korean War," *Political Science Quarterly* 83 (1968), pp. 16-39; Edwin C. Hoytt, "The United States Reaction to the Korean Attack: A Study of the Principles of the United Nations Charter as a Factor in American Policymaking," *American Journal of International Law* 55 (1961), pp. 45-76.

19. For the text of the 1953 Mutual Defense Treaty, see *United States Treaties and Other International Agreements*, vol. 5, pt. 3 (Washington, 1956), pp. 2368-76. For other agreements and declarations see ibid., vol. 7, pt. 2, pp. 2174-78; ibid., vol. 8, pt. 2, pp. 2217-81; ibid., vol. 13, pt. 1, pp. 244-48; ibid., vol. 17, pt. 2, pp. 1677-1831; Johnson-Park Communique, May 18, 1965, *State Department Bulletin* 52 (June 14, 1965), pp. 952-54; Johnson-Park Communique, Nov. 2, 1966, ibid. 55 (Nov. 14, 1966), pp. 777-79; Johnson-Park Communique, Apr. 17, 1968, ibid. 58 (May 16, 1968), pp. 575-77; Nixon-Park Communique, Aug. 22, 1969, ibid. 61 (Sept. 15, 1969), pp. 243-44; Joint Statement on Troop Reduction and Korean Modernization, Feb. 6, 1961, ibid. 64 (Mar. 1, 1971), p. 263.

20. U.S. Congress, subcommittee on Asian and Pacific affairs of House Committee on Foreign Affairs, *American-Korean Relations: Hearings*, 92nd Cong., 1st sess., June 8-10, 1971, pp. 15-16.

21. U.S. Census Bureau, *Statistical Abstract of the United States: 1951* (Washington, 1951), pp. 846, 849; ibid.: 1957, pp. 904, 907; ibid.: 1960, pp. 896, 899; ibid.: 1965, pp. 880, 883; ibid.: 1969, pp. 808, 811; ibid.: 1972, pp. 778-80.

22. Bank of Korea, *Monthly Statistical Review*, May 1954, pp. 62-63; ibid., February 1958, pp. 74-75; ibid., January 1962, pp. 41-42; ibid., January 1964, pp. 47-48; ibid., March 1969, pp. 83-84; ibid., December 1971, pp. 119, 121.

23. See sources cited in Note 22.

24. See sources cited in Note 22.

25. See sources cited in Note 22.

26. For this strategy see Herman Kahn and Anthony J. Wiener, "The

Next Thirty-three Years: A Framework for Speculation," in *Toward the Year 2000: Work in Progress*, ed. Daniel Bell (Boston, 1967), p. 88.

27. Kahn and Wiener, "The Next Thirty-three Years," pp. 75–76, 84–86, 94–95.

28. Ithiel De Sola Popl, "The International System in the Next Half-Century," in Bell, *Toward the Year 2000*, p. 321; Herman Kahn and A. Bruce-Briggs, *Things to Come: Thinking About the Seventies and Eighties* (New York, 1972), pp. 70-71, 77, 244-50.

29. See sources cited in Note 22.

30. See sources cited in Note 22.

31. See sources cited in Note 22.

32. See sources cited in Note 22.

33. U.S. State Department, *United States Foreign Policy, 1969–1970* (Washington, 1971), pp. 36–37.

34. Richard M. Nixon, *U.S. Foreign Policy for the 1970s: Building for Peace; A Report to the Congress, February 25, 1971* (Washington, n.d.), pp. 91–98.

35. See Kahn and Bruce-Briggs, *Things to Come*, pp. 200–01.

36. Kahn and Wiener, "The Next Thirty-three Years," p. 83; Kahn and Bruce-Briggs, *Things to Come*, p. 211.

37. Kahn and Bruce-Briggs, *Things to Come*, pp. 40–42, 45–46, 148–61.

38. Kahn and Bruce-Briggs, *Things to Come*, pp. 46–47, 232–44.

39. Nixon, *Foreign Policy for the 1970s*, p. 97.

40. For strategies of futures research see Marvin S. Soroos, "Some Methods of Futures Research for Investigating Problems Related to Population, Ecology, War, and Peace in the Global System," mimeographed, North Carolina State University, Raleigh, N.C., April 1973.

Notes to Chapter 9

1. Pyun Yung-tai, "What if America Should Fail Us," *Dong-a Ilbo*, Feb. 21, 1948; translated and reprinted in Pyun Yung-tai, *Korea My Country* (Seoul, 1949; third printing with revisions, 1962), p. 79.

2. Alfred Crofts, "Our Falling Ramparts," *Nation* (June 25, 1960), pp. 544–48. Crofts was one of the two in the group of fifty who had seen Korea previously—passing through on the South Manchurian Railway.

3. E. Grant Meade, *American Military Government in Korea* (New York, 1951), pp. 40-52. See also Carl J. Friedrich et al., *American Experience in Military Government in World War II* (New York, 1948), p. 355; Carl Berger, *The Korea Knot* (Philadelphia, 1957), pp. 31-61.

4. Meade, *Military Government in Korea*, pp. 53-58. Other useful assessments of American policies in this period are found in Soong Sung Cho, *Korea in World Politics 1940-50* (Berkeley, 1967), and in Gregory Henderson, *Korea: The Politics of the Vortex* (Cambridge, Mass., 1968).

5. Michael H. Armacost, "U.S.-Japan Relations: Problems and Modalities of Communication," *Department of State Bulletin* 68 (Jan. 15, 1973), pp. 64-72. Reprinted from the January 1973 issue of *Jiyu* (Japan).

6. John King Fairbank, *The United States and China*, 3rd ed. (Cambridge, Mass., 1971), pp. 283-303.

7. Jean-Jacques Rousseau, *A Lasting Peace through the Federation of Europe* and *The State of War*, trans. C. E. Vaughan (London, 1971), p. 91.

8. Gregory Henderson, "Korea and the New Order in Eastern Asia: The United States and South Korea," a paper presented at the fourth annual conference of Korea, Western Michigan University, Kalamazoo, Michigan, November 1972.

9. "Now—A Tougher U.S.," *U.S. News and World Report* 78 (May 26, 1975), pp. 24-27.

Notes to Chapter 10

1. For descriptions of the economic breakdown of post–World War II Korea, see Gilbert T. Brown, *Korean Pricing Policies and Economic Development in the 1960s* (Baltimore, 1973), pp. 30–41; David C. Cole and Princeton N. Lyman, *Korean Development: Interplay of Politics and Economics* (Cambridge, 1971), pp. 18–22; C. R. Frank, Jr., K. S. Kim, and L. Westphal, *Foreign Trade Regimes and Economic Development: South Korea* (New York, 1975), pp. 6–24; and Bank of Korea (referred to as BOK hereinafter), *Annual Economic Review of Korea, 1948*, vol. 1, p. 100.

2. For estimated figures of migration, see Brown, *Korean Pricing Policies*, p. 33, and Chung Jae Park, *Hankuk Kyongje Paeknyon* [One Hundred Years of Korean Economy] (Seoul, 1975), p. 25. For population in South Korea during the period, see BOK, *Economic Statistics*

Yearbook, 1968, p. 6.

3. Frank, *Foreign Trade Regimes*, p. 8.

4. Brown, *Korean Pricing Policies*, p. 35; Korean Development Institute, *Korea's Economy, Past and Present* (Seoul, 1971), p. 13.

5. Park, *One Hundred Years*, pp. 379-80.

6. Ibid., pp. 380–83.

7. BOK, *Economic Statistics Yearbook, 1961*, p. 168.

8. Frank, *Foreign Trade Regimes*, tables 2–8, p. 17. See Brown, *Korean Pricing Policies*, p. 191, for a similar estimate. Investment and productive capacity, however, increased in the 1950s. See Cole and Lyman, *Korean Development*, pp. 155–58.

9. Frank, *Foreign Trade Regimes*, p. 9.

10. BOK, *Economic Statistic Yearbook, 1975*, pp. 268-69.

11. Korean Development Institute, *Korea's Economy, Past and Present* (Seoul, 1975), p. 342.

12. Cole and Lyman, *Korean Development*, pp. 24–55, 78–92.

13. For details of these policies, see Brown, *Korea's Economy, Past, and Present* (Seoul, 1975), p. 342.

14. Seung Hee Kim, *Foreign Capital for Economic Development: A Korean Case Study* (New York, 1970), pp. 115-25, 129–50; Brown, *Korean Pricing Policies*, pp. 213–21.

15. GNP in dollars for the period was estimated from Korean Development Institute, *Korea's Economy*, p. 342.

16. The amounts of property claims settlement agreed are $300 million in grants, $200 million in loans and $300 million in commercial credits. See Cole and Lyman, *Korean Development*, p. 101.

17. BOK, *Economic Statistics Yearbook, 1961*, p. 146; ibid., *1975*, p. 187.

18. BOK, *Chosa Wolbo* [Monthly Economic Report], Nov. 1974, p. 34.

19. Korean Development Institute, *Korea's Economy*, p. 342.

20. Frank, *Foreign Trade Regimes*, pp. 2, 17, 19, 51; BOK, *Economic Statistics Yearbook, 1974*, pp. 271, 277.